Industrial To Residential Conversions

Discover One Of The Best Kept Secrets

In Property

Other books by Ian Child and Ritchie Clapson

Guide To Small-Scale Property Development: And the Rise of the Landlord Developer

Other books by Ian Child

Your Own Personal Time Machine: Get Your Life Back

Industrial To Residential Conversions

The essential guide to converting industrial
buildings for profit

Ian Child & Ritchie Clapson

 Equeum

Disclaimer

The authors and publisher have made every effort to ensure that the information contained in this book is accurate and correct at the time of publication, however they do not assume and hereby disclaim any liability to any party for any damages, loss (financial or otherwise) or disruption caused by any errors or omissions, howsoever such errors or omissions arose.

Any references to planning regulations, legal and accounting practices, options or considerations are given for information only and do not constitute legal or financial advice. Professional advice should always be sought from suitably qualified personnel who are familiar with your specific circumstances before making any decision that may affect your financial or legal position.

First published in Great Britain 2019 by Equeum. This imprint August 2021.

© Copyright Ian Child & Ritchie Clapson

ISBN 978-1-9163267-2-9

Rear cover portraits by Steve Hughes at Retina Photography

Facebook: propertyceotraining
Twitter: Property_CEO
Instagram: propertyceotraining
Website: www.propertyceo.co.uk
Podcast: www.propertyceo.co.uk/podcasts

All profits from the sale of this book go to KidsOut, the fun and happiness children's charity, a fantastic cause that's very close to our hearts.

For more information on the amazing work that they do, please visit www.kidsout.org.uk.

For Beccy,

For whom the thrill of having a book about industrial-to-residential conversions half-dedicated to her will mean so much.

I.C.

For Ritchie,

You've been amazing; I couldn't have done it without you.

R.C.

Table of Contents

Acknowledgements

It's difficult to thank each of the people who have in some way contributed to the writing of this book and to the success of propertyCEO.

So we won't.

Frankly, it's too easy to offend someone we may have missed out, so we'll simply say thank you; you know who you are, and we love you all to bits.

Although it would be totally remiss if we didn't say a special thank you to Tayla, Ella, Dan, Carolyn and her team, all the incredible propertyCEO coaches, and all our equally amazing mentees.

There, that should cover it.

Part 1

1. Introduction

What you will learn from this book

Welcome to the world of propertyCEO. It's great to have you with us for what we hope you'll find is a fascinating insight into the little-known property development strategy known as Industrial Conversions.

So, what exactly have you let yourself in for? Well, in broad terms we hope you'll get to the end of this book and think that:

1. Property development isn't as difficult or challenging as you thought it was, and it's something that you could definitely do yourself (even if you've never done it before)
2. Industrial Conversions is just about the least competitive property strategy there is (at the moment), so you might want to consider taking a closer look before everyone else does
3. There may be some Industrial Conversion opportunities hiding in plain sight near you that you've never noticed before and which will leap out at you (not literally) now that you know exactly how to take advantage of them
4. Now is the best time to get yourself educated and to start taking advantage

This all sounds pretty straightforward and quite exciting, but it would only be fair to give you the flip side as well. So, here's what this book isn't:

1. It's not an end-to-end, detailed, how-to, step-by-step, brick-by-brick, duffer's guide to converting industrial buildings or

developing property. That would be a much bigger book (and more technical by far). In other words, it's not a manual

2. It isn't a vehicle for plugging our property development training (although given that training is our day job here at propertyCEO, we have described who we are and what we do, plus we mention training a smidge late on in the final chapter, although we promise you'll barely notice it. Rest assured, the rest of the book is plug-free)

3. It's not a guide on how to cost or appraise the financial viability of a development project. This merits a separate book in its own right, and in any event, it's not a subject exclusive to Industrial Conversions; the appraisal process applies to any type of property development

4. It's not a dull and boring technical textbook

The reason we've not gone all-in on the technical stuff is that we want to get you interested in taking up property development as a strategy (there, we've said it – our cards are well and truly on the table, and we're only two pages in ☺). Frankly, this won't happen if we let Ritchie unleash all his almost 40 years of property development experience on you in one go, or if we try and give you a Haynes Manual on property development and start banging on about load-bearing capacities and dry lining.

That said, we will be giving you lots of juicy stuff so you can get your appetite well and truly whetted, plus we'll try and give you non-technical explanations of some of the considerations that are by their nature technical.

By the end of the book, you'll know all the fundamental principles that will enable you to take on an Industrial Conversion project yourself if that's what you decide to do, but you'll still need to get yourself a broader education in property development to be able to put it into practice. But, rest assured, we won't leave you high and dry. If you decide that you want to take things to the next stage, we'll explain what your choices are in the last chapter.

In short, the purpose of the book is to allow you to understand the opportunities presented by Industrial Conversion projects, the specific challenges you will encounter, and the concepts you can use to overcome them. You can then decide whether it's a strategy you might like to pursue either on its own or as part of a broader property strategy.

We've tried to avoid using jargon in the book since, like so many industries, property development is not without its very own buzzwords, abbreviations, terminology, and slang. Apologies if you like a good buzzword, but hopefully this way makes it easier for everyone else to follow along.

Before we move on, there's one more resource that you might find useful. One of the challenges with writing a book like this is that there's a lot of potential rabbit holes to dive down. Property development has a lot of moving parts, and to cover them all here wouldn't be practical since we'd end up writing a book about everything. We'd start heading towards Industrial Conversions and then have to dive off into how to raise finance or how to create a compelling brand. So the journey would end up a bit like a Ronnie Corbett monologue, but without the gags.

One solution is to suggest that you do one of our training courses, where you get to learn about all these things. But of course, that comes at a cost. So, we created a resource called 'The propertyCEO Podcast' that's not only completely free; it also aims to be entertaining and educational. Whether it succeeds is open to debate, but we've tried to ensure that each episode provides useful information on a specific subject. Where we come across a potential rabbit-hole in this book, we've included a reference to a particular podcast episode that covers that point. You can then get some further information on it, completely free of charge, courtesy of propertyCEO, and we promise there are no adverts or sales pitches – just information we think you'll find useful.

Where we reference the podcast, you'll see a little sign like this:

You can access the podcast on all major podcasting platforms including Apple Podcasts and Stitcher, or for the more traditional approach, simply listen on www.propertyceo/podcasts.

As we arrived in 2020, the world took an interesting turn, and the property development industry was very much affected, along with everyone else on the planet. Not surprisingly, it focused the minds of many people who realised that events outside their control could so easily impact their financial well-being. Out of nowhere, careers and businesses that had been on full steam ahead were suddenly derailed. And it prompted many to look at property development as a means of creating wealth that gave them a more certain, independent future. That's when we decided to effectively relaunch the podcast as a live webinar show called Open Door. Unfortunately for the audience, it meant they could now see us as well as hear us, but on the plus side, it allowed us to directly answer the questions people were asking about getting into development. You're very welcome to join us for the next Open Door show; just go to www.propertyceo.co.uk/webinars to book your place.

Anyway, we digress; back to the book. We also recognise that some people like technical stuff while others don't. You don't need to be a technical person to be a property developer. But for those of you that like to understand the whys and wherefores, we've included some sections that explain things in a bit more detail. If there's an explanation that might put a non-techie to sleep, we've stuck a box

4

around it, blown a small fortune on a nifty italic font, and called it Technical Corner. Actually, it's not that technical and is often quite interesting; but you at least have the choice to avoid it if you want to.

But all that comes later. For now, let's get started!

So, who are propertyCEO, and why should you listen to us?

This is a very fair question, and like so many interesting business ideas, it traces its roots back to a late-night discussion in a pub. This is where Ian and Ritchie, the two founders of propertyCEO, had a stunningly good idea one evening (one that surprisingly still looked good the following day, which to be fair doesn't always happen).

Ritchie's property CV is an impressive one. It began nearly 40 years ago when he started his nine-year journey to become a qualified structural engineer. He realised he wanted to be his own boss and was running the shadow board for a sizeable £multi-million company whilst he was still in his twenties. He then acquired a struggling structural engineering firm and over the space of the next ten years, turned it into one of the most respected businesses in its sector. The company was ultimately appointed by the government as the peer review engineer for the London 2012 Olympic Stadium, Aquatics Centre and Velodrome and also worked on many iconic projects such as the Wimbledon Tennis Centre Court retracting roof and the Goodwood Festival of Speed sculptures.

During that time, Ritchie worked on hundreds of projects both large and small. He also taught both new and experienced property developers on how to develop property using a system that he'd designed. When he retired still in his forties, he continued to be in demand as a mentor, speaker, and advisor in the property development world.

But to be honest, he found that retirement was, well, fairly dull. He missed the cut and thrust of the property and business world, and he got bored with the trappings of wealth. Owning lots of cars, mucking around on boats, and living in nice houses all sounds fantastic, but at the end of the day, it's nothing like as fulfilling as running a business.

So, Ritchie found himself inexorably drawn back to work. And it's probably fair to say he's not a person who does things by halves. He founded a construction company. He coached SME businesses on turnarounds and exit strategies. He bought a chemical engineering company in the marine industry, and appointed his son as Managing Director to teach him how to run a business. And he also found himself mentoring a small group of private clients who wanted to get into property development (or who were already developers but had learned the hard way that they needed more education). And that's where his path crossed with Ian's.

Ian had got into property some years ago when he'd set up some student HMOs close to where he lived. For 30 years, he'd worked in financial services, and he headed up a pan-European business unit for a large private equity-owned company. It was a challenging role, working with some of the world's most demanding brands and with responsibility for delivering nine-figure top-line revenues each year. But it meant there was little time for too much else. Long hours, lots of time spent travelling around the world and to be honest, not the healthiest of lifestyles. So, at the age of 49, Ian decided to call it a day and retired from the rat race to get his life back.

Around that time, Ian started hearing a lot about a property strategy called Commercial Conversions. In fact, there seemed to be quite a few people doing it very successfully, and he was keen to find a mentor to teach him how to convert buildings while avoiding making any expensive mistakes.

After some exhaustive research, Ian discovered that, for those that could afford his services, Ritchie was the go-to guy for mentoring. So having kicked Ritchie's tyres (metaphorically speaking), he decided to hire him as his property development mentor. What had particularly impressed Ian about Ritchie's CV was that he'd worked on the London 2012 Olympic Stadium. Not only because it was still standing, but because, as the peer review engineer, the government deemed the company Ritchie had built to be competent enough to check and oversee the work of the main design consultants, for what was, at the time, the most iconic and important development the country had ever undertaken. Not everyone has that on their CV. Plus Ritchie was the only property development mentor he'd found that was professionally qualified.

Many months passed, and one thing became evident to Ian; the training he was getting from Ritchie was first-class. In fact, the system Ritchie had built was hugely impressive; the sort of training you can only get from someone who's got decades of experience behind them. But it was also clear that Ritchie could only mentor a small number of people. There were only so many hours in the day, and with his other business commitments, only a handful of people were benefiting from Ritchie's expertise.

Now, as chance would have it, Ian already knew a thing or two about online training and creating digital products, having studied digital marketing on a year-long mentorship following his retirement. So, one evening over several pints in the aforementioned pub, he and Ritchie discussed a plan to turn Ritchie's own systems and mentorship programme into a hybrid online training course that could serve a wider audience. A mixture of digital and one-to-one content that could justifiably be described as the best training of its type available anywhere. That, in turn, became the property training brand called 'propertyCEO', and the two of them haven't looked back since.

Ian had also spent a lot of time during his corporate career studying mindset and personal development, and this had become something of a passion of his. He'd also worked with some of the brightest minds from the world of private equity and learned first-hand how they trained their top executives to be successful. *

There were three things that Ian knew to be true when it came to mindset:

1. The reason most people don't succeed is NOT that they don't have enough information. It's because they lack the right mindset skills to apply it effectively
2. Most great mindset-improving ideas can be written on a single piece of paper. But since one-page books don't sell very well, their authors usually add another 199 pages of filler, which takes (almost) two hundred times longer to read and makes the whole learning process much more boring and time-consuming, so a lot of people don't bother
3. Personal development isn't just about fixing problems like low self-esteem, lack of confidence, and overwhelm; it's also learning about tools you didn't know about, which can supercharge your chances of success

* When a private equity company acquires a new business, they'll often parachute in some highly intelligent (and usually depressingly young) MBA graduates from top US business schools to work with the existing management team. This then creates a powerful mix; a broad base of established industry and market knowledge partnered with some very clever people who have learned the cutting-edge techniques of how to get the best from a business and its senior management. Put the two together, and the business can really go places – it's a powerful combination.

There are too many ideas in the world of personal development for one person to try them all. Since we never do anything we don't want to, the best way of getting people to get the most out of life is to present them with some ideas they may not have known about (on one page rather than 200) and let them choose the ones they like (or at least don't dislike). That way, they're much more likely to do them and get great results. That's the approach we take at propertyCEO.

So not surprisingly, mindset training is included as standard in the training that propertyCEO provides, although Ian's sifted out the dross so not only do you only get the good stuff, we don't make you do anything you don't want to. Believe us; there will be plenty of great tools and ideas out there that you may not have encountered before that could seriously enhance your chances of success.

Interestingly most people that we train come to us thinking they only need property development knowledge, not mindset training. Then they discover that, with the mindset skills in place, the results they want are much easier to achieve.

What makes propertyCEO different?

Of course, there are a lot of training companies out there, including some very good ones. One area in which propertyCEO differs from many of them is in the depth of our experience. Consider this; a development project can typically take between 12-24 months to complete, so a developer who has 5 years' experience may only have completed two or three projects over that period. This differs greatly from many other jobs where 5 years' experience is likely to make you something of an expert. In property development, it's difficult to be a leading authority if you've only done two or three projects because you won't have encountered all the possible challenges that can arise – your sample size is simply too small.

Conversely, Ritchie is professionally qualified and has been involved in hundreds of projects, plus he's also spent much of that time training and advising other developers. As a result, he's seen most of what there is to see, and we ensure that this depth of experience shines through in the training we give.

We also made a rather controversial decision not long after we started, which is that we only wanted to train a small number of people.

On the face of it, this doesn't make a great deal of commercial sense. After all, surely a training company would want to train as many people as possible? Well, rather than train anyone that simply WANTED the results, we decided we would only train those people who we thought are most likely to GET results.

Why would we want to sell training programmes to fewer people?

Well, there are a few reasons. The first is an ethical one; we don't think it's right to take someone's money if we genuinely think they don't have the skills to be successful in property development. Secondly, we're only interested in creating property developers, so selling thousands of places at 2-day workshops is not suddenly going to produce thousands of successful developers. It's much more effective to spend more time working with fewer people because that way they'll get better results.

Finally, the traditional 'sales-funnel' approach to training didn't seem to make any sense to us. Luring people in with a free e-book and then selling them a long list of increasingly expensive training products over a period of months or years may be great if you're a trainer, but it's not very effective for students.

The problem with the approach is that the thing that most people want is results. They want to be a successful property developer making a very healthy six-figure income working part-time. So, if this is the case, why not just give them the training product that has the best chance of getting them the result they want at the outset, rather than create a load of cheaper training materials that, with the best will in the world, can only give them a fraction of the information they need?

So, as a result, propertyCEO only offers a minimal number of courses and mentorships, but we get some great results for our students. People can't buy a mentorship place online – it's an invitation-only process, and we interview people who want to come on our programmes to make sure we're a good fit for each other before we invite them in. As a result, our training isn't cheap, but then we're only working with people who are looking to have the best possible results, and who recognise that the cost of their training is a small fraction of the profit they can make from their first development.

Right, that's enough about us. But before we move on, we'd like to talk briefly about the broader subject of education just in case you were thinking of jumping right in there without a parachute, so to speak. It's not a sales pitch, BUT – we have seen too many people come a cropper when they've neglected to educate themselves properly, so we feel it's only right to mention it and to give you some tips. Here goes...

The importance of education

We're a training company, so no surprises; we're not about to tell you that getting yourself educated in property is a complete waste of time and money. Or that you should read a couple of books, have a chat with that builder you met down the pub and then go for it. Property is an excellent means to become wealthy, but it carries risks like any other wealth creation tool. And that means it can be a great way to become poor too unless you know what you're doing.

11

It is said that all pioneers have broken noses. That's because they have to smash through all the walls since they're the first ones to do it. They also fall down all the holes, since there's no map to follow – they're forced to create the first-ever map as they go. Pick almost any subject in history; the people that have come along <u>after</u> the pioneers have always done it more quickly, more profitably, and with far fewer mistakes.

Now, if you fancy being a property pioneer, we're sorry to tell you that all the broken noses were handed out some time ago, so you've missed the boat. However, you can certainly try and recreate the experience. Simply go out and develop property without getting any training. It will be a lot more exciting because you won't know where all the holes are until you've fallen down them. Also, you'll be slower, make more mistakes, miss more opportunities, and end up with less profit. So, what's not to like?

We once described property investment without training as trying to cross a busy road blindfolded.

- Is it possible to get to the other side in one piece? Absolutely
- Is it quite exciting? We've not tried it, but we should say it probably provides quite an adrenaline rush
- Can you cross without encountering many instances where you have the crap scared out of you? No
- Can you get killed or seriously injured quite easily? Definitely
- Would any sane person walk a hundred yards further up the road and use the pedestrian crossing instead? All day long

Of course, it's still possible to get run over on a pedestrian crossing, but percentage-wise you'd have to say you'd fancy your chances a whole lot better. And when it comes to making money, we can live without all the excitement.

The good news from a property perspective is that there are lots of training materials out there. Books, videos, courses, seminars, mentorships; the list is endless. And of course, there's training available for every conceivable type of property strategy.

However, we would offer a word of warning; you can't learn the end-to-end of property development on a two-day workshop or from a free e-book.

Think about how many hours of study goes into getting a degree (or for that matter, a bog-standard maths GCSE). What would make anyone think that learning properly how to create a successful career as a property developer can be gleaned from a two-day workshop?

Quite recently, we were asked to speak to an audience about property development at the ExCel in London by the organisers of one of the country's leading property shows. Afterwards, a middle-aged gentleman approached us both and having said something complimentary about our talk, his first question was, 'how much did our training cost?'. When we said that a mentorship place cost north of £10,000, he was incredulous. Seriously? How could we possibly justify it being so expensive? Were we trying to rip people off?

In response, we asked him how much a house costs. The man was surprised and to be honest a little indignant – it was after all a silly question. How on earth could he possibly know how much a house cost if he didn't know where it was, how many rooms it had, or what type of house it was? A 10-bed mansion in Mayfair might cost £50m, whereas a two-up-two-down in Barnsley could cost £50k.

So how much does a house cost? The answer is, it depends.

Yet for some reason, it hadn't occurred to him to apply the same logic to evaluating the cost of training.

Consider this hypothetical scenario. Imagine in one envelope we have a voucher for an e-book all about property development which costs £4.99. In another envelope, a voucher costing £100k for 2-years full-time personal one-to-one mentoring with ourselves with full access to our professional team, with the goal of helping you secure your first £1m profit from development. Both constitute property development training.

So, how much does property development training cost?

The answer is, it depends.

The first rule, then, is to find out what the training consists of before you pass judgement. It's all about value, what will get you the best chance of being successful for the most reasonable price. You need to work out what you're trying to achieve, and how much training you think you'll need. If you're looking to get the lowdown on a particular development strategy before you decide whether it's right for you, then please don't spend £10k on a course. If you've decided you want to do development, then get yourself properly educated, in which case expect to pay 5-figures for the best. Clearly, the best training may not be within your reach due to its cost; however, we would always urge you to buy the best training you can afford.

Still not convinced? Here's another perspective. A GP in the UK, on average, earns around £100k a year, and according to the BMA, it costs around £500k to train each GP. Conversely, a small-scale industrial conversion project in the South of England (say 5 x one-bedroom flats) might generate around £250k profit for the developer over 18 months, working part-time. Assuming that the developer might do three of these at any one time, it would equate to an annual profit of around £500k or so per year.

So, if it costs £500k to train a GP who earns £100k a year, how much should the training cost to become a developer who makes five times as much?

Proportionally, the answer would be £2.5m. But of course, that's not the correct answer. In fact, there's no right answer. However, we'd respectfully suggest that you would expect it to cost more than a £297 weekend workshop or a £4.99 e-book.

Here's one final perspective in case your penny is still teetering. Imagine you're feeling a bit dickie one day, and so you toddle off to see your GP. You arrive at the surgery to find your appointment is with a new GP that you've not seen before. During your session, the GP confides that she'd only decided to become a GP last week, having had no previous medical training. But she went on this amazing two-day, £297 workshop to get qualified, and here she is a week later treating you.

Does this sound realistic? How much confidence would you have in a doctor that's only had two-days training that cost three hundred quid?

The other good news is that while good property training is rarely cheap, the returns you get from property can be significant. So, the cost of the training is low in relative terms. A £10k+ mentorship programme is by no means inexpensive. But if it's the determining factor in helping you land a project with six-figure profits and you can then repeat the outcome, it's a pretty good investment.

Also, once you've learned something once in order to do your first development, you don't need to buy further training when you do your second. You pay for the training once, but you reap the benefits time and time again.

You should also make sure you check out the credentials of your trainer(s) and their organisation. Here are some of the questions we think you should ask:

1. How much experience in development do they have?

A depressingly large number of trainers go on a property training course, do their first development, and then start trying to flog their own course. Ideally, you want to be working with people who have real-world experience and plenty of it.

2. What is their track record?

Get them to share some success stories and ask to speak to some of their students. Are they as good as they say they are?

3. What is their current role?

Are they property developers who run a training business as a side-line, or is property development training their main thing?

You want to have confidence that they've real-world experience about what they're training you, but will their main priority and focus be their development projects rather than their students?

4. Who will your trainer(s) be?

Many training companies use their founders to promote their courses, but then the actual training is done by juniors/subordinates. This isn't automatically a bad thing; providing your trainer has the necessary skills, experience, and knowledge to do the job well. If they're simply reciting what they've been told to say, then there's almost no added value. Find out who's actually training you before you sign on the dotted line.

5. How much 1:1 time will you get?

"Mentoring" has a variable meaning in the world of training. In its purest sense, mentoring involves spending some serious time working one-to-one with a mentee face-to-face. However, it has almost evolved to include any training where there is any 1:1 contact at all. At its least generous, this could be a monthly 15-minute phone call with a junior trainer, which can be hugely frustrating if you've got more questions, or the trainer can't answer them. Have an idea of how much 1:1 time you feel you'll want and then get clarity on the mentoring level, expertise, and volume on any given course.

6. Do they have a helpdesk?

How do you pose any questions you might have while you're on the course, and what are the turnaround times? You want to be able to email in questions and get answers on a timely basis.

Always get the best training you can afford since it will pay you back many times over. Cheap training is a false economy (although to be fair, free training is always worth every penny you paid for it).

Which type of training should you go for? Well, it should be relevant to the strategy you're looking to do. Also, the training medium has got to work for you (do you prefer home study or going to seminars, for example). And of course, the trainers have got to be good and the materials top notch. You also need to decide whether you're looking for some high-level training, or do you want the more intensive, fast–track mentorship-type approach? The latter is more expensive but offers a level of support you won't get with the volume-training products.

Also, do you prefer to have one tall trainer and one short one? We hear this can be important for some people. ☺

Our advice is to do some research and ask around. It can be a bit confusing if you're new to it all, so we did a podcast episode on the subject of property training (we don't even try and sell you one of our courses, which frankly we're kicking ourselves about now).

Season 1; Ep 1

OK, that's enough about training; we'll try not to mention it for a while. Let's head off to a very exciting place – the wonderful world of property development.

2. Some Fundamental Principles

Development versus other property strategies

Perhaps you're already involved in property? Or maybe you've not yet started your journey and are still doing your due diligence, trying to find the best strategy.

In our experience, there is no such thing as a 'bad' property strategy, but we quite often come across a property strategy done badly. There's a danger with any strategy that you can have your head turned by all the marketing and spin. Yet every strategy has its failures as well as its successes. You need to do enough due diligence to understand both the risks and the pitfalls and then plot a path to avoid them.

You also need to do your homework before embarking on any property strategy. Some of the things you need to consider are:

1. Do you have the skills (or can you learn the skills) you will need to be successful?
2. Do you have enough time to devote to it?
3. Are you comfortable with the risk profile that each property strategy represents?
4. What is your purpose for doing it, and is it big enough to ensure you keep going even when things get tough?

Another critical area to investigate is the amount of work involved in each one. Some strategies boast great profits. But it may be a full-time job to extract them, and that could be time you don't have, or don't want to have. Passive Income is something that many people look to achieve, particularly through property, but the reality can be somewhat different (we even dedicated a podcast episode to this very subject).

Season 2; Ep 1

So, before we head off to Industrial Conversions, we want to explain how development stacks up against some of the other property strategies out there. And how it can complement those other strategies rather well, as opposed to being an either/or decision.

To do this, we thought we'd share with you a short(ish) story...

The Story Of Old Esmeralda

Once upon a time in a far-off land (OK, it was Southampton), there lived four siblings. Charles was the eldest, then Claire, third was Derek and finally the last man out, so to speak, was Trevor.

Now we have to tell you that there's a sad bit in this story right at the start. But the good news is that things cheer up pretty quickly after that and we actually end up with a very happy ending. In fact, of the six characters in the story, everyone lives happily ever after apart from the sixth person, who dies. So statistically, it's about 83.3% happy.

There are also quite a few numbers involved. Sorry about this, but we do hope you can stick with it (we'll summarise it at the end in case the numbers get the better of you).

But let's get the sad bit out of the way first. The siblings have an elderly great aunt called Esmeralda. And at the ripe old age of 102, Great Aunt Essie, unfortunately, passes away.

Following her demise, each of the siblings receives a letter from Esmeralda's solicitor asking them to attend a meeting at his offices in London. They duly arrive at the appointed hour, suitably piqued with curiosity, and enter a rather austere office filled with dusty old books. Here Mr. Frobisher from Frobisher, Mallard, and Pugh (Commissioners for Oaths) awaits them sitting behind an old leather-topped desk and peering at them over his horn-rimmed spectacles.

After a round of introductions, Mr. Frobisher thanks them all for coming and explains why he has summoned them to London. It appeared that Esmeralda had made a bequest to each of her grandnephews and her grandniece. Unbeknownst to the siblings, their great aunt had died a wealthy woman with an estate worth a very healthy four million pounds. Better still, they were her sole beneficiaries...

Now, you don't get to be worth four million pounds without having some sense about you, and old Esmeralda was definitely not a sandwich short of a picnic. She was actually a very shrewd businesswoman. She knew that there are people out there who, if you gave them a million pounds, would blow it on depreciating assets like cars and boats and holidays. And before you knew it, the capital would all be gone. So rather than leave all her estate to be divided among the siblings who might fritter it away, she did something far cannier.

Mr. Frobisher explained that she had left each of them £200,000 on the proviso that each must invest the money in its entirety in property. This Esmeralda had learned over the years was a very reliable asset. They must then return precisely ten years from now to the day. At that point, they would disclose how much wealth they had managed to accumulate through investing in property using only the £200,000 she had left them. The sibling who had generated the most wealth would then inherit the balance of her estate, a not-to-be-sniffed-at sum of over £3m. There were no other stipulations. Any form of property investment was acceptable, and they had free rein to invest the money howsoever they wished.

So the four siblings left the offices of Frobisher, Mallard, and Pugh that day with some excitement. And they started hatching their individual plans to win old Esmeralda's fortune for themselves through shrewd investments in property.

Let's now roll the clock forward precisely ten years. Our protagonists return to the same dusty office at the solicitors. Mr. Frobisher, who is now somewhat less spritely yet still sporting the same horn-rimmed spectacles, cordially invites them all to take a seat. He turns to Charles the eldest and asks him to declare how he has fared with his property investment activities over the last ten years.

Charles, being older than his siblings, usually thinks he knows best, despite being the least bright of the four of them. He gets up from his seat with a rather smug look and begins to relate to the aged solicitor how his investments had worked out.

"I decided to buy a house with my £200,000," he begins and then pauses for dramatic effect as if awaiting a round of applause from his audience, which doesn't arrive.

"Then – wait for it – I rented the house out to someone! A very nice couple called Mr. and Mrs. Smith. But that's not all – because the rent I received was more than the cost of the upkeep of the house, I made on average a profit of £1,000 each month, which is £12k per year and £120k over the last ten years." By now, Charles is starting to look really smug.

"And that's not all either! I had the house valued yesterday, and it turns out that over the last ten years, it's increased in value and is now worth £400,000! What do you say to that?

Mr. Frobisher writes Charles's figures in a small leather-bound notebook.

"So, Charles, let me see. You started with £200k, and you've now turned that into £520k over ten years. Very good."

Charles's Position

Strategy: Single Buy To Let, Outright Purchase

Initial Investment = £200k
No. of properties owned = 1
10-year Rental Profit = £120k
Current Value of Portfolio = £400k
Mortgages = £0k
Equity = £400k

Total Equity + Profit = £520k

Charles looks crestfallen by the somewhat muted response and sits back down in his chair. Mr. Frobisher turns to Claire and indicates it's her turn to share her numbers.

"Well," she said, rising from her seat. "I bought a house as well, but I only paid £180k for it. And instead of renting it to a family, I spent the remaining £20k converting it into an HMO which is a house of multiple occupation. This allowed me to rent it out by the room to professionals, which meant I generated more income. In fact, I managed to make a profit of £2,000 per month, and so over the last ten years, I've generated £240,000 in profit. Plus, like Charles, the house has increased in value and is now also worth £400k."

Again Mr. Frobisher makes a note in his notebook. "Claire has turned her £200k into £640k, which by my reckoning is £120k more than Charles."

Claire's Position

Strategy: HMO Outright Purchase

Initial Investment = £200k (£180k + £20k)
No. of properties owned = 1
10-year Rental Profit = £240k
Current Value of Portfolio = £400k
Mortgages = £0k
Equity = £400k

Total Equity + Profit = £640k

"I think that places you in the lead, my dear. Very well, Derek; now it's your turn." Derek gets to his feet and starts speaking;

"I decided to buy four £200k houses with my money..." but no sooner had he begun than he's immediately cut off by Charles.

"Hold on a minute, how can you buy four houses that cost £200k each if you only have £200k to spend in the first place? It doesn't make any sense," Charles asks.

"Oh, that was easy," replied Derek. "I got mortgages on each property by putting down £50k as a deposit on each one and borrowing the remaining £150k from the bank. So I ended up with four houses with mortgages totalling £600k, and I rented each of them out as single lets, the same as you Charles. But I only made £500 profit per month on each of them because, of course, I had to repay the mortgages, which ate into my profits. But I still got more rental profit overall because I had four houses instead of one, even though each one made less profit individually. So my rental profit was £24k per year and £240k over the ten years."

"And what about the value of your four houses, Derek?" asked Mr. Frobisher.

"Well, each one is now worth £400k, which makes a total of £1.6m. But of course, I still owe the bank the £600k that I borrowed initially, so my net equity is only £1m.

Mr. Frobisher makes another note. "So, Derek has made £1m in equity growth and £120k in rental profit, so his total is £1.12m, which is, of course, £480k more than Claire. Very well, Derek – it looks like you're now in the lead."

Derek's Position

Strategy: Single Buy To Let With Mortgage

Initial Investment = £200k
No. of properties owned = 4
10-year Rental Profit = £240k
Current Value of Portfolio = £1.6m
Mortgages = £600k
Equity = £1.0m

Total Equity + Profit = £1.24m

"So, last but not least...," he turned to the youngest, Trevor. "What did you do with your £200k, Trevor?" asked the solicitor.

"I bought a knackered old MOT Testing Centre," said Trevor.

There was a stunned silence followed by a snort of derision from Derek, and a mumbled "What an idiot!" from Charles. Mr. Frobisher remained silent, a slight frown creasing his brow before saying, "Please, do carry on Trevor."

"Well, the building was on the edge of a residential area, and I decided to convert it into eight flats. It cost £300k to buy the building, so I had to borrow another £100k as I only had £200k from Great Aunt Essie."

"Right. Well, I think we can all see the flaw with your plan," said Charles rather condescendingly, his nose well and truly put out of joint as a result of his now lying in third place. "If you've spent all your money on buying it, then how on earth can you afford to convert it into flats? The builders aren't going to do it for nothing, you know..."

"Well, I went and got some development finance," said Trevor. "You see, commercial lenders are happy to lend 100% of the development cost, so I didn't need to put in any extra cash to get the flats built. In fact, they lent me a further £300k, and I used that money to build the flats. Then I sold each of the flats for £100k, which generated £800k." Mr. Frobisher regarded Trevor keenly.

"So by my reckoning Trevor, you started with £200k, then you borrowed a further £400k to buy and develop the flats and then made £800k when you sold them. So your net position is £400k. That is, the £200k you started with plus the £200k profit from the development. Would that be correct?"

"Absolutely right," confirmed Trevor.

"Which I think places you in fourth place. So do I gather that Derek is the winner?" Mr. Frobisher looked enquiringly at Trevor with what may have been a twinkle in his eye.

"Well," said Trevor, "here's the thing. It only took me 15 months to convert the MOT Testing Centre. And because it was quite straightforward, I've gone and done another development every 18 months since..."

"Wait, you're saying that you converted six MOT Testing Centres? In ten years?" Charles said incredulously.

"No, not exactly. I actually converted one MOT Centre, then a printing works, two workshops, a small building previously used by a bookbinding business, and finally a building that was home to a hand car wash," said Trevor.

"And how much profit did you make from each one?" asked Claire, as ever one to get to the nub of things.

"After I'd finished the MOT centre, I had £400k in the bank, so I did think about using it all to buy an even bigger industrial property for twice as much money. After all, this could have netted me twice the profit, and then I could keep doubling up every 18 months. But in the end, I decided I wanted to keep doing smaller developments as they were less risky and more straightforward. So, I did one every 18 months and made an average of £200k profit on each one."

"Let me get this straight," Claire interjected, her mental arithmetic whirring through the numbers. "You started with £200k and then did six Industrial Conversions, each of which made you £200k plus it paid you back your original investment each time. So are you saying that you've now got £1.2m, plus the £200k you started with?

"Well, yes and no," said Trevor. As you say, I only invested £200k in each project, but of course, I was getting that back plus a further £200k profit every 18 months. So I wondered what I should do with the extra £200k I was earning that I didn't spend, and in the end, I decided to do the same thing as Derek. So every 18 months, I took the £400k I'd made from the previous conversion project, and I used £200k to buy another project. Then with the remaining £200k, I purchased four £200k houses with mortgages. This cost me £200k in deposits, with each house making me £500 a month in rental profit once it was let out. And after I'd done my sixth conversion, I didn't have enough time to finish a seventh before today, so I bought another four houses instead.

Mr. Frobisher looked at Trevor with an approving eye. "Let me see if I've understood this. You've made a total of £1.2m profit over ten years from converting six industrial buildings, plus you still had your original £200k. And you used all that money to buy four £200k houses every 18 months, and eight houses last year?"

"That's correct."

"So, by my calculations, that would mean you now have 28 houses. And may I ask how much rent these houses have generated?

"Well, it's a bit more complicated to calculate. The first four houses I bought in month 16 after I'd sold the MOT Centre flats. They took me a couple of months to purchase and set up, but then they made me £500 per month for eight and a half years, which is a total of £204k. The second lot of houses I bought made me a bit less because I've only had them for seven years. And so on, all the way up to the eight houses that I bought last year which haven't made me much profit at all yet. But when you work it all out, my total rental profit over the ten years is £708k.

"And of course, you now also own 28 houses. May I ask how much they're worth?

"Again, it's a bit complicated, but the four houses I bought eight and a half years ago have nearly doubled in value. The houses I bought last year have only increased in value a little. All the other ones are somewhere in between. But when you work it all out, the value of my portfolio is now £7.63m."

"But," said Frobisher tapping away at a calculator, "you have a £150k mortgage on each house, so we would need to deduct 28 lots of £150k, which is £4.2m. Which means that your equity is actually £3.43m. So, if I add this to the £708k you've received in rental profit, you've managed to turn your £200k into £4.14m over ten years."

Trevor's Position

Strategy: Industrial Conversions + Single Buy To Let With Mortgage

Initial Investment = £200k
No. of properties owned = 28
10-year Rental Profit = £708k
Current Value of Portfolio = £7.63m
Mortgages = £4.2mty = £3.43m

Total Equity + Profit = £4.14m

He surveyed the four siblings over the top of his glasses once more. Two of them appeared to be looking a little strained; Charles looked positively shell-shocked.

"Let me recap to see where we are. Charles, you are in fourth place with £520k. Claire, you are third with £640k. Derek is second with £1.24m. And that means Trevor is in first place with around £4.14m. Congratulations, Trevor; that makes you the winner by some considerable margin."

At that point, Charles leapt to his feet and started pacing angrily around the room.

"I can't believe it. All that time you told us you had that job at the bank, and instead, you've secretly gone into property development full time. I can't believe you've been so deceitful!" he ranted.

"Hold on, Charles," Claire remonstrated. "There was nothing in the rules that said Trevor couldn't work in property full-time. We both decided not to, but it's up to Trevor if that's what he wants to do. I think he's done a fantastic job."

"Oh, I still work at the bank," said Trevor rather sheepishly. "Although I think I may leave soon to do something else."

"How on earth can you develop property AND have a job at the bank?" asked Charles incredulously.

"Well, I hired a Project Manager to look after all the building work on-site, so I didn't actually need to that much once things were up and running. I did quite a lot of work at the start, finding all the right people and then finding a good project for them to work on. But once the project was underway, it would only take me a few hours a week on the phone with the Project Manager and then the occasional site visit. And then, for the subsequent jobs, I used the same people. In fact, it's quite a nice team now..."

The others looked on in stunned silence while Mr. Frobisher tried unsuccessfully to suppress a chuckle. They all rose to leave, Charles departing somewhat more expeditiously than Claire and Derek. Trevor was the last to rise.

"Well, Trevor," said the solicitor as he walked him to the door. "Many congratulations! We will, of course, have to double-check your numbers, but it looks as though you'll now be inheriting the remainder of your great aunt's estate. Do you have any plans for it? A nice holiday perhaps?" he asked as they shook hands on the threshold.

"You know, Mr. Frobisher, I think I'll invest most of it in property. But I reckon it would be fairest if I did it on behalf of all four of us, don't you? Esmeralda Estates has quite a ring to it – do you think she'd approve?" Mr. Frobisher couldn't resist a smile.

"Do you know, Trevor, I think she would."

And they all lived happily ever after, even Charles.

The 'magic' ingredients

So, what does this story tell us? We've used it to highlight some interesting differences in the way various property strategies pan out. And of course, the numbers aren't going to be absolutely accurate (for example we've not allowed for inflation, or for tax, although that's the same for all the siblings). But even if they aren't 100% accurate, it won't impact the scale of Trevor's success versus his brothers and sister. Even if Trevor's income was only half of that quoted in the story, he still wins by a handsome margin.

In fact, if Trevor had done development only, he would have generated £200k profit a year from working part-time. But by investing the profits in property, he took his financial position into the stratosphere. That said, it's fair to say that finding four new houses to buy each year would have taken up some of his time.

But what if we look at the numbers in a different way? Let's look at the siblings' annual passive income if they stopped doing any more investing after those ten years. We'll also ignore inflation to make life simpler, and you should bear in mind that they all started with the same £200k:

• Charles would have a rental profit of £12k per year from property worth £400k and equity of £400k

• Claire would have a rental profit of £24k per year from property worth £400k and equity of £400k

• Derek would have a rental profit of £24k per year from property worth £1.6m and equity of £1.0m

• Trevor: would have a rental profit of £168k per year from property worth £7.63m and equity of £3.43m

We suspect that Trevor may be looking to quit the bank at some point soon and... well, retire. Whereas the rest of the family may need to stick at their day jobs a little while longer...

So what happened there? Did we perform some sleight of hand? Was there some deft trick that saw Trevor go from zero to hero without doing a great deal? Did we just say that someone can work part-time for ten years, and in so doing, can create a passive income of over £160k a year with £3.5m in assets, and never have to work another day in their life?

And if so, how come they didn't teach you this stuff at school?

Well, it's not quite as simple as that, but let's lift the veil a little so that we can see exactly what happened to Trevor. Einstein famously described compound interest as the eighth wonder of the world, but there's a little magic being weaved by Trevor too.

The ninth wonder in this scenario is leverage. Property has broadly doubled in value every ten or so years. We're not promising it will always do so, just that it has done so historically. Society continues to make more people, but they're not making any more land. So, despite the occasional blip, the long term-trajectory for housing demand and therefore equity growth looks reasonably assured.

Competition-wise, Charles and Claire's mistake was not to buy property with a mortgage. Claire did well to spot that HMOs were more lucrative than single lets. As a result, she generated more rental profit, despite her asset base being the same as Charles's. Plus Claire would have worked a fair bit harder than Charles to get her HMO set up. If she'd purchased using a mortgage, she would have been able to buy another three properties at £200k each. This would have seen her annual rental profits roughly double from £28.8k to £57.6k, plus she would have made a further £600k in equity.

Had Trevor elected to buy his investment properties in cash with no mortgages, he would have purchased only one property per year instead of four. He would have ended up with equity of £1.91m instead of £3.43m, and his rental profits would have been £177k and not £708k. His decision to use mortgages, therefore, netted him more than £2m more than he would otherwise have earned.

If the leverage concept is confusing, the point to remember is that while the value of your property may double in ten years, the amount you owe on your mortgage doesn't change (assuming an interest-only mortgage). As a result, you benefit from the equity growth on the proportion of your property that's owned by the bank as well as on your own part.

So if you use £200k in cash to buy one house costing £200k then in 10 years that house will be worth £400k and you'll have made £200k by sitting and waiting. But if you use the same £200k as a deposit on an £800k house, then you'll be getting a mortgage of £600k from the bank to complete the purchase. In 10 years, your house has doubled in value to £1.6m, but you only owe £600k to the bank, making your equity worth £1m (a profit of £800k). You've put the same money in, waited the same amount of time, but you've got four times the profit to show for it at the end. That's the power of leverage.

The second piece of 'magic' that happened to Trevor is the fact that property development produces cash. Once Derek (the third sibling) had purchased his fourth property using Esmeralda's cash, he didn't have any deposits left to buy any more. He'd used up all his capital buying the first four, which were now producing a profit of £24k per year. So to buy another one (which would need a £50k deposit), Derek would need to save up all his rental profits for 25 months. But Trevor's developments were each making £200k every 18 months plus he also had his own rental profits income. He could afford to buy many more houses than Derek, and this meant his rental profits and leverage were massively accelerated.

This difference between the results of Derek (£1.24m profit) and Trevor (£4.14m) shows the stark contrast between someone who is solely a landlord and someone who is a landlord/developer.

Aha, we hear you say, wasn't there a third piece of magic in play? Didn't the siblings have a centenarian great aunt who happened to pop her clogs and leave them £200k apiece? Perhaps you think that without a couple of hundred big ones, they may not have fared so well? It's a valid point, but here's another small piece of magic for you to consider. You don't need to invest a great deal of your own money to be able to do what Trevor did.

If Trevor had borrowed the £200k he inherited from Esmeralda from commercial lenders and friends or family instead (or indeed from some other private investor), and paid them 10% interest for a year, we suspect he'd have had investors queuing up (how many other investments do you know of that are currently returning 10%?). How would that have affected Trevor's profits? Well, let's say it would have cost him an extra £20k in interest on each Industrial Conversion project and another £2k in overheads. When we look at his numbers, we suspect he may have been able to afford it...

Now, in the story, we had Trevor make his fortune out of converting light industrial buildings since that's the subject of this book. But to be honest, it could have been from any form of property development. New builds, commercial conversions, refurbs, and flips - it doesn't matter which. The point is that they all generate cash rather than equity, and so they facilitate the fast-tracking of property acquisition to build up a rental portfolio if that's the route you want to go down. Or you could take the profit and reinvest it into larger development deals. Or go on a lot of nice holidays. With development, the choice is yours.

Hopefully that's given you a perspective on development that you may not have had before. We've not focused on the extra work that Trevor put in to create his success. His brothers and sister all set up their portfolios as a one-time project, so they had little to do other than in the first year. In fact, Charles simply bought a house and rented it out, about as little work as you can possibly do as a new landlord.

Compare that to Trevor, who was not only finding four investment properties to buy each year; he was also sourcing one Industrial Conversion project per year and overseeing it, albeit with a Project Manager in place. Would he be able to do this while holding down a day job? Yes, providing he didn't mind doing the work in his own time, and that he had some flexibility to be able to visit the site occasionally during working hours. Property development doesn't have to be a full-time job, like being a landlord doesn't. Of course, Trevor missed a trick since he could have decided to go down the HMO route. This would have added a further £1.4m to his 10-year rental profit and taken his ongoing 'passive' income to well over half a million pounds a year.

So, while becoming a landlord/developer remains the most straightforward way we know of creating a £multi-million business, that's not the same thing as saying that it's easy. You've got to want to do it.

And if you don't want to do it? Well, it's interesting that all four of the siblings made money, even Charles, who did the least amount possible. Nothing is guaranteed in life, but even a very passive approach to property investment can yield a healthy return in the long run.

So now our short(ish) story is over, let's look at some of the key aspects of development.

3. The Exciting World Of Property Development

How does development differ from other property strategies?

There are lots of different property strategies out there, and they each have different attributes. Let's take a look at the pros and cons of some of the more common ones. In this section, we mention tenants, voids, broken boilers, and maintenance a fair bit (which sounds exciting, we know – please try and contain yourself). Let's first explain what we mean by each:

Tenants – from a landlord's perspective, these chaps are quite important. There are invariably good tenants and bad tenants. But as any landlord will tell you, having tenants is a big responsibility, and it can also, at times, be quite stressful and demanding. As a responsible landlord, you need to keep your properties in good shape and your tenants happy. But even if you appoint a managing agent, you'll still find that many tenant issues arrive in your inbox, and some will need to be dealt with urgently. Also, tenants can sometimes fail to pay the rent, which causes further frustration and stress as well as financial issues. So, without tenants, you have no rent, but they do bring you considerable obligations and responsibilities too.

Voids – these are periods when your rental property is empty (e.g., between tenancies) during which you have no income. This can be less common with Single Lets, but with HMOs, it can happen more regularly, although the void may only affect one room and not the entire house. To be honest, a well-managed HMO should see very little in the way of voids, but you need to be on top of your game for this to be the case.

Broken Boilers – we'll use boilers to represent any appliance or item of furniture that you've supplied, which need to be kept working/useable. Boilers and appliances are essential, but they're also a liability because they wear out and break down. When that occurs, they need to be repaired quickly and occasionally replaced, and that comes at a cost and often happens out of the blue.

Maintenance – When you buy and hold property, you will need to maintain it. This means fixing day-to-day problems that may arise as well as redecorating the property every five years or so. It can also include some bigger bills such as roof repairs etc.

Let's now look at each property strategy in turn:

Single Lets

This is where you buy a house with cash or a buy to let mortgage, and you rent it out to a single tenant (usually a single person, a couple, or a family). This is the route that Charles followed in our story. Typically, you will make a small amount of profit each month from the rent. Your most significant financial return will be in the equity growth, which you could reasonably expect to double in value every 10-12 years. You'll have tenants, voids, broken boilers, and maintenance to deal with, but your tenants will typically stay for longer than with HMOs. Your voids will be less, plus your broken boilers and maintenance costs should be less as well since the property will get less wear and tear than an HMO.

HMOs

A House of Multiple Occupation is a property rented out by at least three people who are not from one 'household' (for example, a family) but share facilities like the bathroom and kitchen. In a typical HMO, you would be renting the property out by the room, with each tenant on a separate tenancy agreement. By renting it out this way, you get considerably more rental income than for a Single Let. However, you generally have to invest some cash upfront to convert the property (usually by adding en-suites or creating extra bedrooms using stud walls, etc.). You'll also enjoy equity growth in the same way as a Single Let, although your investment in converting the property to an HMO may make it more valuable as a result.

Depending on the size, type, and location of the property, you may also have to be licensed by the local authority. If so, you may have to install upgraded safety equipment such as mains-wired interconnected smoke alarms, fire doors, etc. You'll have tenants, voids, broken boilers, and maintenance to deal with, and each will be a greater burden than with a Single Let because you'll usually have more tenants (and so more tenant issues), and more wear and tear. You'll also have a greater chance for voids since each tenant is on a separate lease, although if a tenant leaves, you'll only have a void for one room rather than for the whole house.

Student Lets

Student Lets are, in some ways, a hybrid of Single Lets and HMOs. The properties are usually configured as HMOs; hence they will need some investment at the outset to maximise the number of bedrooms. They will get trashed a fair bit, which means the maintenance costs will be higher, but at least your house will enjoy some fantastic parties, albeit you won't get invited to any of them. In extreme cases, there may even be a 'chunder chart' attached to a wall in one of the communal areas, which is quite exciting since you may not have one of these at home.

The students will typically be on a single AST (tenancy agreement), and they'll rent the house for one academic year. This often means no voids, assuming the local rental market supports a full 12-month let for student properties. One of the most significant advantages of student lets is that being on a single AST (usually with their parents as guarantors), they are all jointly and severally liable. So, if one student doesn't pay their rent or the house is damaged (through chundering or some other student-related activity), you can pursue all the others for the costs.

Student lets typically command HMO-sized rents, and the increased maintenance cost is offset by the fact that voids are less, and you have the single AST benefit. You will still have tenant issues to deal with, as well as increased Broken Boiler costs and general maintenance costs.

Rent-to-Rent

This involves renting a suitable property from a landlord for a reduced (Single Let) rent and then renting it out by the room, making a profit from the difference. Let's take an example; Gryff is a landlord who has a Single Let house, which is currently available for rent at £1,000 per month. Sarah, a rent-to-rent specialist, asks Gryff to rent the property to her for three years at £800 per month. During that time, Sarah will not only redecorate the house; she will also deal with any minor repairs.

There will be no need for Gryff to pay a management fee to his letting agent. Also, Gryff won't have the risk of any voids or tenant find fees during that period. These advantages make it palatable for Gryff to accept a lower rent since he will be saving on his outgoings. Sarah then invests some of her own cash in turning the house into an HMO (with Gryff's consent). She can then rent it out room-by-room, which nets her £2,000 per month in rental income. She pays £800 to Gryff, leaving her £1,200 profit, which will also need to cover her set-up costs as well as the management and sourcing of tenants.

Rent-to-rent is an excellent strategy for people who want to be able to leverage property but who don't have the cash to buy property themselves. Sarah has all the challenges of an HMO, plus she has a few further considerations:

1. Because she doesn't own the property, she has no equity gain (this accrues to Gryff as he is still the owner)
2. Sarah is on the hook to Gryff for 3 years' rent even if she gets no tenants in
3. Gryff may want the property back after three years, so Sarah's investment in turning the house into an HMO may only have a short-term benefit
4. Gryff may want Sarah to convert the house back to the way it was before it's returned to him, which will mean additional costs for Sarah
5. Sarah is not liable for the mortgage or major repair costs. Gryff will still have to pay the mortgage and pick up the tab for big bills such as boiler replacement, a new roof, etc.

The profit from R2R is typically somewhere between a Single Let and an HMO, and there is the same level of tenant issues as with an HMO. Sarah would most likely still be on the hook for general maintenance costs but not for more significant repairs.

Serviced Accommodation (SA)

This strategy involves renting properties out on very short-term lets. This could be by the night, like a hotel or bed and breakfast, or it could be for longer periods. It may also include renting to contractors who need to live elsewhere for several weeks or months during a project and who would prefer to rent their own place rather than live out of a hotel.

You can do SA either with properties that you own or on a rent-to-rent basis (see above), where you rent them from a landlord. Since the rent you receive per night is far higher than you would get for an HMO or Single Let, you can make some substantial returns using SA. However, the critical risk factor you'll have to manage is your occupancy rate.

This model is more like a full-time job because you're effectively managing a hotel. Your clients may only stay for one or two nights, and they will expect clean towels and the place to be spotlessly clean. You have to arrange to let them in, have the room cleaned, check any feedback or reviews, and deal with complaints. Get any of these wrong, and you're in trouble; you'll get bad reviews, and this will discourage others from renting. The biggest thing to get right with SA is your systems. You need to be bulletproof when it comes to marketing, cleaning, and arranging access. Marketing is particularly crucial since, unlike a 12-month let where you may market once a year, with SA, you may need ongoing marketing. This not only requires managing, but it also comes at a cost.

Development

Development can mean lots of different things, but let's look at it in its simplest form. You buy a building or a plot of land, and you do it up/convert it/build a house, then sell it and make a lump sum profit. Then you do the same thing again (rinse and repeat).

Development is a fundamentally different strategy to all the others in several ways. Firstly, you have no tenants, so there are no complaints, no rent defaults, no managing agents, and no tenant find fees. If you're a landlord, feel free to take a couple of seconds to pause here. Put the book down, close your eyes, and imagine making money from property without having a single tenant to deal with. They will never call you. Not ever. Bliss.

Ok, you're back in the room. Since you have no tenants, you also have no voids. But if your development overruns, you could still find yourself repaying a loan for longer than expected before you get any income, which is a void of sorts.

You have no Broken Boiler costs. Everything is brand new and under warranty, and it won't be getting used (much) anyway. So, no wear and tear either.

There are no maintenance costs. Everything is new, and no one will live in your new units until after you've sold them.

The other key difference with development is a financial one. You don't have any equity gain like you do when you buy a rental property and hold it for ten years. Instead, you get a cash lump sum when you sell your finished units, usually after 12-18 months. The bulk of your profit comes from the value you have added rather than house price inflation. Unlike equity, you can spend the profit from a development project anywhere (try spending equity in Tesco – they're not that keen).

It's tricky to compare the value of equity gain from an HMO or Single Let (for example) with the profit generated from a development project. As an example, we recently bought a small Industrial Conversion project for £180k that generated £230k profit in 18 months. So, if you did six of those over a 10-year period, you'd make £1.38m in 10 years (if we ignore inflation).

If you used the same initial capital and bought a buy-to-let instead, then you'd spend a fair bit of time at the outset, getting it up and running. But after that, you'd only spend around half an hour or so a week looking after it on average, assuming you used a letting agent to manage it. You'd make £500 per month or so in profit, which equates to £60k over ten years. If we also assume that the property doubled in value over that time, then your total 10-year profit is £180k + £60k = £240k (although the £180k is tied up as equity, and not cash).

So, if we contrast the two strategies, the development route produces around six times the profit although it does take more effort (although if you're doing one project at a time, it's far from being a full-time job).

It certainly puts other career choices into perspective. If you'd like to hear some further perspectives about property strategies, check out this podcast episode:

Season 1; Ep 4

Who is property development good for?

By the end of this book, we hope you'll come to appreciate that part-time property development is a strategy that should appeal to quite a broad range of people. Not least because the scale and type of development you can take on is so varied, but also because you are, for the most part leveraging other people's expertise, not to mention their money (we'll come on to that in a bit).

Let's consider each type of person in turn (hopefully you'll fall into one of these categories):

Newbies

We're not sure this is the most flattering term, but most people know what we mean. A newbie in this context is someone who's new to property. They don't own any rental properties (although they may own their own home), and they don't yet do development. Finally, they don't have a property-related business such as rent-to-rent or serviced accommodation, nor are they involved professionally in the world of property.

Development can work well for newbies for two reasons:

1. You're leveraging the expertise of other people while using your existing skills. Don't underestimate how powerful that is. In most walks of life, you'd usually need to build up a great deal of experience and knowledge to create a six-figure income working part-time. With development, not only can you do it with relatively little technical knowledge, but you also actually get to use some of the core skills you already have. These skills are people, organisational, management and decision-making skills

2. You can use other people's money to develop property; you don't need to have any investment capital of your own (although having a small amount will make obtaining finance a lot easier)

Business Owners

Business Owners really do have a massive advantage when it comes to doing property development, even if their current business has nothing to do with property.

For starters, they usually have the key organisational, management, people, and decision-making skills that developers require; in fact, these are the same skills that every entrepreneur needs. If business owners aren't proactive, their business will ultimately fail, whereas an employee typically gets paid regardless. Plus, they already have an entrepreneurial mindset.

Business owners usually have more flexibility than people in a day job, which is key to be able to set aside enough time not only to get things off the ground but also to be able to deal with urgent issues as and when they arise.

Landlords

Well, this is a bit of a no-brainer if you can remember how Trevor got on in Chapter 2.

Landlords usually have more property knowledge than newbies (even though it may not relate to development). They often have more experience of sourcing (and using) property professionals, so it's easier for them to establish a professional team. The problem landlords have is that most run out of cash with which to buy new rental properties. This is where a development strategy can help in a big way.

Since development sits at the 'opposite' end of the property spectrum to renting, landlords can take advantage of two contrasting yet complementary strategies. They don't have all their eggs in one basket since they'll have income coming in from both rental and development profits. Yet they can use the proceeds of development to buy more rental units. And because development doesn't need to be a full-time job, it's possible for them to accommodate it more readily.

Professionals and Other Property Strategists

Here we would include people who don't own a rental property but who operate a property business using other people's assets. This would include rent-to-rent and serviced accommodation specialists. It would also include property professionals (e.g., estate agents, architects, planning consultants, brokers, lenders, contractors, and the like).

These people are often well placed to get into development as they're likely to have excellent contacts in the industry that they can leverage. They may also have a reasonable understanding of the world of property, even if it's specific to one strategy or discipline.

Who is property development not so good for?

Well, it's not a particularly long list if we're honest, but here goes:

1. People who do not have good people, management, organisational and decision-making skills
2. People who lack humility or who find it difficult to take advice
3. People who are very risk averse
4. People who don't like hard work, are not open-minded and are unwilling to learn
5. People who can't operate outside their comfort zones
6. People who aren't action-takers
7. People looking for a get rich quick solution

So, we've established that property development can be lucrative and lots of people have the skills to do it. So why isn't everyone in the country a property developer?

We're reminded of a story we heard a while ago from a developer called Julian, who gave a talk at his daughter's school. Three of the dads were to tell the class what they did for a living. So, Julian rocked up and dutifully listened at the front of the class while an accountant and a chiropodist talked about their typical day at the office. Next, he did his turn, telling them all about life as a property developer, and then there was a spot of Q&A where the kids could ask questions.

At the end, the teacher was rather abrupt with him. Julian seemed to be suggesting that it was possible for someone to earn a six-figure income working part-time and without a huge amount of technical knowledge or experience. How ridiculous! After all, every teacher knows that to be successful, you've first got to pass lots of exams and then try and land the best 9-5 job you can find...

Still, it goes some way to explaining why they don't teach property development in schools, and therefore perhaps why more people aren't property developers.

What's in a name?

Why is it that if you develop property, you're called a Property Developer, whereas if you own some buy-to-lets, you're not called a Buy-to-letter?

Most other property strategies follow the same trend. Got some HMOs? Well, you're known as someone who's got some HMOs; you wouldn't go up to someone and tell them you're an 'HMOer'. Done some serviced accommodation? You'd be hard pushed to find anyone with 'Serviced Accommodationer' on his or her business card. No, they're simply someone who does serviced accommodation.

So, what makes property development so different? And why do we bother bringing up this trifling point?

One of the key differences lies in what springs to mind when people hear the words' property development'. It's such a generic term that it arguably encompasses every other property strategy there is. Yet we often think of it as being rather grand; lots of big projects and £multi-million deals, that sort of thing. Property developers build housing estates and shopping centres, after all, don't they?

Even if you were doing smaller projects, the fact that you have the job title of 'Property Developer' makes it sound like you have a fair bit of experience, don't you think? After all, who'd describe themselves as a property developer if they've never developed property before?

Our point here is that many people think that property development must be some sort of advanced property strategy.

And that they couldn't think about developing a property without first having built up lots of experience. Conversely, most people can envisage becoming a landlord because they can imagine buying a house and finding a tenant to live there. It's not much of a stretch, imagination-wise, quite often because they may already have purchased a home for themselves, so they imagine it must be a similar process.

The reality is that development is not the advanced strategy that many people think it is. If it weren't possible for new developers to enter the market unless they had experience, property development would be a dying industry. And it isn't. Development is one of the most straightforward property strategies there is because it leverages the expertise of others so effectively. Let us explain why.

Property developers don't build houses.

Now, that may seem an odd thing to say, since if there weren't any property developers, then surely no houses would get built? But what we mean is that developers don't physically build houses. They don't lay a single brick; they don't create the drawings; they don't advise on planning. And very often they don't even manage their projects. In fact, virtually all the work involved in building a house (or converting a commercial or light industrial building) is done by other people. So, while property developers don't do that much (sorry), they are still responsible for houses being built.

So, who are these 'other' people, the people that do all the work?

Well, here is a list of the people that typically get involved in a property development project, whether it's a new build or a conversion:

1. Architect
2. Planning Consultant
3. Mechanical & Electrical Engineer
4. Structural Engineer
5. Residential Estate Agent
6. Commercial Estate Agent
7. Project Manager
8. Cost Consultant
9. Commercial Finance Broker
10. Commercial Lender
11. Private Investor(s)
12. Contractor
13. Interior Designer
14. Solicitor
15. Accountant
16. Tax Advisor
17. Asbestos Advisor
18. Warranty Company
19. Insurer
20. Health & Safety Team
21. Lighting Specialist
22. Landscaping Specialist

and potentially several others, depending on the project.

All these professionals have several things in common (none of which will surprise you):

1. They work for an agreed fee (as opposed to taking a slice of whatever profit the developer makes)
2. They will have appropriate qualifications and many years' experience in their area of expertise
3. They are available to hire by anyone (yes, even first-time developers)

4. They are all appointed either directly or indirectly by the developer to work on a specific project

So, now let's consider an <u>actual</u> first-time developer. We're going to call him Clive (for no particular reason), but if you've not done any development before, you can imagine yourself to be playing the role of Clive.

When we look at Clive, we see someone who's keen as mustard but who doesn't have any track record of property development. So, do you think people in the development business will run a country mile when they see Clive coming, due to his inexperience? Do people feel that Clive's new-build projects are likely to collapse within a few weeks of going up because he hasn't got any track record to speak of?

Well, let's take a look at Clive's property development CV. Who exactly is on Clive's professional team, the people that will be advising Clive and physically doing the building work? Clive's selected one person from each profession on the list above, and each one of them has an average of twenty years' experience in their specialist area. So, the team has a total of 400-odd years' experience in property development covering every major area and specialism in the industry.

Where did Clive find all these people? He discovered them in much the same way he found the architect who designed his home extension a few years ago, by a combination of word-of-mouth recommendation, interviewing and shortlisting.

So, did he have to interview hundreds of people? No. Because once he'd appointed the Project Manager (PM), it was the PM who then recommended an architect with whom they'd worked in the past and who had a good reputation. Then the architect he'd selected recommended a lot of other professionals that they'd worked with who had a good reputation in the trade. Before Clive knew it, he had a team of people all keen to work on his project, many of whom had worked together on other projects.

Clive recognised he'd no direct experience of overseeing a development project, and that was why he decided to hire a PM to manage the project for him. A PM makes sure the professionals work together on the project and that the project gets completed. Clive would have regular calls with the PM, but it was the PM that did most of the work on the ground. They would coordinate with the professional team and make sure that any issues got resolved. Of course, Clive had to make some decisions since he was still in charge. But he would usually make these decisions armed with guidance and advice from his professional team.

So now Clive's CV isn't looking too shabby. Would people think that Clive and his team could build a house? Well, between them, they've helped build hundreds if not thousands of houses, so the answer is a pretty resounding 'yes'.

Becoming a property CEO

But what about Clive himself, the hero of our story? Well, he doesn't seem to be pulling his weight if we're completely honest. Yes, he's put together a team of professionals, and yes, he's managed to find a project for them to build. But it's his team that's doing pretty much everything else, all the heavy lifting. The lazy so-and-so's even hired a Project Manager, so he doesn't have to manage things himself.

So what skills has Clive had to utilise to pull this off, bearing in mind his property development experience is more or less zero at this point?

There are four skills that he's had to use, and these are:

People skills – he's had to go and talk to a range of professionals to shortlist and then appoint them. He will also need to be in touch with several of them during the project's build phase and will need to both communicate with them and maintain each relationship.

Management skills – he's had to be able to give his professional team some form of instructions and manage the business plan for the project.

Organisational skills – he's had to make sure that he's got the right people in place and that things happen in the correct order without missing out any critical steps.

Decision-making skills – when his professional team asks him to make a decision (usually with their guidance), he has to make it quickly.

The interesting thing about all these skills is that Clive already has them, despite never working in property development before. That's because they're largely generic, and in fact, most people use these skills to some degree or other in their day job, if not in everyday life.

In fact, you could say his role is very much like that of a Chief Executive Officer or CEO. He's got overall responsibility for everything, but other people do the physical work, and he just facilitates that.

Another analogy we like to use to illustrate the point about the skills you need to be a CEO involves cabinet ministers. This is always a good analogy for people who can't get their heads around the fact that you can become a property developer without having bags of experience.

When we have what's known as a cabinet reshuffle, the Prime Minister plays a game of musical chairs with his or her top ministers.

So, yesterday's Defence Minister becomes today's Health Minister, for example.

Ok, so who is now responsible for the Department of Health? Well, that would be Judith, the new Health Minister who only found out she had the job yesterday and has never worked a day in Health in her life.

Why on earth would the PM appoint someone who knows nothing about health to the top health job in the country? They'd have responsibility for running the entire National Health Service, and they'd be accountable on their first day in the post before they've even had any training? It sounds like a recipe for disaster...

Of course, the answer is that Judith wasn't appointed because of her knowledge of the health sector. Her appointment is based purely on her skills as a politician and her experience of running a government department. So, who does know about health if it's not Judith?

Well, she'll have a huge team of civil servants within the Department of Health who'll advise her on how to deal with all issues arising on Health. She'll need to have a general idea of what's going on, but she doesn't need to get involved in the detail, even though she's ultimately responsible for it. They are the specialists, the experts who make the Department of Health work, but Judith is the person who's in charge.

There are many other examples of the CEO model in action, not least (funnily enough) among CEOs. You may have heard of a chap called Adam Crozier, who for us epitomises the concept of the CEO due to his high profile yet very diverse CV.

His CEO timeline started at Saatchi and Saatchi, where he headed up one of the world's leading advertising agencies. Then he became CEO of the Football Association. Next, he was CEO of the Royal Mail.

And finally, he became CEO of ITV, while also doing a spot of director-ing at Camelot, the National Lottery operators.

Did the Board of Directors at the Royal Mail think they needed to pick someone from the world of football to head up their organisation? Was Adam shortlisted along with Alan Shearer, Harry Redknapp, and the chap who used to read out the pools results? The answer, of course, is that they recognised that Adam was simply very good at leading a large organisation. Apparently, they didn't even ask him to take any penalties at the interview.

Looking at it another way, do you think that Adam was worried on the day of the interview that he'd never worked in a sorting office, driven a red van, or owned a black and white cat? Would they be testing his knowledge of postcodes and envelope sizes? Of course not, the role of CEO transcends the industry. He would learn a lot about the organisation once he started the job, but what they wanted was someone with CEO skills, not postman skills.

Richard Branson is another excellent example of a CEO. He's founded and led many diverse businesses, and while he knows something about each of them, the skills he brings to the party involve getting each business started and then overseeing each one well enough to motivate a team of experts to deliver exceptional results.

You get the picture, and hopefully this demonstrates the point. To be a property developer, you don't physically need to know HOW to build a house. But you DO need to know how a house gets built. You then become the person who leverages a team of people who build that house, and you use your personal skills rather than your technical skills to do it.

And as you've probably already worked out, that's why the name of our business is called propertyCEO.

Risk and reward versus professional fees

This CEO concept is all well and good, but Adam Crozier and Richard Branson aren't exactly talentless or inexperienced as CEOs. And as you're reading this, you may not be sitting there waiting for some blue-chip company to call you about a board-level vacancy. In fact, you might be wondering how a completely inexperienced developer can whip up a team of motivated and enthusiastic professionals with decades if not centuries of experience between them, who are all very keen to work for you. How on earth is that going to happen?

The answer is quite simple. There are hundreds of thousands of people out there who make a living from property. And unlike developers, most of them take a professional fee for what they do.

For example, when you speak to an architect and ask him or her to design you a house, they're unlikely to say, 'Sounds great, tell you what; don't pay me anything, we'll just go halves on the profits when you sell it'. Because if they got paid that way, they'd have to do a lot of due diligence both on you and on the project itself to make sure they'll end up getting any money from it at all. Instead, they'll say 'Here is my fee for designing your house'. You'll then thank them, have a bit of a lie-down, and wish you'd paid more attention to the careers officer when he talked about architecting.

All the professionals you'll need to build a house (or to do any type of development) operate on the same basis – they take a fee. This is important because it means that they get paid for what they do irrespective of whether or not you're a complete idiot. Or if you build a house that you can't sell. Plus, the only way they earn any money at all is when a developer asks them to do some work.

So, do you think they'll be keen to work with you, Mr. or Mrs. Developer? You can bet they're going to be very keen indeed.

So, your professionals get a nice juicy fee for doing their bit, but what about you as the developer? What's your slice of the action? Well, you'll end up keeping all the profit. And if you've done your CEO job well, this will be many times the value of the fees received by any one of your team. This is often hundreds of thousands of pounds, and on larger scale projects can sometimes run into millions. Like any CEO, you command the highest income, but your success depends on how well the team beneath you perform. And of course, by any other factors that might crop up unexpectedly and reduce your profits. Similarly, if you get it wrong (or if your team gets it wrong), you can find yourself making less profit, or worse still making a loss.

In summary, your team gets paid regardless of whether the project is profitable because they're taking no risk. Whereas you get paid a lot more because you're making the project happen and you're also taking all the financial risk yourself.

We'll spend some time a bit later talking about risk and how you manage it, but for now, we wanted to get you comfortable with some fundamental principles:

To be a property developer, you don't need to have technical property expertise or experience. You just need to be able to appoint and manage people who do plus you need to understand the end-to-end process at a suitable level;

The skills you need to do this are skills you already have; and

A property developer gets the lion's share of the reward because, unlike their professional team, they take the risk for the project's financial success instead of taking a fee.

If you're still struggling to imagine yourself as a potential developer, imagine instead that you'd decided to build an extension on your house. How would you go about it? Well, assuming you weren't the

DIY type, you'd go out and find yourself a decent architect and builder based on the recommendations of others. Then you or they would need to hire in a few more professionals during the project to complete the job. You might get a curtain company in to sort the curtains and a flooring company to do the carpets. And let's assume you needed to borrow some money to pay for the work. This would mean either going to the bank to agree the loan and sign all the paperwork or having a chat with a family member who may be happy to lend you the money.

Is this something you could imagine doing? If so, you'll appreciate that it's precisely the same process as being a property developer. The extension wouldn't get built at all unless you organised it. Yet all you did was appoint the team, arranged the finance, and it was then the team who did the physical work. With a development, the scale and risk will be bigger than building an extension, and of course, you may well be selling the end result. But the principle is very similar. In fact, although a development project will involve more professionals, you'll also have a Project Manager to oversee everything. With the extension, you'd probably have been managing the project on your own.

Let's now take a look at how the propertyCEO system works to leverage all of these things and create new property developers.

4. The propertyCEO System

Why you need a system

We mentioned earlier that during his circa 40 years in property, Ritchie developed a system for training new developers. It was quite a simple system, and like all simple ideas, it just worked.

He discovered that most would-be developers worried about having no experience in a field where they'd assumed they'd need lots of expertise. In fact, this was often enough to make them decide to go and do something else instead. Not only were they worried about whether they'd be able to deal with any curveballs that might come up, but they also felt that people wouldn't take them seriously because they didn't have any credibility. So he would sit them down, offer them a chocolate biscuit (he has a secret stash despite what he tells his business partner), and put them straight on a few things.

Firstly, he told them you need to recognise that you need to work with about twenty professionals (and their teams) to build a house. And you can go out and get them on your team within a matter of weeks. In fact, you can do this even if you don't yet know who any of them are. Each one of them will have at least a decade's experience, and they will each have contributed to over a hundred new developments. So, in a very short time, you could have a team at your disposal that has two centuries' development experience and has built two thousand projects. So, the first question is, do you think that this team could deliver a project for you? The newbie developers would consider this, watch Ritchie eat another biscuit, and then agree that absolutely, a team with that amount of experience could pretty much build whatever it liked.

So, where should you go about finding this team? Well, the next part of the system involves finding what's known as a Non-Executive Advisor or NEA. This is going to be a very special person in your business, someone who has been working in property for some time and who has both a track record and credibility. This person is going to act as your mentor and guide — someone who you can turn to when you need guidance. Someone who is happy to be associated with you and your business and so will add to your credibility.

At this point, two questions inevitably come up. The first is; an NEA sounds great, but where can I find this magical person? Let's tackle that one first.

Your Non-Executive Advisor

So who exactly will this person be? Well, it's going to be someone with experience. What you're looking for is a developer (possibly one who's retired or semi-retired), an established property professional, e.g., an architect, financier or contractor, or even an experienced self-builder. You want someone who has a reasonable depth of experience in property development even if it's in one specific area, and you want someone who has contacts that they can share with you. You don't need them to be well known in the property world, but they need to have a CV that convinces you they have experience and a solid track record. If you do your due diligence, then if they can convince you, they'll be convincing to others.

Will you find this person by Googling them? Well, they'll almost certainly have an online presence, but getting their details from an online search isn't going to cut it. You need to get out there and do something called networking.

Good networking is one of the most important aspects of property development. No matter what your personality type, there is a science to it that can make it very straightforward to do. Some people love talking to new people, but most don't. And for those of you for whom the prospect of trying to engage with a roomful of strangers makes walking on hot coals seem appealing, it's actually quite easy to conquer your fears and do a good job of it. Most people are so bad at networking that it's easy to be in the top 5% of networkers in the room, even if you detest doing it.

Now, this isn't a book about networking skills, but it's a great idea to get educated on some decent networking techniques even if you think you're an accomplished networker. We cover networking on our courses, but we also have a podcast episode dedicated to it.

Season 1; Ep 2

The second question that arises is usually, "why would this person want to work with me?" The answer is very simple – you'll be giving them part of the profits from your first deal.

It's up to you how much of your profit you give away to your NEA, and you need to bear in mind the following:

1. You want them to have skin in the game. If things get complicated or worse still, they go pear-shaped, and you need them to devote some time to helping you, then they're going to be much more engaged if they have a more substantial upside for helping bring the project to a successful conclusion

2. In many respects, you can view it as a binary decision. Either you let them have a large lump sum at the end for

helping you win and deliver a £200k-profit project, or you don't pay them anything, and the project won't happen

3. Always pay your NEA through a profit share in your first project and not as a fee. That way their income is precisely aligned with yours and will be dependent on the success of the project

4. For subsequent projects, you can always adjust their fee, or you can do without their services altogether. It doesn't have to be a permanent arrangement

Let's look at it from the NEA's perspective. Assuming you've gone about things in the right way (and we can teach you how to do this), then you'll have established a relationship with this person based on mutual respect. In other words, they don't think you're a complete muppet, and they have some confidence that you're a businessperson who's committed and will get results. Under no circumstances have you lied, blagged, talked up, or otherwise misrepresented your own property credentials to them (or to anyone else). Your NEA must be able to see you for what you are before they agree to work with you.

So when you offer them some of the profits from your first deal, this could be a five-figure or even six-figure sum. Not chump change for most people. But the best part for them is that it's likely to be the easiest five or six-figure sum they've ever earned. So what exactly will they be doing? As your NEA, you need them to:

1. Be associated with you and your brand, although not from a legal perspective. They will not be a director or non-executive director (NED), as this carries specific legal responsibilities. They will merely be an advisor. So no risk or liability for your NEA

2. Answer questions and give support to you when required. This should be straightforward for them since they're giving you the benefit of their experience and knowledge
3. Attend the occasional meeting with you, for example when wooing new investors or meeting planners
4. Recommend good professionals with whom they've worked in the past

You can see that this might be quite attractive to them. Most people enjoy passing on the fruits of their experience to others. And aside from giving you some of their time, there's no actual cost to your NEA in being associated with you or introducing you to his or her network of professionals. And there's no risk for them either, other than a mild reputational one if you turn out to be a complete clown. Plus, YOU will be doing all the heavy lifting and the running around – they don't have to do that much at all.

In return, your business gets instant credibility; anyone checking out your website will be able to see your NEA's CV alongside yours. You'll be able to get them to join you at key meetings if you need support, and they're available to you should you need help on any issues as a project progresses.

And you can access their little black book of contacts. You can get a warm introduction to the professionals that they know to have a good track record. In our experience, what often happens is that the NEA introduces one or two key contacts, and then the rest happens organically. For example, your NEA might introduce you to an architect, and then the architect may give you a recommendation for a planning consultant and a project manager. Next thing you know, the architect is telling you about a very talented designer whom she'd be happy to introduce you to. And before you know it, you have a team. None of them knew you before, but they all know someone who knows you – there's a connection. What's more, many of them will have worked together, and if they've recommended each other, then they're quite likely to get on well.

At this point in the conversation, the newbie developer may ask Ritchie about what happens when something terrible happens. Do all these professionals start looking to the developer for solutions as soon as the going gets tough? This is another area where being a developer is like being a cabinet minister. Like the minister, the developer is at best likely to be able to give a common-sense response to any problem that comes up. But he or she will be reliant on their professional team to make recommendations since the team has a much greater level of understanding and expertise. This is exactly the same as when ministers get advised by their civil servants and industry experts.

The critical thing to appreciate is that, like the minister, the developer needs to make the ultimate decision. But their team will be able to give them enough advice, guidance, and information to make it at least a straightforward choice, even if there's not a right or wrong answer. Will this always be easy? No. Will there be a risk that you could make a wrong decision? Absolutely. Will a bad decision cost you the shirt from your back? Not usually, no, but it may well harm the profitability of your project.

And that's why the developer gets the lion's share of the profits. The buck stops with them, and unlike everyone else on the team, they only get paid when there's a profit. But they will make a decision armed with the recommendations of a team of experienced professionals who are experts at what they do.

Usually, it will take around half a pack of biscuits for the penny to drop with the developer, but it always drops in the end.

OK. We're sixty-odd pages into the book, and you've not seen hide nor hair of an Industrial Conversion. So let's change all that right now.

How much competition is there for Industrial Conversions?

In late 2018, a lady called Sam (who was a student of ours) set out with some excitement to look at a property she'd seen in an auction catalogue. It was a lovely autumn day, and the sun was shining as she sped along the A303 in Wiltshire, thinking about the task in hand and wondering where all the Little Chefs had gone.

As with all property auctions, the auction house had issued a prospectus several weeks in advance detailing the lots for sale. Sam was already on the mailing list, and when she spotted a run-down light industrial building, she immediately saw the potential. The question was, how many others would see it too?

The development opportunity was not what you'd call a looker. It was a small, bluff, and decrepit, light industrial storage unit on the outskirts of a residential area, in a medium-sized town in Somerset. It had been rented to a local builder, and the owner, looking to realise as much cash as he could from the site, had thought to himself that the only way someone could maximise the value of the plot would be to knock the thing down and start again.

So he did what a lot of people in that situation would have done. He got his local architect to knock up a design for two 3-bed semis that would replace the existing structure. And then he applied for Full Planning Permission before putting it in to the auction.

Now, in theory, this would seem a very reasonable approach, but as with so many things, theory only gets you so far. In fact, there was a significant problem - the numbers didn't add up. Sam ran her own numbers and realised that the net profit, having knocked down the existing building and put up two new semi-detached houses, would be minus £35k – not the most appealing prospect.

But Sam's training and experience had taught her that there was more than one way to skin this particular cat. That converting the building would be not only far easier, but it would also make a far greater return than knocking it down and starting again. Using the knowledge she'd gained from propertyCEO, she put together a high-level conversion floorplan and was able to get at least five flats out of it, possibly even six. Working the numbers again revealed that a five flat plan would produce a profit of £180k while the six-flat option generated a profit of £240k.

Just a small matter of £275k more than building the two 3-bed semis...

Fast forward to the auction room. This was a decent sized auction that took place every other month and covered two counties. The catchment area was well over 2 million people in total, so as you'd expect, there was a lot of activity.

Sam's was one of the later lots, and she watched as the earlier ones went through – bidding was brisk on most of the opportunities. The question was: how brisk would it be on hers?

Finally, it was her turn. The lot was announced, and the auctioneer started the bidding low. But no one jumped in. The auctioneer dropped it down a notch, which prompted one bidder to take action. Sam quickly countered, and the battle was on! What became clear was that there was only one other person interested in buying the property, but he seemed pretty keen.

Eventually, the bidding reached the limit that Sam had set herself, and the other bidder showed no sign of slowing down. Reluctantly she called it a day. But what had she learned? That, in a busy auction with a catchment area of over 2 million people, with hundreds of active bidders in the room, everyone had worked out that there was no money to be made from building the new houses. So no real surprises there. But only two people had seen the opportunity to convert the ugly little industrial building into flats.

A few days later, Sam followed up with the auctioneer to see what she could find out about the successful bidder's plans for the property. Was he going to convert it? Did he have exactly the same strategy in mind as she did? It turned out he was a local builder looking for a 'hospital project'* having recently lost a contract. He was still going to build the two semi-detached houses, as he wanted to keep his workforce employed to stop them from going to work for his competitors. This told Sam two things. Firstly, there wasn't much she could have done to outbid a builder who was happy to take on a project without making a profit. And secondly, she had been the only person in the auction house's entire catchment area to see the opportunity to convert the building into flats.

Sam's story highlights one of the most exciting aspects of Industrial Conversions, namely a distinct lack of competition. So why might that be?

Well, the most obvious reason is that industrial buildings don't look residential. You don't immediately look at one and think, 'Wow, that would make a lovely suite of apartments'. In fact, most people don't usually get beyond the idea of knocking it down and starting again. Which in many cases, for small compact sites in residential areas, can be quite a challenging prospect.

*Building contractors will sometimes take on a low-profit 'hospital' job to keep their workforce employed when they've run out of work. If they don't, their best people will go and work elsewhere, and it may be difficult or impossible for the builder to get them back when their next project starts.

Far easier to convert, say, an office building where it's much easier to visualise flats instead of offices. So most developers don't give industrial buildings a second glance and head off to look at offices and shops instead.

Which for Sam and anyone else who knows how to convert industrial buildings, is very good news indeed.

5. Deal Analysis and Due Diligence

So what exactly is deal analysis?

While we did promise earlier not to give you chapter and verse on how to analyse deals, the area is of such critical importance that we couldn't help devoting a quick chapter to it. But no verse, we promise.

It's part of your due diligence, the investigation and calculations that you do to determine whether a deal stacks up and whether you should bid for it, and if so, at what price. It's not a single piece of paper, nor is it a single calculation. It usually takes the form of several Excel worksheets that roll up into an executive summary, and it covers EVERY relevant aspect of a deal that you need in order to decide whether it stacks up.

In this chapter, we wanted to share with you a few of our dos, don'ts, and golden rules when it comes to analysing deals. So here goes...

The golden rules

Deal analysis MUST follow a system

Imagine cooking a recipe with a hundred ingredients that you were serving to someone important. What are the chances that you'd try and remember them all, together with their quantities and method, rather than refer to the recipe? Zero. Why? Because you know you wouldn't get it right – you'd always miss at least one or two out.

There are many parts to a development project, and if you forget to include one, it can be costly. What you don't want to do is to try and remember what to include. Instead, you need a systemised deal analysis process that covers every relevant element.

Time is of the essence

Deals don't hang around; you need to move with speed but never at the expense of errors. By having a system, you're quickly able to work out whether a deal stacks up while being confident that you've considered every relevant factor. You want to have a deal analysed in a few hours and not a few days, to a point where you could make an offer.

Computer says... build your own model

We would suggest that while you could use someone else's model as a starting point, you should build your own deal analyser. Why? Well, other people's spreadsheets and tools are not guaranteed to be error-free. Plus, you may find yourself knowing that you need to put a specific figure in a particular cell, but you don't know why or what happens as a result. You need to understand how your spreadsheet works and that any errors in it can only be yours and not someone else's.

Keep it clean

Some people tend to be rather messy when it comes to spreadsheets and reports. They may have all the right numbers in the right places. And while THEY may know how to decipher the output, woe betides anyone else who tries to make sense of it.

Take the time to structure your analysers in a user-friendly way. Include a page of notes that explains what each calculation does. Imagine that you were going to sell the workbook or give it to a colleague. It would have to be easy to use, obvious where everything goes and what data needs collecting. Plus, when you print it out, it would look comprehensive but clear (and easy on the eye) to whoever is reading it. That's how you should build yours.

Why bother? Three key reasons:

1. Your memory is not infallible, and if you have to revisit the analyser months from now, will you remember what went where?
2. Someone on your team may need to understand how to use the spreadsheet to create, amend or understand what you've done
3. The selected outputs from your deal analyser are a fantastic way to present deals to brokers and commercial/private investors. And this is the last place you want to look like you have a shambolic approach to deal analysis

Evolution is critical

So, is your deal analyser a set and forget? No chance. Your deal analyser is a living, breathing beast that grows with every deal that you analyse. Never get the deal to fit the analyser; always get the analyser to fit the deal.

Again, make sure that when you expand your analyser that you pay attention to the content and output. How easy will it be for someone revisiting the spreadsheet in a year to see what you did?

Also, make sure that you maintain good version control by putting version numbers and dates on each evolution as you update it.

Detail is essential

The detail is where the devil lives, so you need to be able to see him. Never try and build a one-page summary of a deal directly. It should always manifest as a result of the more detailed calculations that are occurring under the bonnet in other parts of the spreadsheet. In other words, let the detail drive the summary; don't try and build a summary from scratch.

You can't outsource deal analysis

Deal analysis is not something you can or should ever outsource to anyone else. Rubbish with spreadsheets? Tough luck – get good at them (you don't need to be a technical whiz). Find numbers confusing? Hard cheese – get to grips with them (the maths is not complicated). Tough love? You bet. Because only YOU can be responsible for doing a deal. You shouldn't delegate that role to anyone else no matter how great they may be at numbers or spreadsheets. By all means, have someone check things over for you, but they're YOUR numbers, and the buck stops with you.

Best guesses are still guessing

A common error we see in deal analysis is where people don't check their numbers. At the end of the day, you need facts or as close to them as you can get. Don't get lazy and stick in ball-park figures or assumptions. Take the trouble to firm them up, particularly as you head toward an offer stage. The fewer question marks you have, the less risk you'll have, and the more profitable you'll be.

We had a situation recently where a mentee had decided to assume the cost per square metre rate from their most recent project. A reasonable assumption? As it turned out, no, it wasn't. Not only was their contractor not available, but the market had also moved in the previous 12 months resulting in a material increase in labour costs. A quick phone call was all it took to find this out. Luckily, they didn't get as far as making an offer before making that call.

Reasonableness testing and double-checking

It always pays to double-check your result by working the deal through manually. Once your deal analyser has given you a result, take a separate piece of paper and work out the numbers manually (rounding as necessary) to make sure the result you're getting from the deal analyser looks reasonable. If you get a materially different number, you'll want to go through your numbers again to find out why.

One of the challenges with a complex model is that we tend to rely on the output. Yet we may have made a silly data entry error somewhere. Doing the exercise longhand, even if you ball-park some of the detail numbers, will allow you to check this. You're not trying to square things to the penny, but it should allow you to spot where there are any discrepancies.

Also, make sure that you have audit checks embedded in your spreadsheet. These will flag where numbers either don't cross-cast or where they're unreasonable.

Finally, it's always helpful to have someone knowledgeable on your team check over the numbers before you make an offer. This will help ensure that you haven't missed or miscalculated anything.

Exercise good version control

You will doubtless end up with several versions of a deal analysis. This will either be because new data requires a new iteration or because you want to compare different what-if scenarios. Make sure that you not only number each version but that you also describe what each represents. There's nothing more frustrating than running many iterations and then losing track of which one is which.

Cashflow is key

Make sure that you have modelled the cash flow of your project on a separate tab to ensure you don't have any shortfall during the project. Many a deal has foundered where the number in the bottom right-hand corner looked great, but there wasn't enough cash available to get there.

Always perform what-if scenarios

Not all your numbers will be glued on. What happens if your Contractor goes bust and their replacement's costs are 10% more? What if your GDVs are affected by a market change that sees them drop by 10%?

You need to run what-if scenarios/sensitivity analyses to see how your numbers look if you encounter a bump in the road. A deal that only stacks up when things turn out perfectly is not a realistic deal. Rest assured, your commercial lenders will be using similar what-if tests to try and break your model. You want to do the same.

Avoid optimism

So, you've finished entering your numbers into the deal analyser, and the computer says 'no'. But hold on a second; it's only a few percentage points off being doable. Maybe you were a bit over cautious? What if you didn't need quite such a big contingency? Or if you could manage to shave another £5 per square foot off the build cost? And who needs tarmac when you can have gravel?

Welcome to the slippery slope that is optimistic assumptions. We can get just about every deal we look at to stack up if we go optimistic on all the assumptions, which should tell you something. Where you have facts, don't try and be optimistic; you'll be basing it on chance. Where you've had to make assumptions because you don't have facts, and you've been prudent, then be sensible. For sure, if every assumption is dialled to maximum prudence, then you'll find that none of your deals stack up. The reality is that some costs will come in higher and others lower, so make sure that you strike a balance.

Only fools fall in love

Never fall in love with a project. The only consideration that determines whether you offer on a deal is the number in the deal analyser. New developers can find themselves prone to wishing a deal would work because they've spent a lot of time on it. They know it would be a fantastic project. As a result, they don rose-tinted spectacles when it comes to their contingency, assumptions, and target margin. That's not relevant. Go with your standard assumptions and let the numbers guide you. Never let your heart rule your head in determining whether to go for a project.

Always target a 20%+ margin

Finally, be aware that your commercial lenders will usually require you to target a margin of at least 20% (on GDV) before they lend. You should always be rejecting deals that do not produce a 20% margin, minimum, in any event. Make it your golden rule. Never be tempted to accept a lower return. A 20% margin gives you a fighting chance of making a small profit even if several things go wrong. More importantly, it means you will be better placed to repay the bank. Working to lower margins gives you far less comfort, and if things go badly wrong, you could make a loss.

While a 20%+ margin doesn't guarantee profitability, it will place you in a much less risky position.

Technical Corner: Contingency

One of the key risks associated with property development is unexpected costs. You can do all the due diligence you like, but when your utility company takes two months to sort out the gas supply or your Contractor discovers some air conditioning plant in the roof void, these costs aren't budgeted for. And the list of possible unexpected costs is virtually endless.

The easiest way to budget for these unexpected costs is to continue to make reasonable but prudent assumptions for the known costs and then add a contingency for unknown costs. How much should this be? In property development, a contingency of between 10%

and 20% of the construction cost is not unreasonable. For Industrial Conversion projects, you can afford to budget a lower contingency than if you were building new since there is less scope for unexpected costs (as you are not going into the ground).

When it comes to analysing deals, contingency is essential. Some people describe it as a buffer, a safety margin that means you've allowed for additional unexpected expenses without impacting your bottom line. We describe it as a cost and not a buffer. Why? Because whilst you don't yet know what the cost will be for, you are 99.9% guaranteed to have at least one unexpected cost hit your project. A buffer sounds like you've built some fat into the deal that you could potentially strip out of you need to make the numbers work. The reality is that you'll almost certainly spend some of it.

So here's one of the Golden Rules of development: ALWAYS allow for a contingency and NEVER think of the contingency as an optional cost that you can strip out if you need to, to make the numbers in your deal analyser work.

6. Sourcing Project Finance and Understanding Risk

Before we cast our fly onto the pool that is Industrial Conversions, let's take a look at the subject of obtaining finance. This applies equally to property development in general.

It's worth us stating here that we cover everything mentioned in this section, in detail, in our training programmes. This includes how to find finance from different sources and how to de-risk the development process as far as possible. In the interest of brevity, our aim in the book is to make you aware of how things work, not to give you a definitive manual. Your professional team (and for this part, your commercial broker and your accountant) will be able to provide you with the advice you need. Not exactly a plug, but we didn't want you getting to the end of the chapter and feeling worried that you don't have enough detail.

We've already mentioned the concept of becoming a property developer without investing your own money. To many, this seems somewhat alien; after all, if you don't have any money, how on earth can you buy or develop property? And since all property developers appear quite wealthy anyway, presumably they always invest their own cash?

This misconception occurs because people tend to view money as an asset and not as a tool. What do we mean by that? Well, you already know (and we suspect it wasn't a complete revelation) that property developers don't actually build houses themselves. They don't know how to lay bricks or do the drawings for Building

Regulations. Instead, they hire people to do this work for them. So, hopefully, no surprises there.

You also need to look at money in precisely the same way. If you can't design a house yourself, you hire an architect. So, if you can't afford to have a house built yourself (or you don't wish to use your own funds), you hire some money.

Ok, you technically borrow the money rather than hire it, but you see the point we're trying to make. You need to think of the money as a tool that you can obtain from a third party that's happy to work on your project. Just as the architect and all the other professionals you'll be using are tools that are happy to work on your project (that didn't sound quite right, but you know what we mean).

Will you have to pay a fee for their services? Absolutely, just as you'll pay a fee for hiring the money. But the money doesn't have to belong to you.

Theoretically, you can build a multimillion-pound development without putting in a single penny of your own funds. That said, many lenders want the developer to have some skin in the game. For example, if you've secured a 30% deposit from private investors in order to buy the asset, you may be required to put in, say, 10% or 20% of that 30% deposit, yourself.

So, if you were buying a building for £200k, the bank might lend you £160k, with £40k coming from private investors. If the lender insisted that the developer put in 10% of the private funding, then you'd have to find £4k yourself.

Some lenders may want the developer to put in 10% of costs or of the asset purchase price – it can vary from lender to lender. Your broker is your friend when it comes to finding the right lender, so make sure you discuss the options with them, based on your personal requirements and circumstances.

Also, be aware that lenders may demand visibility of where your private investment has come from.

Types of finance available

The world of finance can be a little confusing and alien to first-time developers. So, let's have a go at breaking down the concepts and the jargon into something we can all make sense of.

In its simplest terms, there are two elements to the funding that you'll need for any development project:

• Funds to acquire the asset – this is the asset finance, money that you use to buy the building you're going to convert or the land you're going to build on

• Funds to develop the asset – this is the development finance. It's the money that's going to pay for the cost of converting or constructing the building, including your professional fees, the build cost, the loan interest, etc.

You'll most likely use a mixture of commercial borrowing (e.g., banks) and private investors (people with cash to invest) to finance your projects. Commercial lenders will typically lend up to 70% of the asset cost and 100% of the development cost. This means that you only need to find around 30% of the asset finance from another source, and then you'll have all the money you need to complete your project. This 30% can either be your own funds or funds from private investors.

A question often pops into first time developer's heads at this point. "Why would a bank lend me such a big proportion of the money I need to do a development project when I haven't done one before?"

It's a fair question, but first, let's look at it another way. Would a bank be happy to lend money to a first-time buyer, i.e., someone who's never bought a house to live in before? Would they consider that their lack of house ownership experience should prevent them from having a mortgage? Not usually; in fact, they'd simply do their due diligence to make sure the monthly repayments can be repaid.

But perhaps development is rather different? Well, let's consider the commercial lender's position, and we'll use an actual example of a project we've recently completed.

Here are the high-level numbers:

Purchase price of host building:	*£175k*
Development costs:	*£336k*
Total costs:	*£511k*
GDV (selling price):	*£715k*
Target profit:	***£204k***

So, that meant we could borrow 70% of the £175k from the bank, which gave us £122k, leaving us to find the remaining £53k from another source (more on that in a moment).

From the bank's point of view, they're always looking to minimise their exposure to risk. So in return for lending 70% of the asset cost, they insist on having what's known as a first charge on that asset. In other words, if we default on the repayments, the bank can step in and take control of the asset and sell it to get back their money. No one else in this scenario can get a first charge, only the bank.

So how do they know they'll get all their money back if that happens? What if the asset has gone down in value since we bought it? Well, they know the asset was worth £175k when we purchased it, yet they only need to get back £122k (the amount we borrowed from them). What are the chances that the property will have lost 30% of its value in 12-24 months? Slim, we'd say, particularly as property values nearly always increase over time. So, for the bank, it's a fairly safe bet; they should get their money back, even if they sold the property at a discount.

What about the development finance? If the banks are so risk-averse, why are they willing to lend us 100% of the development cost? Well, the clue's actually in the question. It's because they're averse to risk that they want to be the sole lender on the development finance. And so they're prepared to lend you all of it.

This may seem odd until you consider how development finance works. Development finance isn't paid to you as a lump sum when you buy the asset. Instead, the bank pays it to you in instalments as you complete each stage of the project. Up to a point, this is good news. After all, what's the point of borrowing all the money and attracting interest but not yet needing to pay anyone? So, your Contractor will do some work/buy some materials, and then he will need to be paid. You'll ask the bank for a drawdown (instalment), and they'll send a surveyor round to make sure that your Contractor has done the work you say he has.

In simplistic terms, when your Contractor says that he's ordered five bathrooms, the surveyor can see that five bathrooms have arrived on-site and are now in the process of being fitted. When the surveyor is happy, he tells the bank, who then releases the drawdown, and you can then pay your Contractor. The process is then repeated as each part of the project gets completed.

You can see how the bank would be keen to have complete control over this process since it has you by the short and curlies. If you haven't done the work, then you don't get the money. But if you had a second bank involved that was lending you part of the development finance, the first bank isn't in complete control. Hence the bank prefers to be the only lender of the development finance and is quite happy to lend you it all.

The bank doesn't mind if you want to contribute to the development funding yourself. You may have cash available at a cheaper rate that you wish to use. But the bank's development drawdown will only begin once you've spent your own development funds.

So now we can see that the bank's position is very well protected. They're only releasing a small part of the development loan at a time and only after they've made sure work has been done. If the surveyor goes on-site and finds that nothing's happened, there are no bathrooms and not a JCB in sight; then, they won't release a brass farthing.

But what about the bank's security on this development finance? They may have a first charge on the asset loan, but what charge do they have over the development loan? Well, as the project progresses, so its value increases. As your Contractor starts building walls and moving the project forward, so there is less cost to be expended until the project is complete. This means that the value of the asset that the bank has a first charge on has gone up, from £175k (in our example) to an amount somewhere between £175k and £705k (the value of the flats once they're finished).

So if we defaulted, the bank would need to pay our professional team (or another team) to complete the work and then sell the flats. They'll then get back £705k with which to repay the amount we borrowed which was £458k (the £122k + £336k). As a result, they don't need a further charge in respect of the development finance because the first charge they have is enough.

If you fancy a bit more info on the finance side of things (it's many people's number one concern) then check out this podcast episode:

Your credibility

The bank will also want to make sure that the people responsible for the development are up to the task. Aha, you say; that's when they find out you've never done this before, and so they slam down the shutters. Not quite. If that were the case, there'd be no new property developers ever. In which case, when all the old developers die out, no new houses would ever be built again. So probably not, then.

For commercial lending, there are some similarities with how you might get a mortgage for your home. Most commercial finance is only available through a broker. In any event, we would recommend you use a broker if you're a first-time developer. This will give you access to a broader range of lenders through one source. Better still, your broker is also going to be responsible for fighting your corner with the lenders. As you can imagine, it's great to have someone who's on your side when you're trying to arrange project finance for the first time (or any time, for that matter). They can guide you through the process and the jargon.

The second area where there's a similarity to house buying is that the bank will want to check out your credentials, as they would when you buy your own a home. But instead of testing just your earnings and disposable income, they'll also test the numbers behind your project. Will it make the returns that you say it will? What if costs were to increase? Are you paying too much for the asset? How realistic are your selling prices?

They'll also check your personal credibility. But there's something we should now introduce you to which has a bearing on both risk and finance, and it has the exotic title of "Special Purpose Vehicle". Let's first tell you about this before we circle back to credibility.

Special Purpose Vehicles (SPV)

You have to admit, special purpose vehicles do sound quite exciting, particularly if you're a petrol-head. Could it be a distant relative of an All-Terrain Vehicle? Or what about a Sports Utility Vehicle but well, a bit more 'special'? Bigger wheels, perhaps?

Unfortunately, Jeremy, an SPV is none of these things. Instead, it's a company that's formed with the sole purpose of completing your project. Let us explain.

While you personally are a legal entity, you're not the ideal legal entity for a commercial bank to lend money to. Don't take this the wrong way – you're almost certainly a very nice person. But you're a bit too complicated for the bank's liking. The bank has to think of all the things that could go wrong. What happens if you do something unexpected, like die? What if there's more than one developer involved in the project, e.g., a business partner or a joint venture (JV) partner? How does everything get divided up if things go south?

Because a limited company is a legal entity, it's much simpler to start a new one (the "SPV") exclusively for the purposes of this one development project. So instead of lending money to you as an individual (and anyone else involved), they instead lend it to the SPV. You become a director of the SPV, and it's the SPV that purchases the asset. It's also the SPV that employs the professional team and the Contractor, and pays the bills. It's the SPV that owes money to the bank (not you), and it's the SPV that sells the finished units and makes a profit. Once the project is complete, you can wind up the SPV and extract the profit. While it's yourself and any co-directors that are orchestrating all these things as directors of the SPV, it's the SPV itself that is responsible, legally.

Another reason banks like SPVs is because, as a director, you become subject to a set of legal obligations and responsibilities. These require you to always act in the best interests of the company and to ensure appropriate levels of compliance and governance in matters relating to both the company and your own actions. This touches on another subject close to our hearts, which is ensuring people have essential business skills.

Technical Corner: The Training Gap

If you've never been a director of a company before, you will have new legal responsibilities that you'll have to learn and deal with. That said, sometimes you can appoint other people to deal with them on your behalf. But it's not these duties in themselves that cause so many businesses to fail. Instead, it's failing to have a fundamental grasp of what a business is and how it should be run that causes most of the problems.

Part of the problem arises because people don't spot the training gap. They see a goal, and they believe they know how to get there. But they don't appreciate that there's a set of parallel skills they'll need to have as well. Another problem that people often encounter is that their dream isn't based on reality. But it's the reality that impacts their business.

Stella is a case in point. Her passion was baking, and she was very good at it. Her dream was to open her own café and to bake and sell her own cakes on the premises. Nothing fancy, just a local café in her home town. As luck would have it, two weeks after she received a modest inheritance from an elderly relative, the perfect premises came onto the market. Her dream started to take shape. She couldn't believe it – the gods must be smiling down on her, or so she thought. First, the deposit and then the shop! She managed to secure the café and then roped in friends and family to transform its tired interior. Her husband helped out too, as did her two teenage daughters; it was a real family affair. Within two months, she was trading and serving what the local paper described as one of the finest cream teas in the county. Within six months, she'd won a certificate from Trip Advisor for her consistently good reviews. Within 18 months she was bankrupt, her café gone along with some of her health, most of her money and all of her dreams.

Stella's problem is by no means unique. If you do an Internet search for how many new businesses fail within the first three years, you'll get lots of different results. These range from the mildly surprising to the frankly astounding. Even if we keep things towards the mildly surprising end of the scale, the volume is significant. So why did all these people fail?

There are two main reasons. The first is that despite what they thought, there was no demand for their product or services. That's not to say they'd invented the world's first chocolate fireguard or motorcycle ashtray. More often, it's because they didn't do the proper market research to determine if their business model would work. In Stella's case, her cakes were better than the competition, so she was able to get great reviews from the people that visited her. The problem was that there were two household name cafés further up the road that were much easier to get to for the local shoppers and office workers. Plus they also offered free parking, whereas Stella didn't. Very few people would bother to walk the extra 5 minutes to get to her café, so that limited her clientele, and the business became unsustainable.

The second reason people fail is that they don't understand how to run a business. Stella was brilliant at baking, but there was no purpose or vision for her business. She had no financial goals. She had no strategy and no understanding of some of the other essential *skills, such as marketing. These are essential if a business like hers is going to succeed. That's the training gap; Stella thought the ingredients of the cake were having a café and being a good baker. Truth is she only had a fraction of the skills needed to make her business successful.*

Well, on that cheery note, where does that leave you if you've not run a business before? The good news is that running a property development business has some distinct advantages over running a café. Providing you do your homework, you know there will be a demand for your product. People need homes to live in, and there are not enough of them. So, building homes is always going to be a relatively safe bet providing you build the right type in the right place at the right price. Not that difficult to achieve with research and a bit of training.

Also, much of the skills gap you're likely to have is filled by your team of professionals and of course, your NEA, who may also be able to act as your mentor and problem-solver. That said, you are still the business architect, entrepreneur, and decision-maker. You still need to have a vision and both financial and strategic goals for your business. And you also need to understand the essence of what makes a company sustainable and successful. In fact, it's so essential, we hard-wire it into our training courses. However, you learn and develop these skills, please ensure it becomes an integral part of your property development training.

SPVs do not need to be limited companies; they can also be limited liability partnerships, trusts, or even charities. But the rationale for their creation is the same even though the tax and/or legal implications may be different.

The accountant, solicitor, and tax advisor on your professional team will provide you with guidance on the most appropriate SPV structure to select. They will also need to consider the structure of your personal affairs, i.e. whether you have any other business interests and directorships, and in particular, whether you have (or should have) a holding company. Don't worry if this is something you know nothing about; your accountant and tax advisor will set you straight.

We have a podcast episode dedicated to business structuring, if the mood takes you:

Season 2; Ep 8

Your commercial lender will usually insist that an SPV is used (i.e. they will not lend to an individual). But what if you've already got a limited company; could you use that instead? No, the lender will insist that it's a new SPV set up specifically for the project. The trouble with existing companies is that they come with all sorts of history that could make things messy and complicated for the bank, whereas a nice, new, fresh, out-of-the-box SPV has no such baggage.

So that's SPVs – now let's return to credibility.

Back to credibility

So, we got as far as the bank stress-testing your business plan for the project. But how does it go about assessing your credibility as a developer? There are several things it has to go on:

1. *Feedback from the broker:* while the broker is fighting your corner, he or she is not about to burn their relationship with a lender by completely misrepresenting you and bigging you

up as the next Barratt Homes when you've yet to do your first development. So the bank will certainly be getting your broker's opinion about the people behind the deal as well as on the deal itself

2. *Your support documentation:* This is where you can stand out by doing a great job with your deal analysis, due diligence, and research. If you've stress-tested the project and done your due diligence to the max, then that will give confidence to the bank. The more detailed and relevant your analysis, the more credibility you'll gain

3. *Your developer CV:* this will include details of your brand, your NEA, and your professional team. It will include case studies of some of the projects they've worked on and their experience. It will also include your own credentials, highlighting your skills and experience that you will be leveraging as a property CEO

4. *Estate agent feedback:* The bank understands that you believe you can sell the flats for £200k each when they're finished. But if you have correspondence from three local estate agents who each say the same thing having visited the site, then that's a big tick in the box

5. *Sold prices:* The bank will also be looking at recently sold prices and may be more inclined to base their valuations of your finished units on these, since it's likely to be more prudent. It can be useful to include some recently sold prices in your own analysis. This is particularly true if you're able to highlight any reasons why your units would be worth more than similar units sold in the last year or so. Similarly, it can pay dividends to point these factors out to the bank's surveyor when he or she initially appraises the site.

The bank will also want to know your personal circumstances, your employment history, and your financial status. While it's the SPV that they'll be lending to, it's you as a director that will be calling the shots, and they'll want to know that you're not a liability. This may sound intrusive, yet it's not dissimilar to the process you'd go through when getting a personal mortgage for your home.

We've mentioned credibility a fair bit, mainly because it's hugely important as a developer, and we cover it in this podcast episode:

Season 3; Ep 3

Personal Guarantees

The bank also has another level of protection that it will almost certainly require of you as a developer. And that is the provision of a Personal Guarantee (a PG). This is where you give an undertaking to the bank that you'll use your own assets to repay the bank if required to do so. Does this mean that your home is on the line? Yes, and any other assets you may have.* If you are working in partnership with others within the SPV, then they, too, will have to give PGs on the same basis.

The bank doesn't have to call on a PG as a last resort. It may well call on it first if it thinks it's easier to get money out of you than trying to get money out of the SPV. And it doesn't have to call on all PGs. If it decides it's easier to get the cash owed from you rather than your fellow co-owners/shareholders, it's able to do that since you are all jointly and severally liable.

Unlike your mortgage company, the lender can't usually come and repossess your home. However, it could technically take you to court to force you to sell your home.

Now, at this point, new developers who've not heard of PGs often start to get a bit sweaty and start envisaging a worst-case scenario. This is a good reaction because it shows they appreciate what's on the line here. But before we start rocking in a corner, let's get some perspective.

Why do banks want you to give a Personal Guarantee? The main reason is to protect them against their own worst-case scenario, which is you hot-footing it to the hills if the going gets tough. Banks are great at lending money but completely rubbish at property development. They have no ambition to pick up the pieces after you've decided you're out of your depth and want to hand back the keys. So the easiest way for them to make sure you push through every challenge without giving up is to have a nuclear deterrent at their disposal. Basically, the PG is there to deter you from doing a runner.

It's not commonplace for banks to call on a PG. However, the best way of avoiding them is good communication and a proactive approach to problem-solving. Commercial lenders are not naïve enough to think that developments always go smoothly. So, when you encounter bumps in the road, they'll want you to be up-front about telling them and proactive about taking remedial action. It's when you keep problems a secret or bury your head in the sand that they start to have concerns.

Another thing to bear in mind here is that the lenders will insist on a minimum developer margin of 20% (or possibly more) for the project before they'll lend on it. This means there is already a 20% buffer in place before you reach a loss-making position. The chances of you getting things that wrong (or circumstances changing that dramatically) while not impossible, are still slim.

Expect to be asked to sign a PG when securing finance. It's a case of getting comfortable with the level of risk and understanding what's expected of you and your fellow directors. It's an integral part of being a property developer.

While it's important to get a perspective on PGs, it's critical that you talk the PG document through with your solicitor. Once the bank has sent you their draft wording, make sure your solicitor is in the loop (in fact the lender will insist you have a solicitor advise you). You need to know what you're signing up to.

It's also advisable to discuss the loan agreement itself with your solicitor as well.

De-risking by the bank

You can see how the bank has almost entirely de-risked the project as far as they're concerned. It's difficult to see a scenario where they won't get their money back. That said, the last thing the bank wants to do is to have to take control of the site or pursue people for payments. That's nothing but hassle and cost for them. At the end of the day, you're the one taking the risk, and you're getting paid handsomely for the privilege. The downside is that you're putting your personal finances on the line. Yet the scope for that to be an issue is minimised if you're educated and diligent in your approach.

Returning to the original question, why would the banks lend to a first-time developer, you can now see it makes sense for them to do so. They charge fees and interest on the loans, which generate a healthy profit for them. Not only have they de-risked their position, but they also recognise that after you've done your first successful development, you'll most likely do another. Consequently, they have a view to creating a long-term relationship from the outset.

Private Investors

It seems like quite a while ago now, but at the start of this chapter, we talked about the bank lending 70% of the asset finance. That means you need to find the rest from elsewhere. In the case of our example, it meant we had to find £53k from somewhere other than the bank.

The easiest way to fund this amount is to do it yourself. You should be on good terms with the lender, plus they also happen to know the project inside out! Now you may not want to do this for any number of reasons, not least because you don't happen to have that kind of money just lying around.

Why would anyone want to lend you money at all come to think of it? After all, the bank has got first charge on the asset, so it's not as if you can give them the same level of security. You may be able to provide them with a second charge, or a first charge over another asset that you own. But for the most part, these lenders are going to have little or no security.

Well, the reason they'll want to lend you money is that you can afford to pay them around 8-10% interest per annum. And you'll be borrowing their money for around 12-18 months.

There are very few places that can beat that level of return, particularly in the current economic climate. So whether you have one source lending the entire amount, or ten people lending £5k each, there are going to be many people interested in lending you money. The icing on the cake for them is that property is an appreciating asset; it can't lose all its value instantly as stocks and shares can. Plus, there's a bank involved in the deal which will be doing its own due diligence on you. They know that you'll have had to have had a credible project for the bank to lend you money, even if they have no first charge security.

So, where do you go to secure a loan of that size? Well, there are several places to look, so let's run through them now.

Friends and family

It's often surprising who has money within your circle of friends and family. People usually keep very quiet about their net worth and savings. Some just want to avoid setting large Christmas present expectations, but for the majority, their personal wealth is just something they want to keep to themselves. But when word gets around that you're looking to borrow funds at a highly attractive interest rate, that's when people can come out of the woodwork.

For them, there's an added advantage in that they know you, and presumably trust you. Plus, they may genuinely want to help you, albeit the 8-10% interest softens the pain somewhat and rewards any altruism on their part.

The key here is to advertise what you do and what you're offering; get the word out that you're looking for investors and see who responds. Who knows, you may even get bigger Christmas presents from some of them.

Private Investors

These are people with cash who are happy to invest in property developments. Usually High Net Worth individuals, they're attracted by the higher interest rates. They're also likely to want to do their own high-level due diligence on your project before investing. At the £50k level, this would be regarded as a small loan.

Angel Investors

An angel investor is an affluent individual who provides capital for a business start-up. This is usually in exchange for convertible debt (debt that can later be converted into stock) or equity in the business.

Crowdfunding

These are lending platforms that comprise capital obtained from a large number of small lenders. There are several property crowdfunding vehicles available that will lend money to developers.

Pensions

Following changes to UK pension rules, individuals are now able to transfer their existing pensions to a scheme that they themselves administer. They may then invest as they see fit subject to certain rules. There are many individuals who have such pensions but who lack the appetite or skill to create a property development business themselves. But they may be happy to lend some of their pension pot to a developer.

Technical Corner: Pensions

If you have a reasonable-sized pension pot, we would urge you to check out a type of self-administered pension called a SSAS (a small, self-administered scheme). You'll be surprised by not only how flexible it is in terms of what you can invest in, but also how you can avoid your hard-earned pension pot simply reverting to the pension company after you die. Instead, the benefit can be passed on to the next generation. You can even lend money from your SSAS to your business.

If SSASs are new to you and you do have a pension, make a note to do some further SSAS research. If you've no idea how big your pension pot is, ask your pension company for a valuation plus a projection of your income at retirement. Many people are surprised by how much is in their pension pot.

From our own experience, we would recommend speaking to a SSAS specialist when doing your research, as many pension advisors are not that knowledgeable about SSAS.

Joint Venture (JV) Partners

This is an individual who has cash to invest and who wants to get involved in development projects. There are many different scenarios, but a common one is where the JV partner supplies the funds, and you provide the development skills.

A friendly word about JV partnerships

Please be very careful when considering any JV relationship. We hear more tales of woe from JV partnerships that have gone wrong than any other issue. Why is this? The problem usually arises because either the partners didn't know each other well enough or that they didn't bother to find out whether they had the same values and goals. In some cases, the other partner turned out to be a wrong' un.

Think of a JV partnership like you would a marriage. Everything is all sweetness and light during the honeymoon, but somehow over 40% of all marriages end in divorce later down the line. Assume that the same likelihood for downstream incompatibility exists for any prospective JV partnership.

How can you de-risk things so that you can take advantage of a partnership without all the grief of a later 'divorce'? The easiest way is to have a one-off commercial arrangement with them on your first project. This is where you each have your own separate company (and brand) that contributes to that project. That way, you're not in business together directly; you are merely working for two firms/brands that are contributing to the same project. Each of your individual companies will then own 50% of the project company (assuming it's an equal split). It's a lot easier than having to work out who keeps the cat later down the line, if you split up.

Ok, isn't it about time we talked about Industrial Conversions?

We know we've taken a bit of a trip around the houses so far. That's because we felt we needed to set the scene. You can't take on an Industrial Conversion project without understanding the other moving parts and how they all fit together. But you'll be glad to know there's no more mucking about – in fact you're one small page turn away from...

Part II

7. Industrial Conversions

What do we mean by 'converting' an industrial building?

In a nutshell, we mean taking a building that has industrial use and converting it into residential apartments/flats or houses.

In most cases, this will mean:

1. Keeping the basic infrastructure of the existing building
2. Increasing the specification of the walls and roof to meet the standards required for residential use
3. Inserting some more door and window openings as necessary
4. 'Beautifying' the exterior to make it look more attractive as a residential property
5. Creating apartments or flats, rather than houses (although houses are by no means an impossibility)

The 'opposite' of converting is demolition – replacing the existing building with a brand new one. Most people think that the idea of starting with a blank canvas sounds attractive. By the end of this chapter, you'll discover that doing the opposite of what most people think can be a far more profitable route to take.

Understanding the use class system

Let's start by taking a look at the planning 'use class' system in use in England and Wales. We'll start at the bottom and work our way up, so apologies if you already know some of this stuff (although no harm in having a refresher).

Before we kick things off, we need to mention that there were some rather dramatic changes to use classes that took place in September 2020. We'll explain what these were shortly, but as it's recent history, we felt it would be helpful to describe the original use class system first (which was around for many years) and then explain the more recent changes afterward. That way, you'll not only understand the impact of the changes, but it will also give you a reference point should you see mention of an old use class in some pre-2020 planning documentation and wonder why it's not mentioned in Ian and Ritchie's book. Right, here goes:

It's not possible for a building to perform whatever function you want of it. You can't, for example, decide to turn your living room into a grocery store by merely putting in a shopfront, buying a cash register, and taking a few trips down to the cash-and-carry. You would first need to get Full Planning Permission from your local council, and this would involve what's known as a 'change of use'. In this example, you would be proposing to change the use of the building from a dwellinghouse (which has the use class C3) to a shop (which has the use class A1). Here is a list of the planning use classes that existed pre-September 2020 to get your juices flowing;

Part A

Class A1 – Shops
Class A2 – Financial and professional services
Class A3 – Restaurants and Cafés
Class A4 – Drinking establishments
Class A5 – Hot food takeaways

Part B

Class B1 – Business
B1(a) – Offices excluding those in A2 use
B1(b) – Research and development of products or processes
B1(c) – Light industry

Class B2 – General industrial
Class B8 – Storage and distribution

<u>Part C</u>

Class C1 – Hotels
Class C2 – Residential institutions
Class C2A – Secure residential institutions
Class C3 – Dwellinghouses
Class C4 – Small houses in multiple occupation

<u>Part D</u>

Class D1 – Non-residential institutions
Class D2 – Assembly and leisure

<u>Sui Generis</u>

So, those are the use classes. Here are a few thoughts by way of further explanation:

<u>What is Sui Generis?</u>

Not all uses of land or buildings fit within the use classes order listed above. When no use classes order category fits, the use of the land or buildings is described as sui generis, which means 'of its own kind'. The government gives examples of sui generis uses that include: scrap yards, petrol stations, taxi businesses and casinos (this is by no means an exhaustive list).

<u>Mixed Use</u>

Where land or a building has several uses that fall into more than one class, then this is deemed to be 'mixed use', which will usually be considered sui generis. The exception to this is where the building has a primary overall use to which the other uses are ancillary. For example, where a light industrial building has a small office attached, the office would typically be regarded as ancillary to the light industrial building.

Note that Scotland and Northern Ireland each has a separate use class system, which differs to that of England & Wales. To find a list of each, check out the website www.legislation.gov.uk which has details of all UK enacted legislation.

You could also try the following web searches:

1. Scotland: The Town & Country Planning (Use Classes)(Scotland) Order 1997
2. Northern Ireland: The Planning (Use Classes) Order (Northern Ireland) 2015

Use class changes from September 2020

Right, it's now time to tell you about the rather exciting changes to the use class system that occurred back in September 2020.

The government decided that it wanted to make it easier for non-residential buildings to be repurposed. After all, there were lots of empty retail, industrial and commercial units all over the country, and their owners would need Full Planning Permission before they could change, for example, a bank (use class A2) into a shop (use class A1). This Full Planning Permission requirement was something of a barrier, given it introduced cost, delay, and uncertainty for the business looking to do the conversion. So, the government devised a cunning plan to tackle this.

It involved creating a new use class called Class E, which has sometimes been referred to as a 'super-use-class,' given its breadth. In essence, the government changed the use class of a wide range of non-residential buildings and put them all into Class E. Here is what the use class system looks like post-September 2020:

Part A

Class A1 (now Class F2) – Shops less than 280m² mostly selling essential goods, including food and which are at least 1km from another similar shop
Class A1 (now Class E) – Shops, retail warehouses, hairdresser, undertakers, travel and ticket agencies, post offices, pet shops, sandwich bars, showrooms, domestic hire shops, dry cleaners, funeral directors, and internet cafes
Class A2 (now Class E) – Financial services such as banks and building societies, professional services, (other than health and medical services) and including estate and employment agencies
Class A3 (now Class E) – Restaurants and Cafés
Class A4 (now Sui Generis) – Drinking establishments, public houses, wine bars or other drinking establishments (but not night clubs) including drinking establishments with an expanded food provision
Class A5 (now Sui Generis) – Hot food takeaways, for the sale of hot food on or off the premises

Part B

Class B1 – Business
B1(a) (now Class E) – Offices excluding those in A2 use
B1(b) (now Class E) – Research and development of products or processes
B1(c) (now Class E) – Light industrial
Class B2 – General industrial
Class B8 – Storage and distribution

Part C

Class C1 – Hotels, Boarding, Guest Houses, (where no significant element of care is provided) (excluding hostels)

Class C2 – Residential institutions including care homes, hospitals, nursing homes, boarding schools, residential colleges, and training centres

Class C2A – Secure residential institutions including prisons, young offenders' institutions, detention centres, secure training centres, etc.

Class C3 – Dwellinghouses

Class C4 – Small houses in multiple occupation, occupied by between 3 and 6 unrelated individuals as their only or main residence who share basic amenities such as a kitchen or bathroom

Part D

Class D1 (now class E) – Clinics, health centres, creches, day nurseries, day centres

Class D1 (now F1) – Learning/Non-residential institutions including schools, non-residential training centres, museums, public libraries, public halls, exhibition halls, places of worship, law courts

Class D2 (now Sui Generis) – Assembly, Leisure and Sui Generis, including cinemas, concert halls, bingo halls and dance halls

Class D2 (now class E) – Assembly, Leisure and Commercial/Business/Service, including indoor sport or fitness, gyms, indoor recreations not involving motorised vehicles or firearms

Class D2 (now class F2) – Assembly, Leisure and Local Community Uses, including hall or community meeting places, swimming baths, skating rinks, outdoor sports and recreations not involving motorised vehicles or firearms

Sui Generis

For clarity, here are the types of property that now fall within Class E – Commercial/Business/Service:

Shops, retail warehouses, hairdressers, undertakers, travel and ticket agencies, post offices, pet shops, sandwich bars, showrooms, domestic hire shops, dry cleaners, funeral directors, internet cafes
Financial services such as banks and building societies, professional services, (other than health and medical services) and including estate and employment agencies
Restaurants and Cafés
Offices excluding those in A2 use
Research and development of products or processes
Light industrial
Clinics, health centres, creches, day nurseries, day centres
Indoor sport or fitness, gyms, indoor recreations not involving motorised vehicles or firearms

As you can see, there are now a significant number of properties included within Class E. The original use classes ran in parallel with the new Class E from September 2020 to 1st August 2021, after which they were dropped. This was primarily because there was lots of legislation that referenced the old use classes, and it wasn't possible to change this overnight.

As planning news goes, this was something of a bombshell. Suddenly, the scope to repurpose non-residential property became a great deal easier. Fancy turning your shop into a restaurant? You no longer needed Full Planning Permission. You could now change any building in Class E into any other type of building in Class E because you were no longer changing its use class.

The eagle-eyed among you will have spotted that Light Industrial class B1(c) also changed to Class E, which, as we will see later in the book, becomes highly relevant when we're contemplating industrial conversions.

However, as it transpired, that wasn't to be the government's most significant announcement. In December 2020, they announced a further change that had HUGE ramifications for anyone considering converting non-residential properties into residential:

From 1ˢᵗ August 2021, we would be allowed to convert Class E buildings up to 1,500m² to residential under permitted development.

We'll be walking you through all the details in Chapter 11, but for now please just make a mental note that Light Industrial now sits in Class E, and Class E properties up to 1,500m² can be converted to residential using a brand-new PDR, effective from 1ˢᵗ August 2021.

Right, let's get back to where we were, which was telling you about what the planning system is and why it exists.

Planning considerations

The planning approval process is very welcome because it ensures that some very relevant questions are asked before any conversion takes place. What parking provision have you made for the cars that will visit your new shop? What will be the impact on local traffic? How will your neighbours' properties be affected? And will you have any two-for-one offers on those chocolate biscuits that Ritchie really likes? All but one of these issues (and many others) will be considered by the planners in determining whether your application will be approved.

Converting an industrial building to residential use is no different. Here the planners will establish whether there are any material considerations involved. A material consideration is a matter that should be taken into account in deciding a planning application or on an appeal against a planning decision.

Material considerations can include (but are not limited to):

1. Overlooking/loss of privacy
2. Loss of light or overshadowing
3. Parking
4. Highway safety
5. Traffic
6. Noise
7. Impact on listed building and conservation area
8. Layout and density of building
9. Design, appearance, and materials
10. Government policy
11. Disabled persons' access
12. Proposals in the Development Plan
13. Previous planning decisions (including appeal decisions)
14. Nature conservation

Introducing Permitted Development

As you can imagine, this planning approval process requires a reasonable amount of work on the developer's part. It can often also take a fair amount of time. However, the UK government has decided that for certain types of development, the change of use would not need full planning consent. This is because the government realised that there was a shortage of housing stock and a surplus of non-residential buildings that could be converted, and so it was keen to make the process as straightforward as possible.

For this type of development, the government created something called 'Permitted Development Rights' (PDRs). With a PDR, there would be no need to apply to the local authority for permission to carry out the work.

However, for certain types of Permitted Development, the government requires that approval is obtained from the local planning authority prior to the Permitted Development being carried out. This process (known as 'Prior Approval') is not the same as securing Full Planning Permission. The local authority is only able to judge the application against a small number of criteria. Also, in certain instances, their planning department must consider the application within 56 days, and is obliged to respond within that time.

There are several types of scenario where Permitted Development Rights exist, including:

1. Commercial Conversions – converting commercial buildings, e.g., office blocks, etc. to residential use
2. Residential Extensions – extending your home subject to various restrictions on size, etc. This may not require Prior Approval

It is worth noting that up until 30th September 2020, a PDR existed that allowed us to convert a building with a use class B1(c) 'light industrial' (but not B2 'industrial') of up to 500m^2 to residential use. While there was much speculation that the government would extend this right indefinitely (as they had previously done for commercial buildings), late 2020 saw several new PDRs introduced that impacted industrial conversions but did not extend the original PDR. Then, as we mentioned earlier, from August 2021, it again became possible to convert light industrial buildings to residential use under Permitted Development.

We cover the Permitted Development Rights that exist for Industrial Conversions in greater detail in Chapter 11. For now, what's important to know is that the pathway to converting any building is a lot simpler and quicker thanks to Permitted Development Rights. Is it an essential requirement to have a PDR to convert an industrial building? No, but it helps, and we should take advantage of it whenever we can, as we'll discover in Chapter 11.

What do industrial buildings look like?

Ask someone to picture an industrial building, and they'll often think of a factory; lots of smoking chimneys and substantial brick buildings housing all kinds of industrial equipment. While that would definitely fall into the industrial category, the reality is that industrial buildings come in many different shapes and sizes, and they can be used for many different purposes.

In this case, pictures tell a thousand words, so here are some examples of buildings that would fall into the 'industrial' usage classes of B1(c) (now Class E) and B2:

Figure 7.1: Industrial buildings come in many shapes and sizes

What's striking about the pictures is that:

1. There's no consistency – industrial buildings come in all shapes and sizes
2. Many of the buildings are quite small – industrial buildings don't need to be large factories
3. They don't generally have chimneys. Some of course do, but many of these buildings have relatively few distinguishing features – they blend into the background.

A phrase that we use quite often at propertyCEO about Industrial Conversion opportunities is that they 'hide in plain sight'. Unless you live in the middle of nowhere, we guarantee there will be dozens of them within striking distance of where you live. Many of them you may not have even noticed, let alone thought about whether you could convert into residential use.

These buildings will have many different types of use in the light industrial sector; unfortunately, there's no definitive list.

The basic approach to converting a building

To think about converting an industrial building, we should first understand the 'building-within-a-building' principle.

Figure 7.2: The BRE Cardington Research Establishment

Here is a rather extreme example of the principle in action. These huge hangars were built at Cardington in Bedfordshire in 1915 and later housed the massive R101 airships. As you can imagine, they not only had a vast internal area; the base/floor had a massive load-bearing capacity to withstand the weight of the equipment that was being used. So much so that it enabled a brand new seven-storey building to be built directly off the slab. There was no need to dig foundations; the first layer of bricks was laid straight onto the concrete base.

Now we know what you're thinking; this looks like a developer who hasn't really thought through the marketing strategy very well. After all, who on earth would want to live in a house built inside an airship hangar? Mind you; you could always close the doors any time it rained...

This was actually a project that Ritchie worked on. This building plus two others were constructed to test the structural integrity of new building materials and techniques. By building them inside the hangar, they could be erected very quickly (with no foundations to dig or rain to stop play) and in a controlled environment (they could conduct experiments while still being 'inside').

So why is the 'building-within-a-building' principle so important?

Let's scale things down a bit so you can see how the principle applies to Industrial Conversions.

On the following pages you can see some drawings taken from one of our own development projects. It's an old printing works that we converted into five 1-bedroom flats. It had the usual conversion issues that you encounter when converting an industrial building, including:

1. The walls were solid and without insulation so were not suitable for residential accommodation

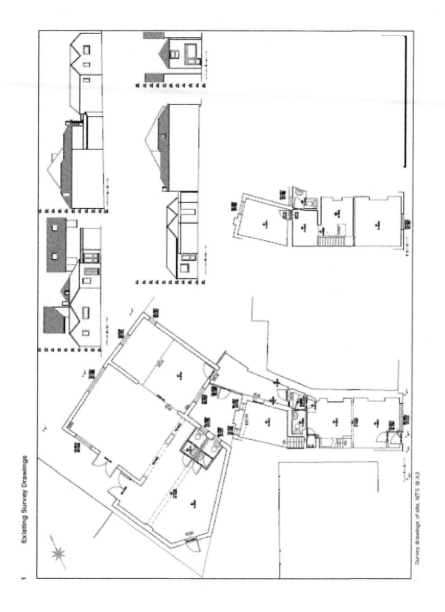

Figure 7.3: Printing Works Conversion – existing layout

Proposed Ground Floor Plan 1:100 @ A3

Figure 7.4: New Residential Ground Floor Flat Layout

Proposed First Floor Plan 1:100 @ A3

Figure 7.5: New Residential First Floor Flat Layout

2. The roof was uninsulated and so was unsuitable for residential accommodation
3. Similarly the floor was also uninsulated

As a result, the architect has tackled these challenges by:

• Building a new insulated wall immediately inside the external wall. This was both easier and cheaper than building a new external wall from scratch since half of the job was already done

• Adding a layer of insulation immediately below the existing roof. Again, this was cheaper than building a new roof from scratch. In the case of this project, we decided to replace the roofing materials as well and to give it a new slate roof

The net result, as you can see from the architect's drawing, is effectively a building within a building. Unlike the airship hangar, this new 'building' fits snugly within the existing one. The new structure abuts the walls and ceiling of the existing building, making maximum use of the available space.

What you end up with is a building that is now entirely up to modern residential specifications, but which has utilised the industrial structure that was already there.

While this building within a building approach allows us to tackle some of the obvious problems with bringing an industrial building up to residential spec, it doesn't solve them all. Later in this book, we'll be showing you some tricks of the trade that allow us to address the other common problems involved in these types of conversion. For now, though, let's look at why Industrial Conversions are such a good idea in the first place.

The significant advantages of Industrial Conversions

Conversion projects always have some distinct advantages over a demolish-and-rebuild approach. Industrial conversions are no exception. We'll cover each of these in more detail later, but for now, it's useful for you to understand the high-level benefits. So here goes:

No demolition costs or problems

An obvious one this, but if you're not knocking anything down, then you won't incur any demolition costs. Interestingly, it's the headaches involved with demolition that can be more painful than the actual costs. Many light industrial units were built to the limit of their plots, which would mean having to gain access to neighbouring properties in order to demolish them. It can often involve closing the road or diverting access during the demolition process, which is not always straightforward and can add a significant layer of cost. So, zero demolition is definitely a good thing.

Working indoors

Bad weather can be a real curse when it comes to development. It's not only the fact that rain can stop play – it can also make it more difficult and time-consuming. Contractors faced with a new build project where they know they'll be digging the footings during the winter won't find it anything like as appealing as the same job over a nice dry summer (clearly the appreciation that English rain-free summers are rarer than hen's teeth is usually ignored in this assessment). But with an Industrial Conversion, almost all the work takes place inside. There are no muddy footings to dig or external walls to build. Most of the work is under cover from day 1, which makes it the ideal winter project from a contractor's point of view.

New-build certainty

As any builder or developer will tell you, most of the problems they encounter on a project are in the ground. What might look like a nice, unassuming building plot can have all manner of nasties lying under the surface waiting to ruin the developer's plans. This can include the discovery of existing service supply pipes and cables, unstable ground, old wells, and the like. With a conversion project, the groundworks required are either zero or minor at worst, so you should have few hidden surprises.

Permitted Development Rights

Light industrial buildings fall under the 'super' use Class E, which means that since 1 August 2021, such units up to 1,500 square metres in size have the benefit of Permitted Development Rights (subject to Prior Approval). Consequently, Full Planning Permission isn't required to convert them into residential buildings. We'll talk about this in more detail a little later, but why is this a big deal? Well, the planning process is one of the more challenging aspects of property development because it introduces two key challenges. Firstly, there is no guarantee that it will be granted. This can mean that at the point the developer acquires the project, he or she runs a risk that the council may decide to reject the application. The second challenge is that the planning process itself can eat up a lot of time, with no guaranteed end-date. With Permitted Development, both challenges largely disappear.

Getting started quickly

Linked to the previous point, if you can make use of PDRs, then since you don't have to wait for Full Planning Permission (albeit you will still need Prior Approval) your Contractor can get started on site relatively quickly. This shortens the length of the project and means that you get your profit more quickly, plus your finance costs are lower.

Design flexibility

One of the significant advantages of industrial buildings is that they tend to contain large open spaces. This means that there are fewer internal walls to demolish, pipes to dismantle, or trunking to rip out. You have a relatively blank canvas from the outset, which is much easier to work with.

Building off the slab

The 'slab' is the floor of the building, and in the case of industrial buildings, this can be a very substantial piece of concrete. The reason is obvious – industrial buildings need to be able to house much heavier items than residential buildings (which only have to accommodate people, furnishings, and appliances). This can include things such as heavy machinery, vehicles, printing presses, and the like. Since the load rating of the slab is far higher than the rating needed for a residential building, there is often no need to rip up the slab and put in new foundations. The new construction can normally be built straight off the existing slab.

Contamination containment

The 'C' word is a common concern with industrial premises for obvious reasons. This can include things such as oil and petrol, and other chemicals that have may have been used, stored, or spilled on site. Much of this contamination, if it exists, will be in the ground, hidden under the slab. But if you're not digging up the slab, then the contamination might be able to stay where it is. It's often only if you remove the slab that you have to deal with the contamination.

It's important to note that should there be any contamination issues after you acquire the site, you will be held responsible as the building's owner. It may have been the previous owner who caused the contamination; however, you now have the responsibility to deal with it. In extreme cases where, for example, contaminants leak into an aquifer and affect the water supply, the costs involved in addressing the problem can be significant. For that reason, we usually advise against developing buildings with obviously high contamination potential e.g., old petrol stations.

Being able to use the existing structure

Since you're starting with a building already, you often don't need to build new outer walls. You may need to upgrade or insulate the existing walls, but that's usually less expensive and time-consuming than building new walls from scratch, depending on the existing construction.

Create more interesting living spaces

One of the benefits of industrial buildings is that they can have some interesting design features that you can incorporate into your finished flats. Examples include vaulted ceilings, exposed brickwork, steelwork, and trusses. These all add unique features that are missing from the usual 'shoebox' small apartment. At best, these features can command a price premium, but as a minimum, they should make units easier to sell.

Less competition

Most developers ignore industrial buildings believing that they can't readily convert them. They imagine they'll encounter all the costs and challenges we've mentioned above, so surely it would be better to find an easier site on which to work? This means there will not only be fewer people wanting to buy the site, but the site also may have been significantly undervalued by its present owners.

So, lots of advantages then, both in terms of the speed and ease of construction. But please don't underestimate the value of having a lack of competition. In fact, let's explore that in a little more detail, as it really is a huge plus.

Creating a competitive edge

Imagine a piece of land that is available for sale on Rightmove. It has Full Planning Permission in place for two 3-bedroom semi-detached houses.

Depending on the experience/boredom threshold of the estate agent, there will either be a single image of a patch of grass or five images of the same piece of grass taken from different angles. There will also be an aerial or plan shot of the plot, with a jaunty red border around it to show you precisely what you're getting. They may even have included an artist's impression of the finished scheme. This image will often contain some unrealistic vegetation, various women holding the hands of small children strolling aimlessly around the property and an expensive-looking car of an undeterminable make parked in the driveway.

The problem with a new build project that's for sale on the open market is that it's quite often a straight shoot out on price. The vendor is going to be looking for the best price, and no one should be under any illusions that there's a different agenda. What if he likes you? Doesn't matter. What if you're a local and your kids go to the same school? No dice. What if he's your brother-in-law? See previous answer.

That, coupled with the fact that every developer in the country can see the opportunity (it's on Rightmove), means that the opportunity is 99% likely to go to the highest credible bidder.

The problem is exacerbated because with new-builds, what you see is pretty much what you get. If there's Full Planning Permission in place for two 3-bed semis, then that's what'll most likely be built. You could have a debate about their ultimate selling price. Or how much they will cost to build. But it's not going to make that much of a difference to what you can afford to pay for them. The only other alternative is to lower your margins, which is a very slippery slope indeed.

Basically, it's a level playing field. The winner will be the person who can afford to build it with the lowest costs or the lowest margin expectations. And that shouldn't be YOU. It follows then that there are two key areas where it's possible to get a competitive advantage when developing property:

1. Find off-market opportunities

How much easier would it be to secure a deal if you were the only one negotiating on it? If it wasn't plastered all over Rightmove with every Tom, Dick, and Harold gawping at it and running their numbers? It's a much better proposition for you as the developer, although it's a lot more challenging to find off-market deals than simply firing up your laptop and going onto a commercial property portal.

2. Find a way to add value that others cannot see

What if you could see a way in which you could squeeze an extra bedroom into each of the units? Or if you could get Full Planning Permission to build another unit in the back garden? Would anyone else have spotted that opportunity? If they haven't, then you can afford to outbid the competition because your profit will be greater than theirs. Wherever you can get an angle that will allow you to add value that other developers may not have seen, that's where you can get a significant advantage.

If we now turn to Industrial Conversions, most people can't see the conversion opportunity at all. The buildings don't look remotely residential. They're nothing like as obvious a prospect as turning an office block into flats. In fact, most people would think the only way to do it would be to start from scratch by demolishing them, which is expensive, time-consuming, and often quite tricky, particularly on smaller city-centre sites.

As a result, you don't see many people marketing industrial buildings as 'conversion opportunities'. It's because it hasn't occurred to them that they are actually convertible. The audience isn't looking at the picture of that old printing works and thinking, "Wow, what a great conversion opportunity...". They're merely thinking, "Oh, what a crappy-looking old printing works..."

Better still, many of these buildings don't go on the market at all, because their owners can't imagine there's much money to be made from selling them. If they knew there was a lucrative opportunity to convert them into flats, they might well be interested in having a conversation with a developer who's knowledgeable about Industrial Conversions (that'll be you, then). And that would probably be a discussion that doesn't involve any other developers.

We hope you can now see the extent of the opportunity. A lack of competition, a marketplace that doesn't know these opportunities exist plus the ability to approach business owners directly. It's a powerful combination, particularly when you consider that only around 1% of eligible buildings are on the market. Or in other words, 99% of your opportunity is out of plain sight.

8. How To Find Opportunities

Different types of industrial conversion

In the previous chapter, we looked at what industrial buildings look like. In this chapter, we want to show you what an Industrial Conversion looks like. Showing you some before and after images is all well and good, but it doesn't convey the scope. What we want you to see is the different types of conversion that are possible.

Figure 8.1: Single-storey conversion

As you'll see from the images in this section, Industrial Conversions come in many different shapes and sizes. Many of these features are interchangeable, so we tend not to try and classify them by type. However, you should get a good idea of what's possible.

1. Standard single-storey residential conversion

Figure 8.1 shows a small (sub-500m^2) building that's been converted into five flats. This is about as straightforward as they come. As the host building was small, internal light wasn't an issue, so the space has been divided up without introducing an internal courtyard (we'll explain more about these later). Some window sizes have been changed to give a more residential look and feel, and the roof covering has been replaced with new slate tiles.

2. Two-storey residential conversion

Figure 8.2: Two-storey conversion

Here we have a two-storey conversion (Figure 8.2). Since many industrial buildings have significant headroom, there's often scope to build more than one floor. This can maximise the use of the available space.

3. Duplex residential conversion

Figure 8.3: Duplex conversion

A duplex apartment is a two-storey flat. Creating duplexes can be useful when you have significant headroom in certain parts of the host building. Instead of creating a second complete storey, you have individual stair access within each apartment. Duplexes can give you a lot of flexibility because the upstairs area doesn't need to mirror the shape or size of the downstairs space. It makes use of the void that exists above each apartment, which in industrial buildings can be quite sizeable. If the second-storey headroom is too low to allow accommodation space, it could still be possible to create storage space which is invaluable in smaller apartments.

Figure 8.3 shows a duplex apartment in a large industrial conversion scheme. One of the key points about duplexing is that the staircases are created within the individual flats. Whilst this takes up internal floorspace, it avoids the need to create communal stairwells and walkways, which can often be beneficial.

4. Conversion with an internal courtyard

Figure 8.4: An internal courtyard scheme

Internal courtyards are a great way of solving the problem of how to get light and access to your apartments (we'll talk more about them later). Since many industrial buildings are built up to the boundary of their plot, it can be challenging to gain access to your proposed flats. You're often forced to use the existing main entrance to get to each unit.

Also, it may not be possible to insert windows on the perimeter wall because it overlooks a neighbouring property. By carving out the centre of the building, units can get both access and light without creating new doors or windows on the perimeter walls. Note how the courtyard scheme in Figure 8.4 is completely inwards facing, including the first floor dormers.

5. Conversion with external walkways

Figure 8.5: Conversion with external walkways

External walkways can provide a novel way of giving access to second storey units.

The image in Figure 8.5 is from one of Ritchie's previous projects. As you can see, an internal courtyard has been created, and an external walkway used to provide access to the upper-level flats. Dormers have been added to create duplexes, and light filters down to the storey below via gaps to the side of the walkway, creating a striking scheme.

6. Conversion to houses

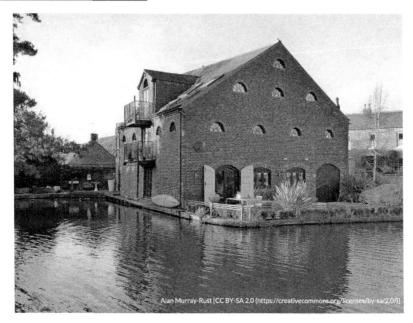

Figure 8.6: A conversion to a residential house

While it's more common to create flats when converting commercial and industrial buildings, it's also possible to develop houses. This can be particularly useful where there isn't as much demand locally for apartments, or if you have some outside space that would provide a garden. Figure 8.6 is a good example of a house conversion, in this case a substantial single unit in an attractive waterside location. Depending on the space available on your site, it would be equally possible to create multiple houses e.g. a pair of semis, a row of town houses, etc.

7. Conversion with dormer extensions

Figure 8.7: Dormer windows on an industrial conversion project

Dormer windows can be a great way of getting light and space into the building, albeit they will need Full Planning Permission (we'll cover this in detail a little later).

Figure 8.7 shows another of Ritchie's projects that incorporated dormers as part of the design. Note how the building still retains its industrial character visually, even to the extent of retaining the old chimney. Attractive planting around the perimeter softens the impact and lends a more residential feel to the exterior.

8. Mixed use or commercial only scheme

Diana Batchelor & Jonathan Smith [CC BY-SA 4.0 (https://creativecommons.org/licenses/by-sa/4.0)]

Figure 8.8: The Metropolitan Wharf building in London

There is no reason why industrial buildings can't be converted into a use class other than residential. Figure 8.8 shows the iconic Metropolitan Wharf building on the north bank of the Thames in London, which has been converted into a mixture of workspaces and luxury loft-style apartments. In locations that are less suited to residential development, it may still be a good location for offices or retail.

9. Pod scheme

Image © Benjamin Benschneider courtesy of ZGF Architects LLP

Figure 8.9: Pod units in a larger converted industrial building

Figure 8.9 shows how a very large industrial building can be converted into pod-style office units. The roof has been opened up while still retaining the cross-members. This allows the central part of the building to be both inside and outside at the same time.

What does a good opportunity look like?

As you can imagine, not every industrial building is ripe for conversion, not by a long way. So, what are the hallmarks of an ideal Industrial Conversion project? What do good buildings have that bad buildings don't? Various factors influence the answer, so let's now look at each of these in turn. We're going to be focusing on the most common type of opportunity, the small-scale flat conversion project.

The question of size

In theory, there's no limit to the size of the unit that can be converted, but we want to zoom in on the sweet spot. In Chapter 7, we mentioned the 500m² threshold of the Permitted Development Rights that existed for Light Industrial buildings before October 2020. This used to be a major consideration, as it made converting larger buildings less attractive, since full planning would be required. But from August 2021, we can now convert light industrial buildings (Class E) up to 1,500m² in size (we'll cover this in greater detail in Chapter 11). It's useful for us, then, to get a perspective on what 1,500m² looks like because it's quite difficult to visualise it when it's just an abstract number. The best way to do this is to consider how many flats you can fit into 1,500m².

The first question then is what size flat are we talking about? There are rules that govern the minimum flat size you can build. Following a regulatory change, all permitted development applications made after 6th April 2021 must comply with National Space Standards (see Technical Corner for details). National Space Standards detail the minimum flat sizes (and certain other parameters) that can be built. These previously did not apply to Permitted Development schemes, but they have now been extended to include them. National Space Standards dictate that the minimum size for a 1-bed flat (with a shower room) is 37m², (or 39m² with a bath) although your local authority may have set this higher – check their website or directly with their Planning Department.

Technical Corner: Apartment Sizes and National Space Standards

As we start this section, it's worth noting that, as a rule, the smaller the flat, the more valuable it is per m². So, if you had 200 m² of floor space to convert, then building 5 x 40m² flats would typically generate a greater GDV than building 4 x 50m² flats or 3 x

$65m^2$ flats. Does this mean it's always more profitable for the developer to develop smaller flats? Not necessarily, as it means the host building is more valuable, so competing developers can also pay more to acquire it.

Until 6 April 2021, National Space Standards didn't apply to Permitted Development Rights, so we could build units smaller than $37m^2$. Realistically, the minimum flat size we would have considered building would be $30m^2$, as this is the minimum size that generally makes a residential property mortgageable. Building units that are smaller than that (e.g., for short-term occupancy, etc.) would have technically been allowable, but then your buyer(s) may not have been able to get a mortgage on them from a high street lender, which would severely limit your market. More importantly, as one falls below $30m^2$, the space starts to become uncomfortably small as a home. The government elected to make National Space Standards applicable to PDR schemes due to unscrupulous developers taking advantage of the absence of Space Standards on historic PDR schemes. They built cramped, low-quality 'rabbit hutches' well below $30m^2$ to maximise their profits (in some cases an unbelievable $16m^2$ with no windows).

Fortunately, the application of National Space Standards now prevents this. Is this good news all round? In the main, yes, however, one side-effect is that units that sit between $30m^2$ and $37m^2$ can now no longer be built under PDRs. These flats are more affordable than their space standard-meeting $37m^2+$ counterparts, yet are far from being 'rabbit hutches' and so would allow more people to get on the housing ladder in decent-sized accommodation. Does it penalise developers who would otherwise have built these smaller units? No, because it's a level playing field, and all developers must play to the same rules, so there's no advantage. It does mean that developers won't be able to pay quite as much for a building to convert since they won't be able to *create quite as many units. So, the value of the host building becomes cheaper (bad news for the building's seller), and the number of more affordable flats will be reduced (bad news for young people looking to buy their first flat), but neither of these directly affects the developer.*

One frustration of the political storm that forced the government to adopt National Space Standards for PDR schemes was an apparent assumption that any flat less than 37m² must automatically be unsuitable for habitation and therefore shouldn't be built. Anyone who has ever visited a 30m² apartment would understand that this is far from the case. The changes have done a great job of ensuring that tiny flats with no windows can no longer be built, but they've also meant that smaller, entry-level apartments can't be created either, and this pushes up the cost of getting on the housing ladder.

So, if we're looking at building 37m² flats, the next assumption we have to make is about communal spaces. The nature of flats means that there will need to be some shared areas, which will include walkways, bin storage areas, cycle storage areas, and so on. While the volume of communal space will vary by project, it would be prudent to assume that 20% of the building will comprise communal space.

So, if we take a 1,500m² building, then 20% of the space will be communal, which leaves us 1,200m² to convert into flats.

If we were building 37m² flats, then we would be able to create 32 units with 16m² to spare. There are a few variables here; you could build larger 1-bed flats or indeed 2-bed flats. You could build duplex apartments, or you may need larger communal areas, and so on. For now, though, let's stick with these 1-bed flat numbers and see what they look like in financial terms.

The GDV of each flat (its retail price) will vary around the country. According to the government's 2018 House Price Index statistics, the average apartment price in England is £230k. This figure will include studios, 2 and 3-bed flats and maisonettes, as well as 1-beds. It will also include more expensive areas like London. In general, most Industrial Conversion apartments will tend to sit towards the lower end of the market. This is because the types of neighbourhood in which their host buildings sit are unlikely to be on Millionaire's Row. So, with that in mind, let's go with a 37m² 1-bed flat GDV of £150,000. You'll get variations to that figure project by project, but for now, we'll use it as an example.

So, if you've got 32 x 1-bed flats at 37m² selling at £150k apiece, then your total GDV will be £4.8m

The next step then is to work out what sort of return you'd be likely to make on that sort of project. Using some very broad-brush calculations, you'd expect your profit margin to be somewhere between 20% and 25% of the GDV (although larger returns are certainly possible). Industrial conversions typically have a better return than new-build projects because both the development costs and site acquisition costs tend to be lower.

So, if we look at 32 x 37m² flats, a 20% margin would make the developer a profit of £960k, while a 25% margin would return £1.2m.

Now, we're not for one moment suggesting that taking on a 32-unit scheme is an ideal first-time development. But, using these numbers as benchmarks, we can then scale them to fit smaller projects. At 250m², a host industrial building will only produce 5 units and return the developer between £150k and £188k, and so on. A 1,000m² host building would deliver 21 units and return a profit of between £630k and £788k.

Hopefully this calculation of what can be created with a 1,500m^2 host building gives you a broad rule-of-thumb calculation that will enable you to work out approximately how many flats (and profit) you can get out of any given project. The formula is effectively:

A) Total Area in m^2 multiplied by 80%

B) Divide A) by average flat size e.g. 37m^2

C) Multiply B) by average retail price per flat

D) Multiply C) by target profit (min 20%) to give profit £

However, it's worth noting that the flat type and size you elect to build will be determined by local demand (we'll get into this later). You will also need to remember to adjust to reflect the retail cost of a flat in your specific area.

There are a few further points we need to make here:

• We'll talk a little later about creating internal courtyards. This is where we carve out a part of the centre of the industrial building to gain access points and let in light. This is more likely to be necessary on a more substantial development, but it may take up more than 20% of the available space. This will reduce the number of units that you can build, which will affect your profit calculations

• One advantage of converting industrial buildings is that it's often possible to create vaulted ceilings. While this doesn't alter the square meterage of a flat, it does increase the volume. This will not only make flats easier to sell, but they may also command a slight premium as a result

• Please remember that the figures we've quoted are examples. Every project is different, and while a 20-25% margin range is possible, it can't be guaranteed. Should a project encounter unexpected costs during the build phase, then this can impact the overall margin. That said, as the work is being done above ground on an existing structure, the scope for unexpected costs is often less than on a new-build project

Technical Corner: The development management fee

Many people are surprised to discover that a developer can earn a fee during the construction phase of a project. This is separate from the Project Manager's fee and can be up to 10% of the build cost. If we assume a build cost in our examples above of £600k, the developer would be earning £60k in fees from the project. Note that this fee is included within the project's professional costs, so if you claim it, you'll reduce the profit of the project by £60k. Think of it as an advance profit.

The ability to charge a Development Management Fee will be dictated by the commercial lender, and you should check this with your commercial broker. Why do some lenders allow you to take a fee, and others don't? Well, it comes down to mindset. Some lenders want you to focus on getting the project completed and believe that the best way of focusing your mind is to ensure you can only take any profit at the end. Other lenders worry that if you've got no income and your circumstances change, then you may be forced to defer working on the project in favour of putting food on the table. So, by allowing you to have a small advance of the profits, they ensure you don't need to down tools (so to speak) to work elsewhere.

What is the ideal project size?

We now have some perspective on what a 1,500m^2 industrial building looks like as a development project. But what is the ideal size of project?

For someone attempting their first conversion project, we would recommend going for a scheme that has the benefit of Permitted Development Rights, coupled with a reasonably low GDV. This makes it a much more manageable project on which you can cut your teeth.

It's also worth noting that you'll get diminishing returns as your host building gets smaller. If you were only getting two 1-bed flats out of your project, then you're only going to have 20% of the GDV of a project with ten apartments. However, it will take you a lot more than 20% of the time. Hopefully, that's obvious; a site visit for ten flats doesn't take five times as long as for two flats. Similarly, a meeting or call to discuss the project doesn't take five times longer just because there are five times as many units. Also, some of your professional fees will not be proportional to the number of units.

However, you need to bear in mind that developing these projects is not a full-time occupation. So doing a relatively small job that returns you £30-40k in your spare time while allowing you to cut your teeth/learn the ropes is not a bad strategy at all. Ultimately, it's up to you, but for a first-timer, we'd be recommending the PDR route all day long.

Remember also that your first job will have some unique challenges as you'll be doing things for the first time PLUS you'll be establishing your professional team. Why not make it a more straightforward project that you can get successfully across the line and save the larger, more complex projects for later?

Location #1

There are several factors to consider regarding the location of your project. The first is where it should be relative to where you live. We'd strongly advocate having a Project Manager on your team, so you do not have to manage the project yourself. However, you'll still want to visit the site regularly and of course, to be on hand if there's a pressing need for you to visit.

If the project is in your backyard (figuratively speaking), then you're also going to have a much better knowledge of the locale. When you venture off your patch, you become reliant on the Internet and other people for your local knowledge; not a showstopper but something to be mindful of.

Another angle here is that you'll want certain members of your professional team to be based reasonably near your project. Your Contractor will need to be in striking distance if the project is to avoid incurring lots of travel costs. Also, there can be a benefit in having a planning consultant who knows the foibles of the local planning authority, etc.

For all these reasons, we would suggest looking reasonably close to home for your opportunities; let's say within a one-hour drive of where you live.

Location #2

The second location issue is, of course, much more closely related to the end result of your efforts. We know that the three most important aspects of a property's value are location, location, and location. To a certain degree, Industrial Conversions are no exception.

The first thing you need to think about here is your end customer. Who's going to live in the homes you're going to build, and what would they think about its location?

Now some of these points are obvious, but they serve as a useful checklist:

• Don't consider buildings that are slap bang in the middle of an industrial estate. No matter how beautiful your flats are, no one will want to live there. There are no amenities, the neighbourhood's a ghost town after dark, and there's next to zero entertainment or dining venues on your doorstep

• Since industrial zones often adjoin residential areas, there may be scope to develop industrial buildings that are on the edge of an industrial estate. Again, you've got to view the living environment through the eyes of your customer, but this approach can often pay dividends

• Your ideal host building will already be in a mostly residential area. Often these are single one-of-a-kind units that have been built alongside existing residential properties.

Ugly Is Good

Without wishing to offend any industrial-building owners, it has to be said that very few industrial buildings are what you'd call 'lookers'. In fact, many of them can make brick outhouses appear aesthetically pleasing in comparison, and of course, there's a reason for that. Large multinational brands with massive budgets who care about the kerb appeal of their premises didn't build these things. These were usually created by small business owners who were looking to get the maximum amount of space for the minimum amount of expenditure. So the architect never got as far as discussing his or her thoughts on kerb appeal. In fact, quite often there may not have been an architect on the project at all. As a result, these buildings are often butt-ugly, bland, and utilitarian both outside and in.

Now you may be thinking that this lack of beauty might be a bad thing when it comes to creating a residential property. Surely we want it to look more, well, residential? The reality is quite different. When someone looks at an eyesore like that, they often can't get their head around anyone wanting to live in it. So they don't get as far as ever considering the idea. Whether they're the owner, a developer, or a commercial agent, the only use they can see for the building is industrial. Unless, of course, you knock it down and start again. And with you now knowing what you know about Industrial Conversions, this is very much a good thing. Long may everyone think it's impossible – it means far less competition for you.

When it comes to the end game, you will undoubtedly need to factor in some beauty treatment for your new baby. However, you'd be surprised by the level of exterior beautification that can be achieved. For now, we want you to stick by the mantra "Ugly is Beautiful", at least as far as Industrial Conversions go.

Run-Down, and his good friends; Derelict and Empty

Now you may be thinking we have an unhealthy predisposal towards ugly things, which this next point may serve to reinforce. When you look at an industrial building, it will fall into one of these four categories.

1. In use and looks very smart
2. In use and looks run down
3. Not in use – empty
4. Not in use – derelict

Every building has an owner, so let's think about what assumptions we can make about the appetite of the owner of each of these buildings to sell their property to you.

1. In use and looks very smart

The owner has clearly invested money in the building. If he's the business owner, it's unlikely that he's going to be moving out any time soon, having spent time and money in the upkeep of the building. If the landlord doesn't own the business himself (i.e., he only owns the building), chances are he's not going to be rushing to sell having sunk cash into the property to bring it up to a very smart standard.

2. In use and looks run down

These landlords and business owners may represent a great buying opportunity for you. They've not invested in their property, which could mean one of several things;

1. They're struggling financially – money's too tight to spend on the premises
2. They're nearing retirement – the business owner will be retiring in a few years and so sees little point in sinking money into the building
3. They're going to be upsizing or downsizing – as a business expands (or contracts), so its space needs change. If a company sees a change of premises on the horizon within the next few years, they're unlikely to spend time and money doing up the existing building

All these scenarios are potentially good for you since there could be a real appetite on the owner's part to sell the property and realise some cash.

3. Not in use – empty

Empty buildings are clearly going to be of interest to you, although the status can often be very different from the properties in 2 above. The main reason is that an empty building is often (ironically) a sign of action. A vacant building costs money; it doesn't make money. No one is going to leave a building empty long-term because it hits them in the pocket. As a result, there's a strong likelihood that some action is being taken somewhere to alleviate the situation. It may be that the property is on the market (or about to go on), either for rent for sale. Or it may be about to be renovated or have new tenants move in. You definitely want to investigate and find out what's happening, but you should recognise that the situation is likely to be different compared to buildings that are still occupied.

4. Not in use – derelict

Derelict buildings can be a mixed bag for several reasons. Firstly, the fact that they've not been used for some time may point to more complex issues under the surface. Is there a legal dispute? Is the ownership complex or in doubt? Because empty buildings cost money, there's usually a reason why they've not been used, and this will not always be a positive one from your perspective.

The second challenge is that the structural quality of a building starts to suffer over time. A derelict building is likely to have all manner of structural issues that would need to be resolved as part of its conversion to residential. Possibly nothing that would be a showstopper, but you will need to be aware.

Finally, if a building has been derelict for a while, it's unlikely you'll be the first to think about approaching the owners to develop it (although you may be the only one thinking about converting it). Again, it's always worth investigating the status of derelict buildings to find out the lie of the land, literally.

It's also worth noting that there's a sliding scale between type 1 and type 2 buildings in the above assessment. Buildings are not either very smart or run-down. Most fall somewhere in the middle, and common sense will determine where any specific opportunities sit on the scale.

So, we now know what an opportunity might look like; let's look at how we can go about finding one.

The McDonald's influence

The McDonald's fast-food chain is one of the greatest business success stories of all time. But what has it got to do with Industrial Conversions?

On face value, not a lot, but dig beneath the surface, and you realise that McDonald's extraordinary success is built primarily on its ability to systemise its business. As it started to roll out its franchise model in the late 1950s, the biggest challenge the company faced was consistency. How could it ensure a burger sold in Utah was as good as one sold in Florida? The answer was by systemising everything in the business so that the end product was the same everywhere. Since everyone was using the same ingredients, the same equipment, the same recipe, and the same processes, uniformity was automatic.

This was no mean feat, but they achieved it on a massive scale. Everything in a McDonald's restaurant is a system. Very little is left to the employee's discretion. They can't cook the fries for a bit longer or change the ingredients. Every single process is the same in every single restaurant. And as a result, whenever you go to a McDonald's restaurant, you know exactly what you're going to be getting. The dining experience is more or less the same irrespective of which restaurant you visit.

Another facet of this systemisation was an attention to detail. McDonald's senior management would study the minutiae of every aspect of the service delivery to see how it could improve things. Speed was critical. If they could shave one second off the preparation time of a burger, then that would equate to around 75 years of reduced wait time annually across the whole organisation – simply because they sell billions of hamburgers every year.

The business lessons from McDonald's are fascinating, but let's get back to property and in particular property systems.

One of the common failings we see with new developers is that they don't have a system. They'll think to do a particular analysis on one property, but they'll forget to do it on a second property. Or they'll go and view a property without doing some basic due diligence to see whether it's a viable opportunity. This problem reduces significantly if you have a system.

There are two potential challenges you'll encounter if you don't have a decent system in place for vetting potential opportunities. The first and most common is that you'll waste your time. You'll spend an age reinventing the wheel or looking at deals that don't stack up. And you'll only find this out after you've spent hours looking at them.

The second challenge is rare but can be much more painful financially. This is where you buy a property, having forgotten to perform part of your due diligence.

Let's use the sales funnel analogy, as it's one that's used in lots of different businesses. As a developer, you're trying to put as many opportunities in the top of your sales funnel as possible. The more frogs you kiss, the more princes (or princesses) you'll find. The trick is to have a big enough funnel so that what comes out at the bottom are cast-iron opportunities.

To take an extreme example, Arthur has 100 opportunities to look at in his sales funnel. Arthur's funnel is very short – he just prints off the particulars and goes and views every property. As a result, he wears out a lot of shoe leather, he wastes a lot of his own time, and all the agents have him down as a total timewaster because he rarely buys anything.

Martha, on the other hand, has a system. She puts the same 100 properties into the top of her sales funnel, but what happens next is very different. Firstly, all the opportunities are assessed against some pre-determined high-level criteria that immediately identify over half of them as unsuitable. They quickly get ejected from the funnel. The remainder then gets evaluated in more detail against slightly more stringent criteria, and here nearly three-quarters of them are discarded. Martha's now down to about 10-12 of the original 100 that she started with, which she now begins to take a more serious look at. Again, she uses a predetermined system. She whittles her shortlist down to 3-4 properties that are worth running more serious numbers on and potentially viewing.

An important point to note here is that while Arthur's been wearing out his shoe-leather (and the patience of his local estate agents), Martha's been sat at home in her PJs. She hasn't spoken to anyone, and she hasn't left the house. She's simply sat in bed with her laptop, an Internet connection (and if we know Martha, a cheeky glass of Pinot), and followed her system to arrive at a shortlist. As a result, she minimises the number of viewings she has to do, and estate agents much prefer her to poor old Arthur because she doesn't waste their time.

So, having a system is critical, but what sort of system should you have?

Creating a deal assessment checklist

This is an obvious point, but you don't want to be relying on your memory when it comes to calling up the factors you need to consider as part of your deal assessment process. Even if your total recall ability is elephant-like, using your memory is NOT a system (plus you've possibly forgotten that your memory isn't as good as you thought it was ☺). Instead, you need to put together a good, old-fashioned checklist covering every aspect of the deal assessment. You can then use this checklist day in, day out, for every deal, plus you'll almost certainly refine it over time. This is the only sure-fire way of making sure that you don't inadvertently forget to consider something.

Where to find potential projects

In this section, we're going to be looking at the primary sources of potential deals. Some are very much desktop activities that you can do at home in your spare time. Others involve laying down some shoe leather, getting out there and speaking to people.

Let's ease ourselves in gently and start with the desktop approach (you're welcome to do this in your PJs, with or without a glass of Pinot).

Rightmove

The Rightmove website (rightmove.co.uk) has become a dominant force in online property searching in the UK in recent years. There are other consumer portals about, such as onthemarket.com, zoopla.com, and primelocation.com, but Rightmove is the daddy of them all.

What many people don't realise is that Rightmove has a commercial property section. Just scan along the top menu until you find 'Commercial' and then click on 'Commercial property for sale'. *

From here, everything is relatively intuitive. Enter the county, city, town, or postcode and then choose the search radius. We suggest that you start to look at opportunities within a 60 to 90-minute drive of your home. Since the radius options are mileage-based, you'll have to be the judge of what radius works best for you.

You can then start applying some of Rightmove's filters:

* We should point out that Zoopla's commercial property listings are sometimes more comprehensive than Rightmove's, presumably due to the relative cost of advertising for agents. Whilst we'll focus on Rightmove for brevity, you should make sure that you check out all the commercial property portals as a matter of course.

1. Leave the 'Property Type' drop-down as unfiltered. Not all the opportunities we're looking for will be listed in the Industrial/Warehousing category, so we need to cast the net wider
2. Select 'no preference' for 'Business for sale'. Some vendors are selling both their business and the property. We don't want to buy the company, but there could still be an opportunity to discuss the premises
3. Leave the price range settings untouched
4. Set the 'Size' tab to 'square metres' and then set the maximum size to whatever you feel comfortable with, bearing in mind that 500m^2 will net you around ten 1-bed flats
5. Leave 'added to site' as 'Anytime'
6. Leave the 'Include Under offer/Sold STC' box unchecked

Finally, hit the green 'Find Properties' button, and you're away. Websites have a habit of changing, and you may find that Rightmove has reformatted its filters page or added some extras since this book was last updated. It shouldn't have changed out of all recognition, and you'll still be able to work out which filters to apply.

It's now a case of scrolling down the page, scanning each of the results to see if anything suitable comes up. Here are some key points to remember:

• Ugly is good. Don't discount any property based on looks alone. The only exception is where you can see that the building is one of a row of 'terraced' units on an industrial estate. In this case, it's safe to assume that a residential conversion is unlikely to work, although a conversion to some other commercial use might

• Make sure you save your search (you'll need to sign up/sign in to Rightmove to do this – it's free) and set email alerts to 'On'. That way, you'll get an alert each time a new property that matches your criteria goes on the system.

One point to make here is that Rightmove is not going to be the best place to find opportunities. It's merely ONE of the places to look. There won't be hundreds of industrial or light industrial units all screaming out for conversion. If you're lucky, you may find one or two, but please don't lose faith if you don't. The same goes for the other consumer portals like Zoopla.

Estates Gazette

Estates Gazette has a website called Propertylink which can be accessed at:

https://propertylink.estatesgazette.com/

It's not too dissimilar to Rightmove in many respects. Its prime focus is commercial and industrial property, and there are no residential properties on the site.

It's simple to use, and you should pull up more opportunities than on Rightmove since it's a commercial property only search portal. One mistake that's easy to make is to forget to click the 'For Sale' tab at the top of the home page. At the time of writing, the home page defaults to properties that are for rent. To change this, you need to click on the For Sale tab.

You can then enter your search parameters for location and radius, plus you can also set the target size of the property. You'll find that the information contained in Propertylink is more spartan than on Rightmove. That said, most agents have included a link to the listing on their own websites where you can access further information.

Google

Where would property developers be without Google Maps and Street View? It's undoubtedly made desktop analysis much, much easier, and you should use it when evaluating any opportunity at a more detailed level, particularly once you've found some potential candidates on Rightmove or Propertylink.

You can also use Google Maps (in satellite view) to find light industrial buildings straight off the bat. Admittedly this can be a little hit and miss, but the process is straightforward. Commercial and industrial buildings are usually reasonably easy to spot on Google Maps due to the size and shape (and sometimes colour) of their roofs. You'll need to ignore buildings in larger industrial estates (these are easy to spot), but what you're looking for is an industrial-looking roof in a sea of residential properties. Once you find one, switch to Street View and take a look at the outside of the building. Does it look like a contender? You'll need to assess it against your criteria; however, this quickly becomes automatic. In many non-rural areas, Google has thoughtfully included an option to display its satellite view in 3D, and this can be very insightful. Remember to check by clicking the 3D button and seeing what comes up.

A word of warning; Google Maps and Street View are not always up to date. The images in Street View can be up to ten years' old or so, and a lot may have changed in the interim. How do you tell? Google usefully includes an "image capture" month and year at the bottom of each page in the small print. Many an aspiring developer has looked at a fantastic opportunity on Street View only to find that when they eventually drive by, the building has been demolished or already converted.

Now we need to be realistic here. You're not going to be able to look at a building on Street View and determine its use class without doing some subsequent investigation. However, it does give you a means of identifying potential prospects and creating a shortlist for further research.

The best approach (as ever) is to be highly systemised. Pick a defined area to scan, and break it down into numbered, bite-sized chunks. That way, you can scan each chunk in one session and will always know what area has been scanned and what is still left to do. If you don't, you may find yourself experiencing a strange sense of déjà vu as you re-scan streets that look curiously familiar…

Another way of using Google (or for that matter, any business listings website such as yell.com) is to search for businesses in your target area that typically reside in the sort of building we're looking for. Remember that the vast majority of ideal properties are not actually on the market. But that doesn't mean that their owners are not interested in selling.

The basic approach is straightforward:

1. Search for a particular business type in your preferred business listing website (e.g., printing works) in your target area. We'd recommend starting with a smaller area, before doing a broader search
2. Enter the postcode into Google Maps and then locate the building using Street View (the postcode will get you close, but you want to pinpoint the exact building)
3. Once you've found the building, look at whether it gets past first base using your assessment criteria. You can zoom out from Street View to get the satellite view, which will enable you to see what else is nearby:
    a. Is it in a residential area or close to one?
    b. What sort of area is it?
    c. What amenities are nearby?

4. Make a note of both the address and the business name in your list of potential prospects. Later in the book, we'll be showing you how you can start a conversation with the building's owner

Commercial Agents

As you are probably aware, estate agents come in three primary flavours:

1. Residential only
2. Commercial only
3. A hybrid of both

The commercial real estate world is quite different from the residential one. However, some agents have both a residential and commercial department within their offices.

The world of the commercial agent is rather more 'corporate' than that of the residential agent. Residential agents typically have a high street presence where customers can pop in off the street or browse properties for sale in the window. It's effectively a shop in many respects, and its customers are predominantly private individuals buying their own homes, rather than business customers looking for premises. With a commercial agent, there is no Joe Public to deal with; their customers are almost exclusively businesspeople. As a result, you're more likely to find yourself meeting in a boardroom, office, or meeting room rather than in a shop. Also, you will need to have made an appointment rather than simply popping in on the way back from Sainsbury's.

Commercial agents are certainly a great source of industrial properties, and whilst you can view their wares on their website and on the property portals, just like residential estate agents, you can often get an early notice of an opportunity if you've taken the effort to establish a personal relationship.

There are, however, a few points you need to consider:

1. Be very wary of disclosing your role as an industrial-to-residential developer. Commercial Agents work for the seller and their goal is to get the best price they can. If they sense there's an opportunity to convert their client's run-down industrial building into swanky new residential apartments, you may suddenly find the price goes up. Your job is not to educate the world on the benefits of industrial conversions (you can leave that to us). Instead, your job is to buy an industrial building as cheaply as possible. As far as the agent and seller are concerned, you're just like any other industrial building buyer; there's absolutely nothing special about you whatsoever. You only dive into the metaphorical phone box and change into your spandex one-piece Super Industrial-Conversion Man or Woman outfit AFTER you've secured the property.

2. Similarly, whilst you have no obligation to disclose your business or plans for the property, you may want to think about a suitable response or even a cover story since you're likely to be asked. Try and go for something unelaborate and non-specific, and make sure you think about it in advance rather than having to think on your feet. Don't be afraid to give a polite but firm brush-off if the questions are too intrusive for your liking.

3. You're likely to be looking in a broader geographic area than if you were buying a residential property, so don't try and befriend every single commercial agent over three counties. Instead focus on a small number of reputable agents in that area who have a track record of offering the type of property you're looking for. Bear in mind that whether you proactively look to establish relationships or simply respond to property ads, you're still going to find yourself talking to

a commercial agent, so it's a question of 'when' rather than 'if'.

4. Remember that the engagement is likely to be far more 'business meeting' than 'informal chat', so you should dress and behave accordingly. Remember that the trick to a great relationship is establishing rapport, so focus on that. Every customer a commercial sales agent sees is looking to buy a property, so simply telling them what you're looking for isn't going to make you stand out from the crowd.

5. Make sure that you're specific about what you're looking for. Just like residential estate agents, people who say they want 'anything that makes a profit' get immediately filed in the time-wasting idiot drawer. So, property type, size, location, and value are the minimum spec you need to give them.

One of our very favourite podcast episodes is (in our view) a must-listen for anyone that ever talks to a residential or commercial estate agent, even if it's only to buy your own home. In it, we interviewed a leading independent estate agent, and they gave away so many tips on how to approach and deal with agents, it was amazing. During the interview, our estate agent shared that he sometimes gets investors and developers, whom he's never met before, come in off the street and ask him whether he has any below market value (BMV) deals they could see. "Yes," he replies, "I'm so glad you asked – I've been saving up a whole drawer-full just on the off-chance someone I don't know from Adam comes in off the street without making an appointment and asks me."

The words "you idiot" were surprisingly absent from the end of his response, but you can somehow sense they're there. So, we'd certainly recommend listening to him on the podcast if you want to learn how to avoid looking like a muppet in front of the estate agents you'll meet on your journey.

Season 1; Ep 3

Residential Agents

Residential agents are a less likely source of deals since they don't on the whole sell industrial buildings, although many of them are very well connected locally, and may get wind of deals or at least know of potential sites. Generally, however, your engagement with residential agents is likely to occur once you're looking to assess values and specification of a potential deal, rather than when you're hunting for opportunities.

When you meet a residential agent, always make an appointment first – don't just wander in off the street – and be very clear on your elevator pitch. These guys see a lot of people and you need to distinguish yourself from the typical residential home buyer that usually crosses their threshold.

Auctions

Auctions are another excellent potential source of opportunities, and there is bound to be an auction house close to you that covers your area. One advantage of auctions is that they tend to have quite a broad geographic spread, plus they tend not to take place that frequently. This means that you don't need to spend a lot of time visiting a lot of auction houses to be able to take advantage of them as a source of projects.

Most auctions work the same way. The auction house will issue a catalogue (either hard copy or online), and you'll have an opportunity to view the lots before the auction date, often at open day viewings. It's always worth getting yourself on the mailing list of your local auctioneers so that you get to see the catalogue as soon as it's issued.

There's a whole other book we could write about buying property at auction, and this isn't it. What we will urge you to do is to get yourself clued up before you try and buy something. There are doubtless bargains to be had in an auction room; however, there's risk there too. Given that the auction process and experience is somewhat unique, you should do your research before you go. In fact, we always tell our students to go to an auction room first without trying to buy something so that they get a feel for the environment and what's involved.

A final point we should make is that many buyers fail to think outside the box when it comes to auctions. They'll do all the right research, get all their ducks in a row and rock up at the auction room keen as mustard. Only then do they find that the lot they were going to bid on has been withdrawn. What's happened there? Well likely as not some more enterprising developer had thought to approach the vendor directly before the auction date and made them an attractive offer. Will they have paid over the odds? That may make you feel better if you've lost out, but actually, there's no such thing as paying over the odds.*

* You can't pay 'over the odds' for a development property (unless, of course, you've made a balls-up of your profitability calculations). That implies that all development property has a market rate, whereas the value of a property is specific to each developer. Remember the example of Sam, who missed out on the auction opportunity when only two people bid? Imagine she'd secured it and gone on to make a £200k profit. Yet all the other developers in the room would have smiled wryly to themselves and thought 'she's paid over the odds for that one'. That's because the value of the building was worth more to Sam than it was to them because she knew a way of making more out of it than they did. So, a building is worth what

you can make of it, not what other people think it's worth. With Industrial Conversions, you can create an edge that allows you to pay more for a property than other people. So why wouldn't you approach a vendor pre-auction and make them an offer?

Have they sealed the deal and got rid of all the competition? You bet. So as a strategy, you definitely want to bear it in mind when you spot a prospective project in the auction catalogue.

Deal Sourcers

Professional deal sourcers are people who earn a commission from finding deals for property investors and developers. Typically they will take a percentage of the purchase price, and they'll often 'package' the deal in return for a higher fee. A packaged deal is typically one where the sourcer has agreed on a price with the vendor, all terms are in place, plus all the analysis and numbers have been run and cross-checked.

There's also likely to be a contract in place between the vendor and the sourcer, giving the sourcer a fixed period in which to find a buyer.

At the other end of the scale, there are some dubious property sourcers out there who do little more than share details of available properties that are on the open market. Useful to a degree, but you then have to do all the hard work in securing the deal.

At the end of the day, it's a case of buyer beware when it comes to deal sourcers. A good place to find deal sourcers and check out their credentials is at property networking meetings (see next section). Ultimately, you'll want to get some references or feedback from people who have used their services successfully before.

Another way of looking at property sourcing is as an outsourcing strategy that leverages your time. After all, you only have so many hours in the day, only one network and only one pair of eyes. Finding a deal sourcer you can work with and trust could get you access to more deals and save you a lot of time. This comes at a price, but if you're only paying their fee on deals that progress, you can treat the sourcing fee precisely as you would any other professional fee.

Networking

The more people who know what you do, the more chances you'll have of finding a deal. Networking takes many forms. There are property networking meetings all over the country, and these are a great place to meet other property people. Even if they don't have a property opportunity themselves, they may know other people you or they could talk to who do. Networking meetings are also a great way of meeting potential business partners and funders.

If we think for a moment about the type of person who will typically own the host properties you're looking for, then it's likely to be local business owners. There are many networking events involving local businesspeople. These represent another excellent opportunity for you to get your message out there.

As with so many things, networking works best when you have a system in place. And of course, a well-practised elevator pitch that allows you to convey what you're all about succinctly and professionally.

Friends, family, and acquaintances

It never ceases to amaze us how many times we've heard of new property developers having an unexpected property connection with friends, family, and acquaintances. This often manifests itself when family-members prove to be surprising sources of finance;

however, your personal network can also be a source of property opportunities as well.

We had an example of this recently when one of our suppliers, knowing that we were involved in property development, asked us for some advice. It turned out they owned an old industrial building, and we ended up joint venturing with them on the conversion.

Have a think about the tradespeople you use. Would any of these have an industrial building that could be converted? You can also ask your family and friends to be on the lookout. Many developers offer a 'reward' to friends and family who introduce them to projects that they take on. It's a win-win arrangement, and it means you have more eyes on the ground.

Businesses for sale

There are some interesting angles to think about here. Finding businesses for sale is not difficult. Many online portals and agencies advertise them. The circumstances that are driving the sale could be many and varied:

1. The owner is retiring and wants to sell up
2. The business is failing, and they're looking to cut their losses
3. The owner no longer wants to be in that business
4. The company is in great shape and has been primed for sale so that the owners can take a windfall profit and reinvest
5. And many other reasons

Clearly, some of these businesses will operate from industrial buildings. Based on what you already know from this book, you would suspect that the value that the owners have placed on their building (assuming they own the freehold) is potentially going to be less than what you'd be willing to pay to convert it. The complication then is that you're not looking to buy a business, you only want the property. However, the business is unlikely to be sellable without its premises, so surely the business owner isn't likely to compromise the value of his or her company by selling you an essential asset?

Without a doubt, this will more often than not be the case. But there will be scenarios where it can work quite handsomely. Usually, this will be where the value of the business is relatively low compared to the size of the conversion opportunity, and so the profits on offer from selling the building can outweigh the profits from selling the business.

Also, just because a business is for sale doesn't guarantee that there's anyone out there willing to buy it. You may find that many owners have had their businesses for sale for some time without the whiff of a potential buyer. For them, the prospect of a definite profit from selling you their building (or joint venturing) versus the long and possibly infinite wait for a business buyer may be highly attractive. At the very worst, you can leave them your number so they know whom to call if they change their mind.

A final consideration here is one about tax. We're not going to go into the ins and outs of it because it's complicated, and we promised we wouldn't get all technical on you. But what we will say is that there are circumstances where it may be tax-efficient for the owner to sell you the business, including the property, rather than selling you the property on its own. As you can imagine, this is very much one for your professional team to advise you on, your accountant and tax advisor in particular.

Advertising

Facebook ads are increasingly popular and the most targeted advertising there is. Creating an advert that could be put in front of business owners in a particular area can be a great way to get your message in front of would-be vendors who had not thought about selling their property.

Facebook advertising is straightforward, although you'll need to have your own Facebook page and ad account. It's crucial to follow Facebook's stringent advertising guidelines; however, all this information is readily available on Facebook.

An alternative approach to the DIY method is to enlist the help of a digital marketing agency. There will be a cost to this, but at least you won't have to learn the ropes, nor should it take up too much of your time.

Social Media

Social media can be a way of creating awareness of your property development brand, where you can also make it clear that you're looking for deals. However, be wary of creating a monster that needs constant feeding. Social media depends on ongoing content to maintain credibility and interest, which means curating material to put out there (in our view not the best use of your time from a deal-sourcing perspective). If we had to pick a favourite, we'd say LinkedIn had the most relevant audience and demanded the least content.

Old-fashioned shoe leather

Despite all our access to property websites, Google Maps, deal sourcers, and network contacts, the old-fashioned approach is often the best, namely walking the streets.

These buildings often hide in plain sight, yet we've had many cases where the building in question couldn't be seen from the road – it was only visible on foot. Getting out and about is an excellent way of rooting out these opportunities.

The best way to do it is (as ever) to have a system. Plot an area that you can cover in a specific time (however long you intend to take) and then stick to the roads in that area. If you do extend your search further, make sure you keep a note of which roads you walked along. Also, make sure you check out both sides of each road. You should check out Google Maps and Street View first to get some idea about the number of industrial units in that area and start with the most obvious candidates.

Take a notebook with you so you can jot down any addresses that are possible opportunities, together with any other relevant information. This would include the company whose name is above the door, whether it looks empty or in use, and its general state of repair. You should also take a camera (your phone camera is fine) so that you can match your notes to the image (it's very easy to forget which was which after you've seen a few!).

Doing this exercise by car is quicker and for the less mobile, a lot easier. But it's not as good for two reasons. You're not going to be the safest person on the road if you're crawling along looking left and right while also trying to avoid oncoming traffic and pedestrians. Plus, you're too low down in a car to see much, so you'll miss some opportunities that you'd otherwise see when on foot. If a car is the only option, see if you can persuade someone to drive you so that you have more time to focus on looking instead of driving.

Finally, for the health-conscious, this shoe-leather approach is one of the few methods of property sourcing that's also good for you!

9. Contacting Owners Directly

A story about a direct-to-owner approach

One of our students recently visited a small bookbinding business that was located quite centrally about a quarter of a mile or so from his local city centre. He'd made an appointment to discuss some bookbinding he needed doing for his business with the owner. While he didn't go there with the express intention of looking at a potential building project, we teach all our students to be on the lookout for opportunities – you never know when a great deal might present itself.

So, as he pushed through the narrow double doors at the front of a white-painted brick Victorian building, his developer's radar was well and truly switched on. Certainly, the location was good for residential units being only a short walk from the town centre. The area was regarded as an 'up-and-coming' neighbourhood; not the best but not the worst. The building was two storeys tall and sat on a corner plot. It abutted the pavement on both streets and sat between two modern buildings. It looked tired both inside and out, but structurally there weren't any obvious signs of problems.

As the doors closed behind him, he heard a bell ring in some distant corner of the building. After a few moments, the owner emerged and introduced himself. The man appeared to be in his late 60s or early 70s, and having first offered our man a cup of coffee, led him through to a meeting room where they began to talk about his bookbinding requirements

As their discussions drew to a close, he asked the owner about his history. How long had he been a bookbinder, and how did he end up in this particular building? Now one thing that is true the world over is that given a quarter of a chance (and often less than that), people like nothing better than to talk about themselves. Sure enough, the owner obliged and began recounting the highlights of his working history, how he had bought the building outright back in the 1980s and had been there ever since.

The student explained that he was a property developer and asked whether the owner had ever thought about selling the building. The owner explained that he hadn't, but as he intended to work for a few more years yet, he wasn't interested in selling up any time soon.

He then asked whether he could see where the bookbinding was done. Pleased to have an attentive audience, the man showed him into a large open-plan workshop with a vaulted ceiling. The room was stacked to the gunnels with boxes, bookbinding equipment, and books. He could see through some rather grimy windows that there was a small parking lot immediately to the rear of the building. He commented to the owner that it must be a godsend given the lack of free parking in the immediate vicinity. He also made a mental note of the layout of the building, and roughly where the doors and windows were.

He then thanked the man for showing him around, and soon found himself back on the street outside. He took a few external photos of the building on his phone, and then drew from memory the internal layout on a piece of paper while it was still fresh in his mind.

That evening back at home, he spent a couple of hours doing several things. Firstly, he drew a more accurate plan of the building's footprint. Using this quick sketch, Google Maps, and Google Street View, he was able to estimate the floor area of the building. He had to make some assumptions about the second storey, as he hadn't seen it. But he knew where the two-storey workshop was in relation to the rest of the building and so could reasonably estimate the available space and the approximate shape of the upstairs area. At this stage, though, he didn't need to be 100% accurate; he only needed to have a rough idea of how many flats he could fit into the building.

Having done this, he then scoured Rightmove looking to see what was on sale in the local area and what sort of prices they commanded. Using one of propertyCEO's analysis tools, he was able to establish that there was quite a strong demand for 1-bed apartments, and that parking came at a premium. There was also a reasonable market for 2-bed flats, but studios seemed to be very few and far between. He was also able to establish the approximate price per square metre for the apartments currently on the market, as well as their average selling price. We'll talk some more about this market area comparison approach in the next chapter.

Fortunately, the building had windows on both the front and rear elevations, so there were no major light issues to deal with. The workshop area was more of a challenge since it was two storeys tall. He felt that the best way of dealing with the workshop would be to insert a floor halfway up it and make the building two levels throughout.

With the workshop floor in place, he could see he would be looking at a total floor area of around 290m^2, which sat comfortably within Permitted Development Right territory. He would need to allow approximately 20% of the space for communal areas (access, walkways, bin and cycle stores, etc.). This left him with around 232m^2 of accommodation (116m^2 on each floor). Having studied the shape of the building, he decided that the best approach would be to have two x larger 1-bed flats upstairs each at 58m^2. Downstairs he could fit in three x smaller 38m^2 1-bed units. In addition, he considered building into the roof void but decided against it, as the roof height didn't look tall enough.

Then he calculated his GDV by multiplying the unit sizes of the five flats by the current market rate for flats that he'd found out earlier. He then tweaked the results so that they looked reasonable compared to the other properties currently on the market (including what had sold recently). This gave him a total GDV of £900k, which suggested he would be looking at a target profit figure of around £200k.

His final task was to estimate the likely build cost. This is something that requires significant focus when you get close to making an offer. However, at this stage, he only wanted to know that at a high level, the numbers looked reasonable. After all, if the build cost came to £700k and the GDV was £900k, he would need to secure the building for next to nothing, which was never going to happen. If this were the case, he'd know not to waste any more time on it.

Since our student had both a system and the right tools, he was able to do this quite easily. He also rang up his preferred quantity surveyor (QS) to ask questions about the likely cost of putting in a new floor in the workshop. This meant he had a reasonable estimate for the extra cost this would entail. After a couple of hours' work in total he arrived at the following ballpark numbers:

GDV: *£900k*
Margin: *£200k*
Cost To Convert: *£400k*

If these figures were accurate, it meant that he could afford to pay around £300k for the building.

The next day, he wrote to the owner. He thanked him for his time and said he appreciated that the owner wasn't looking to sell at the present time. However, he'd worked out some very rough numbers that suggested he might be able to offer the owner something in the region of £250-300k for the freehold, should he ever decide to sell. He also made it clear that this would be a cash sale since he had funds from private investors already lined up.

Almost immediately, he received an email back from the owner. He thanked him for his interest but again reiterated that he had no plans to sell at the current time. This wasn't a problem. He knew from his conversation with the owner that the business would have to either close or be sold when the owner retired, as he had no family to pass it on to. Plus, he'd hinted that the building and the business were a big part of the owner's pension pot. The man was 70 years' old, and so with retirement on the horizon, hopefully, when the time was right, our student would be the first person he'd call.

Then, almost exactly one week after that email had landed in his inbox, he received a call from the owner out of the blue. He explained that he'd been surprised by the size of the offer that might be on the table. He'd previously thought the building was worth around half that figure. He explained that a few years before, he'd had some estate agents around to value the building. They'd made it clear that any potential purchaser would need to invest a lot of money in getting the premises into a useable condition. The owner had even asked whether there was scope to build houses or flats, and the agents had dismissed it. They suggested it was unlikely to be the best route since any developer would need to demolish the building and start again. The implication was that a developer would be willing to pay less than someone who was going to keep the building as a light industrial unit.

He explained that our student's email had caused him to reconsider his retirement strategy. He felt he'd needed to work a few more years to build up more of a nest-egg. But if these numbers were achievable, there would be an opportunity for him to retire sooner than expected. However, he was naturally suspicious; why would our man be able to offer so much more money than anyone else?

Our student didn't explain that he'd be converting the building to residential units. Instead he said that it was just the type of property that he needed for one of his business ventures, so he was happy to offer a good price. He suggested that the next step would be for him to revisit the owner at the building. He could then have a proper look round with his professional team and take measurements. That would enable him to put together some firmer numbers ahead of making a formal offer.

The owner agreed, and they decided to meet later that week.

So, what does this story tell us about making offers to owners directly? Here are a few things to consider:

1. A large proportion of industrial buildings are not currently on the market, but that doesn't mean they are not for sale at any price

2. There is a strong likelihood that you will be valuing an owner's industrial building at a higher price than they think it's worth or than other people are willing to pay for it

3. The scale of your offer may allow the owner to rethink their plans; often an unexpected six-figure windfall can make quite a difference to an individual or a small business

4. Your offer is on the table NOW. It's one thing for an owner to think about putting their property on the market in the future. But when someone presents an offer today, it forces them to consider it and to make a yes or no decision

5. There's no competition when you contact an owner directly. That's not to say they won't go to the market to check out whether yours is the best deal. But we know that for Industrial Conversions, the chance that another developer would be considering the same route (and therefore able to offer the same price) is slim

6. Don't feel obliged to tell the owner that you'd be planning to convert the building into residential units

Note that no formal offer was made; he only gave the owner an indication of the sort of figures that were in scope. This is critical because, as a developer, you need to minimise the time you spend on deals that don't progress. He could have spent a couple of days poring over the numbers and firming things up. But if the owner had said no straight out of the blocks, then it would be a wasted exercise. Far better to go in with a ballpark figure that is a reasonable best-guess (or an offer range). You can then explain to the owner that you would need to see the building and take measurements etc. to firm up your offer.

A property developer or investor who only ever considers properties that are currently on the market is missing a big trick. Most properties in the UK are currently for sale; it's just a question of how much it costs to buy them. You may have no intention of moving from your beautiful £500k home anytime soon. But if a developer knocked on your door tomorrow and offered you £750k cash for it, you may surprise yourself with how quickly you have Pickford's on speed dial.

You can see that our student spent around two or three hours getting to a point where he had a ballpark figure to present to the owner. Would every three hours spent this way produce a deal? No, not by a long shot. But when the upside is a project generating £200k plus he was able to do the work at home while his family watched X-Factor (he's not a fan), it all makes for a very worthwhile exercise. The worst that can happen is that your numbers don't stack up, in which case you forget all about it. Or perhaps the owner doesn't want to sell in which case they've got your number should they ever decide to. And as we always tell our students, it's also great practice. The more of these calculations and approaches that you do, the better you'll get at doing them.

Identifying a building's owner

In this example, our student stumbled across the opportunity by accident, and he was able to engage with the owner immediately, one to one. But what if you've spotted a potential building but have no connection to the business that occupies it? What's the best way of getting the owner's attention? Well, the great news is that most of what you need to do can be done at home in your PJs. You simply need to unleash the power of the Internet.

You need to approach owners only after you've done your initial calculations. You won't have the benefit of seeing the internal layout of the building, but you will be able to estimate its size and the number of floors. Your market area analysis can tell you what types of unit sell well locally and what price they command. If you make your approach to the owner without doing your basic analysis, you'll end up wasting several people's time, including your own.

We mentioned earlier that industrial buildings generally come in four different flavours:

1. Well-kept and in use
2. Run-down and in use
3. Run-down and not in use
4. Derelict

The approach for contacting owners is generally the same for each. But we wanted to remind you that different scenarios can present different challenges.

The first step is to make sure you can identify who owns the property. Many industrial properties are leased by the businesses that work in them. But it's the landlord you're looking to make contact with, not the leaseholder/tenant. In fact, if the tenant was to get wind of your plans to buy the building and convert it, they may be a little concerned. Or they may decide to make an offer to buy the freehold themselves, so it's best not to have that conversation with them if you can help it.

For buildings in England and Wales, you can find out the identity of the owner using the Land Registry's online portal. Many businesses have web addresses that can easily (and deliberately) be mistaken for belonging to HM Land Registry. The safest way of accessing the correct portal is to do a web search for the term "Land Registry". You can then click on the .gov website that should appear at the top of your search results (the Land Registry is a government body). Once on the .gov site, you can then click the link, which will take you directly to the portal.

You will need to register on the portal before you can use it, which is free. There are two ways of searching. You can use the postcode (if you know it), or you can use a map search. The portal gives full instructions for each within its 'Find a Property' tab.

There are three documents available to download via the portal:

1. *Title* – this tells you the name and address of the owner of the property plus details of any mortgage company. It will also show any covenants, rights of way, easements, etc. that may exist for the property
2. *Title Plan* – this is a map showing the boundary of the property, plus it will highlight any areas referred to in the Title
3. *Flood Risk Indicator* – which shows the probability of flooding using a relative score

You have to pay a small fee to download each document. At the time of writing, it costs £3 for each of the Title and Title Plan, and £9 for the Flood Risk Indicator.

Not every property title is available through the Land Registry portal. More detective work may be needed if your search on the portal draws a blank.

Having downloaded the Title document, you will usually have several outcomes:

1. The owner is shown as a private individual, and their address is listed (it may be different to the property address, and you can look on Google Maps' Street View to see if it's a residential or business address)
2. The owner is more than one private individual
3. The owner is named as a company at the address of the property
4. The owner is a company at a different address

In instances 3 and 4, your next stop should be the Companies House website. This is another government agency, which provides details of all companies that are registered in the UK and their directors.

Again, countless websites want to charge you money for accessing company data that's free on the Companies House website. So, to make sure that you end up on the correct portal, do a web search for "Companies House", and the .gov website should appear near the top of your search results. You can then click on the 'Get information about a company' option.

There is no need to register to get access, and all the information you need is free. Search for the name of the company that's listed on your title document, and it should appear on a list with others of a similar name. Select the one you want, and you'll be presented with three tabs:

1   The Overview section shows the status of the company including when it was formed

2. The Filing tab provides information about the company's filing history
3. The People tab lists all the directors or partners of the business, including their correspondence address. This is the tab you want; if you click on a name, you should also be able to see any other companies they are connected to

You may also be able to see their month and year of birth, which can be useful (are they close to retirement age, for example). By looking at the co-directors and their ages, you get a good picture of the type of organisation you're dealing with. As an example, the bookbinding owner showed on Companies House as the only director in his early seventies. This suggested a small business with one decision-maker, and there would be no doubt who to approach. If there had been another younger person listed as a co-director and with the same surname, it might have pointed to the fact that a son or daughter was working in the business. If there were ten directors and they were all connected to lots of other companies, then you can imagine a more corporate environment where any decision to sell the building would be discussed around the boardroom table. In itself, the information isn't valuable, but it allows you to build a picture of who you'll be dealing with and to gauge your best line of attack.

As a result of your labours, you should now have the name and address of someone who is either the owner of the building or is a director of the business that owns it. One point to note is that the correspondence address given on Companies House may not be the home address of the owner. It could be a business address, the address of their accountant, or a virtual office address. However, any correspondence sent to that address should reach them, although it may not reach them quickly.

How to approach owners

So you now have a name and an address. What should you do next?

The first thing you need to appreciate is that your next move is not going to secure you a deal. We've not yet experienced a scenario where a student fires off a letter, and the owner writes back and says, 'sounds great, send the paperwork to my solicitors'. It doesn't happen like that for obvious reasons.

Instead, you'll be performing a series of steps where each step has only one aim, which is to secure the next contact. In other words, when you write to the owner for the first time, the objective is NOT to try and buy the property. Your aim is only to get a response from the owner. You want to start a dialogue.

Why is this point so important? Well, it's because a lot of people screw it up royally. They keep thinking that their goal is to try and buy the property. So they make every contact more about purchasing the property and less about getting some form of engagement. It's a bit like going fishing. If you want to catch a fish, you need to think about what fly to use to catch it, not what type of sauce you're going to have with it when you eat it.

So, your first step is to write a letter to the owner. Not an email, a letter. And where you think it is appropriate (and if your handwriting is up to it), a handwritten letter rather than a typed one (or find someone who has neat handwriting if you don't). Go for decent stationery as well, without going overboard.

Mark the envelope 'Strictly Private & Confidential: To Be Opened By Addressee Only'. The aim is to avoid the letter being intercepted by a personal assistant or office clerk if it's going to a business.

By all means, use your branding on the letterhead to give you credibility. However, there's no harm in presenting yourself as a private individual if you prefer. There's no right or wrong answer here. Let's go back to the work you did on Companies House to establish the type of company you're dealing with (corporate or single owner). You can imagine that a letter from a property development business may be better received by the board of directors in a larger company, whereas our student's bookbinder friend may have preferred a personal approach. In the end, only you can decide.

So, what do you say in this letter? Well, here are some pointers:

1. Introduce yourself and try and establish a personal connection to the property. "... I've lived in the area for many years and have often thought as I passed by your building that there would be a great opportunity to... ". Better still if you've got a connection to the business or are connected to someone who has, then that might be worth mentioning

2. You want to avoid sounding like one of those stock-in-trade letters that estate agents send out that says, "are you thinking about selling your property?" These get sent to every man and his dog and end up in the bin within about 4 seconds. Make sure your letter is perceived as being unique and specific to that one building

3. Explain who you are and what you do, "I'm a local developer building homes in the area..."

4. Hint at the positives "...we've been able to offer owners of similar properties a very significant uplift..." or "we've often been able to offer owners a price that is in excess of their expectations of what the building was worth..."

5. Keep it brief – remember, you're trying to hook a fish; you're not trying to eat it (yet). So re-read your letter after you've drafted it and ask yourself whether it could create a spark of interest. If you received it, would you want to get in touch, or would you put it in the bin?

6. If you have the phone number of the company (it doesn't have to be the owner's direct line), you can say in the letter "I'll give you a call next Thursday at 5pm to see if it's something that's of interest." That way, if you call at that time and reach the owner's assistant, you can legitimately say that you had an arrangement to call at that time. There are no guarantees, but every edge you can get that increases your chance of getting the next contact will help

Finally, let us reiterate that as good as your letter will be, you're only trying to get a response. You're not yet trying to buy a building. On average, it takes seven touch points for people to do business together, and at this stage, you're only trying to get to second base.

Assuming you receive some form of response, your next step is to angle for a meeting. This can either be at the building, at the owner's offices/home, or in a coffee shop. It's worth remembering the often-abused statistics surrounding how we communicate with others. Only 7% of communication is transmitted verbally. The rest is conveyed by body language (55%) and tone of voice (38%). So, the sooner you can get in front of them, the higher your chances will be of making progress. If you can't procure a meeting, a phone call is the next best thing.

Always approach every encounter with a prospective owner through their own eyes. What would you think if you received a letter from a person you've never heard of who might be interested in buying your house? You may be interested enough in having a call or meeting with them. But what are the main interests and concerns that you're likely to have? At the top of most people's list will be credibility (are they reputable, experienced, trustworthy) and price (how much will they be prepared to pay). Make sure that you go into those meetings well prepared, particularly on the credibility front. This is where you may find yourself referencing your NEA or some of the other experienced professionals with whom you would be working. You could even ask your NEA to join the meeting.

One word of caution. Never try and blag it; you will always get found out, and that will be the end of the opportunity.

Technical Corner: Avoiding the 'blagging it' minefield

Ok, so blagging isn't a very technical term, but we wanted to make an important point. By blagging, we mean presenting yourself as someone who you're not. More particularly, presenting yourself as an experienced developer when you've never done a development before and may not yet own a hard hat, let alone stepped foot on a building site.

It's human nature - the tendency for some new developers is to try to look more experienced than they are to compensate for their lack of experience. They don't necessarily lie outright, but they try and convey an impression of experience. They believe that this is necessary in order to be credible. In fact, it does the opposite. You need to understand that to do this is a massive own goal. It's an accident waiting to happen.

As a new developer, you'll need to inspire confidence in those you need to make your business successful. Your NEA, your professionals, your private investors, and your commercial lenders included. None of these people are idiots, and all will potentially have decades of experience working in an industry that you're new to. If you try and blag your way through it, you will be found out. It may not happen at the first meeting. But it will happen. And then you'll be regarded as a pretender or a chancer, which will mean that people are far less inclined to work with you, let alone lend you money.

The good news is that you don't need to fake it 'til you make it. You are a CEO who's pulling together an experienced team of people that will be making things happen. Your credibility is your entrepreneurism, your CEO skills, and the leveraged experience of your team. You really don't need to pretend to have skills or experience that you don't have.

So please don't!

Preparation is critical

When you have your meeting/phone call with the owner, make sure you come well prepared. Have a list of questions, and don't try and remember all the things you want to ask – you'll forget some.

You should also be very prescriptive about the next steps. Again, you're only ever thinking about the next touch point. An obvious next step is to arrange to go and see the building in person. You want to take measurements and to see the lie of the land and get a rough idea of the layout and floor space. Be sensitive to the fact that the building may not be vacant. The owner may not be keen on a property developer with a tape measure going around their tenanted building. The owner may also have floor layouts of the building that they can send you. These will be good enough for you to put together a high-level plan, albeit you would still want to see the building before making an offer.

At every touch point, you should have a well-drilled answer to the question, "What are the next steps?" Never let the owner see you have to pause, scratch your head, and try and think about what the next steps should be. Whether it's the first touch point or the twenty-seventh, make sure you always know what the next steps are.

Try always to make your next touch point a face-to-face one. Yes, you could send an offer by email, but you'll miss all those non-verbal communication signals and opportunities.

Finding a connection

One of the biggest challenges with the cold-call approach is that you have to work hard to establish a relationship with the owner. It's a real standing start. Life's made a lot easier if you already have a personal connection to the owner (or even their business) even if it's an indirect one. For example, if you and the owner had a mutual acquaintance, you could see if they'd be prepared to introduce you.

You need to find a decent Industrial Conversion opportunity first and then find a connection to its owner. Once you have the name of the owner, you can then give some thought to who might know them and who could get you an introduction. It may be that you have a contact who knows someone else within the business and that you could get an 'in' that way.

Googling the owner is another way in which you can glean some useful information. You can also look at the company's website to see if they mention any other activities that the company is involved in. We had a student a little while ago who discovered via Google that the owner had played at a charity golf event at a particular golf club. Our student wasn't the world's greatest golfer, but he had a friend who played golf at the same club. So he mentioned seeing the article and asked him whether he knew the owner. It turned out that he didn't, but he did know that the owner was on the committee that was organising a dinner event at the golf club the following month. So our student bought a ticket for himself and his friend and went along. Sure enough, he was able to strike up a conversation with the owner at the event and got himself a business card and the offer of a coffee in town the following week.

A similar but more obvious approach may be to become a prospective customer of the owner's business. In our earlier example, our student was looking for a bookbinding solution. But the outcome would not have been any different if he'd gone there with the aim of striking up a conversation with the owner about the building.

Now you may be thinking that this all sounds a little duplicitous – a bit cloak and dagger. After all, don't you want to be upfront with people? Ok, let's be clear on what we're advocating here. People do business with people. You're never going to secure a deal without meeting the person who owns the building or their agent. It doesn't happen any other way. That means you need to get to a face-to-face meeting as soon as you can. That's the only way you'll move forward in progressing a potential deal.

Bear in mind that the outcome for the building's owner in meeting you can only be positive or neutral for them. Why wouldn't they be interested in talking to someone who might pay them more money for their building than they thought it was worth? However, if they're not interested, then they can say so, which is what happened to our student in the first instance. What's important is that you get an opportunity to speak to them. Whether you do that by sending them a letter, leveraging a mutual acquaintance, or engineering a situation where you can introduce yourself to them, then there should be no harm caused. Stalking and kidnapping would be a different matter. Arranging to be in the same room as someone is harmless (so long as you didn't first break in).

The power of networking

Business networking can be a good way of getting connections to building owners, both directly and indirectly. We've covered the benefits of networking elsewhere; however, networking in the business community, as well as the property community, can significantly increase the breadth and depth of your network.

We hope this chapter has helped you get a perspective on what's involved in establishing contact with building owners whose properties are not currently on the market. It's a little difficult to be prescriptive here since all situations and opportunities are different. But whether you've found something by going direct, or on the open market, you'll need to know what to build, so that's where we'll head to next.

10. Knowing What To Build

So now we've found an opportunity, we need to understand the following information:

1. What types of residential units should you be building?
2. How much will you be able to sell these units for at the end of the day?
3. How many units can you get into the site?
4. What is the likely development cost of the conversion?
5. What is the maximum you could afford to pay for the host building?

Let's start at the top.

What type of residential units should you build?

Two factors will influence your decision here. First, let's take a step back and look at the fundamental principles. The following story will help illustrate the point.

A little while ago, the owner of an industrial building approached us. He was looking to dispose of the property as he no longer needed it and was trying to establish the most profitable approach. He'd already thought of redeveloping the site and had engaged the help of an architect that he knew. He'd paid the architect £10k to have some plans drawn up. These predictably involved knocking the existing building down and building some flats. The proposed units were four 2-bed flats and one studio. When the architect asked for a further £10k to take things to the next stage, the owner became worried about the path he was being led down. That's when he approached us to get our views.

When we studied the location of the property and the local market conditions, something became very clear. The market for 2-bed properties was almost non-existent, and studios weren't that popular either. The biggest demand was actually for 1-bed flats. This took us about an hour to find out by researching online, and we later ratified it by talking to some local estate agents.

The architect (being an architect and not a developer) had looked to maximise the space in the building, whilst creating an attractive and usable living area. But no one had thought to find out what local customers would want. As a result, it would have been all too easy to develop four lovely 2-bedroom flats and a studio that nobody particularly wanted to buy.

You can imagine the building owner's problem assuming he'd gone ahead and built the units. Until all of them were sold, he would still have finance costs being incurred, and he wouldn't be able to realise his profit. And it's not as if he would only have one flat to sell – he'd have five of them to shift. It may well take a while, or alternatively he might have to sell at a discount – either way, it's an outcome that's far from ideal.

Now you may be feeling somewhat aggrieved on the building owner's behalf. After all, why would the architect have designed some flats that wouldn't sell, the wretched so-and-so? But we must stop you there; this poor choice of scheme wasn't really the architect's fault. As a developer, you're the one that needs to dictate what type of units get built. If you give free rein to your architect, you may get what he or she wants to design, not what will necessarily sell easily.

In this case, the architect was from an award-winning practice that designed high-end houses and apartments. They did a stunning job, but it wasn't appropriate for the local market which in this case demanded cheap, entry-level accommodation. Unfortunately, it happened to be the only architect that the building owner knew, so he'd approached him, mistakenly assuming that all architects are the same.

We usually like to bring the late Pablo Picasso and the even later Vincent van Gogh in at this point. Both were artists yet if you gave each gentlemen the same set of oil paints, brushes, and an easel, and asked them to paint a picture of a house, they'd come up with two completely different paintings. Similarly, architects have different styles and specialisms, and you need to adopt a 'horses for courses' approach when choosing one. You can normally get a pretty good steer from looking at their website and their project portfolio. If it's full of award-winning developments and glitzy corporate constructions in the City, then designing some entry-level flats in an old industrial building in Grimsby is probably not their bag.

So, the first thing you need to do then is to identify what your target market is looking for. There are three steps to the process. All are relatively straightforward, but each needs to be done in the right order.

At propertyCEO, we developed a system called a Market Area Comparison (MAC). This allows our students to identify the local demand in any area in the country. It tells them what sort of property sells well and what doesn't. How many bedrooms work best and what features are must-haves versus those that are unnecessary. Critically it also looks at the size of properties that have sold recently and that are still on the market. This means you know what size units you're competing against.

Before we show you how to get this information without spending a single bean, we'll have a brief word about the various paid-for data applications that are currently available on the market

A word about premium property data applications

There are various software applications available that allow you to take shortcuts to obtain property market information on any given geographical area. They provide details on sales values and market values, as well as trends. The main advantage they give you is in saving you time, since the information itself is usually in the public domain, just not in one place. Most of these applications charge a monthly or annual subscription fee, in some cases, quite a significant one. We're not going to explore the pros and cons of each one here, and if you can afford them, they will certainly make life easier/quicker for you, plus they can give you some additional information that could be useful to you. However, we would offer some words of caution if you were thinking about exclusively using them for data analysis:

1. Most of these apps don't provide a qualitative assessment of properties. An old two-bedroom ex-council flat that sold for £100k might be in the same data pool as a brand new two-bedroom penthouse flat with parking and gym access that sold for £500k. Not only is their average sales price of £300k essentially meaningless, you probably wouldn't want to include either property in your analysis, as they are outliers. Conversely, the MAC process allows you to see each property individually so you can decide whether or not to include it in your analysis

2. Similarly, because you're not seeing any images of properties currently for sale when you look at app data, you're not getting a picture of the quality of finish, style, or kerb appeal of the competition

3. Many apps don't offer the degree of granularity you need, e.g. they give you average values for 2-bed properties, but don't distinguish between flats and houses, let alone penthouses and bedsits

4. Finally, we'd suggest you still need to know how you can get the data manually, even if you also use other tools

If you don't have access to our MAC tools, you can still create a version manually. Here is an overview of the information you'll need to establish the demand for any given property type in your target area.

The 3-step MAC process

The easiest way of getting this information is to go on the rightmove.co.uk portal since it has the largest repository of homes for sale on the market. It also has some handy tools and filters that you can use to wring out the maximum amount of information.

There are 3 steps to the MAC approach, namely:

1. Collate data from the Rightmove website
2. Establish the ideal unit type for your host property
3. Double check with several local estate agents

Using Rightmove

The basic approach is to look for properties for sale that are similar to the units you will be building and that are in the same area as the host property. By similar we mean 1-bed flats, 2-bed flats, etc.

1. Go on to rightmove.co.uk and select properties for sale in your target area. Make sure the radius of your search is sensible, as you want to pick up properties that are a direct comparison. If your search radius is too large, you'll pick up properties that are in better or worse areas, and they will skew your analysis
2. Make your life a bit easier by using Rightmove's filters to remove retirement properties, buying schemes, etc. before you start

3. Once you've captured the number of properties for sale in a) and b) below, obtain the data for each property that appears on Rightmove for items c) through to g) – the easiest way is to enter it all into a spreadsheet

   a. Number of properties for sale – note the number of properties for sale for each of the property types you're interested in (e.g., 1-bed flats), making sure that the radius of your search picks up a reasonable sample size. You don't need to count them manually as Rightmove gives you a total

   b. Number of properties including sold, etc. – as above but with the "include properties sold or under offer" checkbox ticked. Leave this box ticked when recording the data from c) onwards, below

   c. Price – note the cost of each property

   d. Area – note the area in square metres or square feet of each property. This is often shown on the floorplan, or it can be obtained from the property's EPC report, which is available online via the EPC Register

   e. Relevance – note how similar the property is to the units you would be looking to build. The easiest way is to have a scale (1 = very similar, 5 = very different, etc.)

   f. Proximity – how close is the property to your units? Again, use a scale

   g. Features – what features does the property have, e.g., parking, balcony, garden, etc.

You need to repeat the exercise for each different property type (e.g., studios, 1-beds, 2-beds). Remember that we're using the exercise to find out what the market demand is, not just how much 1-bed flats sell for. So don't assume that your development will be 1-bed flats. If your analysis tells you that studios are a better way to go, you'll want to know this. This means that you need to pull the data on every flat type, not just 1-beds.

While we collect quite a bit more info in our own MAC analysis tool, the above will be a great starting point for working out the demand in your area.

So, now you have this information in a spreadsheet for each relevant property type, what on earth do you do with it? Some of the fields you've collected are useful for direct comparisons, while others provide averages. Ideally, you want around 20 properties in your spreadsheet for each flat type to have some meaningful averages, however, think twice about including any outliers. You may find that some properties are twice the size of everything else or half the price. This may be for a very obvious reason that has no correlation with your own units, in which case you should exclude them.

Also, be wary of location. Two flats can be within a street of each other, but because one's at the top of an ex-council tower block and the other is a posh Victorian conversion, their numbers can differ wildly.

Here are some of the metrics you can glean from this data:

A. Average size (area) – add up the sum of the square meterage of all the 1-bed flats and divide by the total number of flats (making sure all your figures are in metres or feet and not a mixture of both!)
B. Average price – the total asking price of every unit combined divided by the number of units
C. Cost per m^2 – B divided by A

If we look at these three metrics for studios, 1-bed flats, and 2-bed flats in your area with a sample size of around 20 for each, you already have some incredibly useful information. So, what exactly have you learned?

Size: You now know the average size in m² of the competition. You can see how large your units would be compared to the rest of the market. It can be tempting to fall into the trap of using working assumptions for market apartment sizes (e.g., a 1-bed flat is 40 m²). However, if the average 1-bed flat size on the market in your area is 55m², then you know your 37m² flats are going to be up against some stiff competition unless this is reflected in the price.

Cost: You now know the average, upper and lower range of the 'for sale' prices of the competition. What GDV did you have in mind for each of your units? If the average is £150k and you were planning on £175k, then you know you've got to be able to justify the uplift in terms of quality, size, features, or location. If you're at £175k and the most expensive on Rightmove is at £170k, you need to ask yourself whether the price is achievable. Can you justify being the most expensive?

Cost per m2: This is a calculation that many people overlook, but it's critical to understanding one aspect of how your units stack up against the competition. Since a property's floor area has a direct correlation to its price/value, you want to be able to see how the cost per m² of your units stacks up against everything else on the market.

But just because your unit may be bigger or smaller than average, how should that affect the price you charge?

Imagine you were comparing:

<u>Flat 1:</u> A 40m², 1-bed flat you intend to build with a GDV of £200k, and

Flat 2: A 50m^2, 1-bed flat currently on the market at £250k

Which is better value?

By comparing them at a cost per m^2 level, you can instantly see that they both cost £5,000 per m^2. However, let's imagine Flat 1 was now 45m^2 instead of 40m^2. Now it's only costing £4,444 per m^2, which would make Flat 2 seem a lot pricier in comparison.

Conversely if Flat 2 cost £230k instead of £250k then its cost per m^2 is now only £4,600 which makes Flat 1 at £5,000 per m^2 seem quite expensive. Obvious? With a calculator, yes. But what you want to avoid is making a blanket assumption that just because your flat is bigger and it costs more, everything is ok. If it's 10% bigger but 50% more expensive then everything is NOT ok!

Another great way of benchmarking your proposed GDVs is to multiply the floor area of each of your units by the average cost per m^2 for that property type in your area.

To use an example, let's say that the average selling price of 1-beds is £160k and their average size is 50m^2. Divide £160k by 50m^2, and we get £3,200 per square metre.

If you're going to be building some 40m^2 1-bed flats, then if we multiply 40m^2 by the £3,200, we get £128k. This would be the GDV of each unit based on the retail market average per square metre cost.

While it's not an exact science, it can make for an excellent 'reasonableness test'. If the calculation produces £128k and you were hoping to sell your units for £160k, you need to have a compelling reason why your cost per square metre is so much more expensive (or alternatively invest in some unbelievably expensive taps).

If we look at some of the other data you collected in your spreadsheet, you will be able to build a picture of some of the key features:

1. Do most units on the market have parking, and if so, what sort of premium does it attract?
2. How many units have gardens or balconies?
3. What types of flat are available, e.g., conversions versus purpose-built?
4. How do prices change as you move further away from the street on which your units are located?
5. How close are your units to public transport links? Can you walk into town?

One mistake we come across is where the developer wants to incorporate parking spaces, but the target audience doesn't want or need them. A parking space could easily add £10k to the cost of a flat. But if your customers are young professionals who are a stone's throw away from the bus stop and the train station, they're not going to want to pay a premium for a parking spot they're not going to use.

However, you should also be aware that parking will be a consideration when Full Planning Permission is being sought on a project. The council will have minimum parking space requirements and will also consider the availability of local on-street parking. In theory, this should not be a consideration with a PDR application as parking is not normally one of the criteria that the council can use to assess it. However, there is enough wriggle room for them to make it an issue if they want to. As with all things planning-related, the Planning Consultant on your professional team will be able to give you the best advice.

Finally, another area you should consider is demand. You will recall that when you collected the data from Rightmove, you captured the number of 1-bed flats that were available for sale. Then you ticked the box to include the number INCLUDING those that were recently sold, which gave you a second, larger number. What does this tell us? Well, in isolation, not a great deal, but consider these results (where the first two columns are taken from Rightmove, and the third is simply the difference between the two):

Type	No. For Sale	No. Including Sold	No. Recently Sold
Studios	20	25	5
1-bed	50	100	50
2-bed	2	2	0

You now know the following:

1. There appears to be a much bigger demand and supply for 1-beds; in fact, they dominate the market
2. There's only a negligible demand for 2-beds and what stock there is doesn't seem to be shifting (so you probably won't want to be building any 2-beds then)
3. Studios have more demand than 2-beds but aren't as popular as 1-beds, nor are they selling as well
4. 1-beds appear to be selling like hot cakes

You can also perform the same analysis for neighbouring areas to see how your target area stacks up in comparison. You don't need to get data for every property. Just select the area and property type, then apply the same filters and then check and uncheck the 'sold' box to get your two numbers. Remember that this is not telling you how long it takes to sell a property; it's only a relative comparison between property types.

You would always look to confirm your findings from this exercise with local agents before buying the property (see step 3 below). However, this is a great desktop exercise that allows you to not only test your theories on the selling price of your units; it should also give you a steer on what type of units the market can best support.

Matching the ideal unit type to your host property

This is the second step, and there are two considerations to bear in mind here. Let's say that the local market favours 2-bed flats based on your MAC analysis above. The first question then is, 'can I build 2-bed flats in my host building?' While some buildings are blank canvases into which you could put almost any type of unit, others can have some limitations due to their layout. So, if your building isn't going to be a good fit for 2-bed flats, then you need to consider a Plan B (and even a Plan C). Remember, just because plan A isn't feasible, it doesn't mean that Plan B won't work, but at least you now know.

The second consideration is that industrial buildings tend to have a particular style due to their architecture, and this may not appeal to everyone. You may also find that people who are buying flats locally wouldn't want to live in your converted building because it's not swanky enough. What if all the 2-bed apartments locally are on luxury, gated communities, whereas yours are on the rear end of an industrial estate overlooking the gasworks?

Again, you need to do a reality check here. If the local market is asking for a premium product, will you be able to deliver? Or will you be polishing the proverbial turd? In which case you need a Plan B...

You're not after a definitive view here – it's quite unusual for the analysis to determine that only one solution will work.

By now, you'll be forming a good picture of what the market is looking for, so now it's time to see if you were right...

Check with local estate agents

Now we move to the third and final step of the MAC process. Residential estate agents are your friends when it comes to development, and they have a pivotal role to play throughout your project.

1. At the beginning: they advise on what type of unit to build, the target market, the best fit and finish, and the ideal selling price
2. In the middle: once they know they'll be selling the end units for you, it's helpful to invite them on site during the project. They can see how things have moved on and start to get excited about the end units they'll be selling. They can also give some thought to marketing strategy. Imagine that your estate agent was showing YOU around one of your units. How much more engaged would they be if they'd been involved in the project personally not only at the start but also as the building was transformed?
3. At the end: these are the people who'll be selling your units for you, advising on the best marketing strategy and the best way to dress and advertise the units.

You want to get some advice and feedback on what your analysis is telling you, and your local estate agents will be the best people to ask. At this stage, the conversation can be at a relatively high level. The agents should be happy to help as a) it's no skin off their nose, and b) you will need to appoint one of them to sell the end units, so they will be viewing you as a potential customer.

Having explained who you are and what you're looking to do (you don't need to provide details of the actual property involved if you don't want to), ask them what types of people want to live in that area. What is the demographic, and of course, what types of property are they looking to buy? Ask them the question; what kind of unit will sell the quickest, in their opinion.

Once they've given their initial view, feel free to discuss your findings, particularly if you arrived at a different conclusion. You don't want to present your MAC findings first because you run the risk of leading the witness.

Another point to consider is volume. It's one thing to establish that 2-bed flats have the highest demand. But if you then flood the market with ten 2-bed apartments all at once, you may find it takes a long time to shift them all. Again, this is where your estate agent can provide guidance. Would you be better off having a mixture of 1-bed and 2-bed units so that you're able to sell them more quickly as your combined target audience is larger? Yes, you'll make less profit on paper, but if you can't find enough buyers then it could be a great move to mix things up. You'll have noticed that when large housebuilders build a new development, they nearly always create a mix of house types, even though only one house type will be their most profitable one. That's partly because they want to appeal to as many buyers as possible and thereby sell the units quickly.

We encountered an example of this very recently with one of our students. She had been to view an industrial building that ticked all the right boxes, on paper at least. The numbers stacked up, the property was easy to convert into 1-bedroom flats, and no other developers seemed to be in the frame. However, after the viewing she went to meet with some local agents to get their view on the potential project, just as we'd trained her to do. It was then that she discovered a fatal flaw. There was a glut of 1-bedroom flats about to come onto the market from two large new developments. Plus, even more were being built that would be coming on in the next 12 months. This would mean one of two things. Either her unit price would need to be reduced to try and get a quick sale, or the units would stay on the market for a long time before being sold. Neither option was appealing, and our student decided to pass. There are plenty more projects out there with better prospects. However, it goes to show the importance of getting guidance from the people on the ground that know the local market inside out.

When you speak to an agent, make it clear that you're converting an industrial building. Will that skew their thinking in a particular direction? Are older professional couples buying the 2-bed properties, whereas your funky Industrial Conversion might appeal to younger couples that can only afford a 1-bed?

Fit and finish is another critical question to ask; what sort of standard should you go for? There's no point in having gold taps and marble floors in a modest 1-bed flat. But your 2-bed flat customers may want premium appliances and fancier tiling in the bathroom. This is all stuff you need to know before you buy because it has a bearing on the cost.

Bathrooms should be on your list of things to discuss. We try and get larger shower cubicles and wet rooms in our more basic flats as they add a hint of luxury that people appreciate. Let's face it; everyone hates a poky shower. But what if your agent thinks that you need to fit a bath rather than a shower? Again, you don't need to take his or her advice, but it's a factor you need to consider.

Parking is another question you should always quiz estate agents on. There are several considerations here, not least of which is whether your development has any parking spaces. If it doesn't, where will people be able to park? Does the agent think that it could be a deal-breaker for many customers, or are most of them likely to commute or put up with street parking? We've seen deals come unstuck on the issue of parking because the developer didn't ask the right questions before they purchased the site. They assumed that buyers would be able to live without parking when, in fact, they couldn't. All the competition had parking, and so people bought those units instead.

If parking is a deal-breaker, can you change the plan to incorporate it? And if so, what sort of premium does that put on your units? How will it affect the price? Again, your residential agents will have a view.

We also mentioned quirky features and vaulted ceilings. If you think this is a possibility with your project, be sure to mention it to the agents. Get their view on whether it adds value or isn't worth the cost or effort.

The final question you need to get the agents' views on is what your units will sell for. You've discussed the unit sizes, the number of beds, the fit and finish, and the parking. You know who your ideal customer is. So, at what price should you be marketing the finished product?

This is critical since it's coming from an independent source that you don't already have. Cynics will recommend caution, as an agent may be inclined to be optimistic in their pricing (perish the thought), particularly if they're trying to win your business. That's all fine; you can bear that in mind when you compare their views with your own market analysis. But if you've got three separate views and valuation estimates, then you've also got a bit of a spread (and with a bit of luck they won't all be lying through their teeth ☺).

Ask the agents if they could share some comparables with you. What has sold recently nearby that would lend credibility to their valuation of your units? They may even be able to give you some particulars, in which case, feel free to challenge them on the differences, as there will be some. We've often found agents who share their opinions very eloquently on local market prices but who, when asked for actual examples of properties they've sold there recently, start squirming a bit and start looking at their shoes.

Which agents should you ask?

Make sure you speak to local agents who know the area, otherwise, you can't rely on what they tell you. It will be generic advice and not explicitly related to that location. Some estate agents cover a large geographic area but may not have in-depth knowledge of the area in the immediate vicinity of your project. A good way of discovering who might be the more knowledgeable agents in your area is to go onto Rightmove and use the map view. Make sure you zoom in on your target location (as before the radius needs to be big enough to pick up 20+ properties ideally) and filter by the appropriate property type (e.g., houses or flats – but ignore bedroom count). You should also tick the box that says, 'include recently sold properties'. Then simply count the number of properties that are listed against each agent. You'll usually find that one or two agents have more entries than the rest. You can reasonably assume that their local knowledge is decent, plus they should have more recently sold examples that can back up their assessments.

You need to make sure you speak to at least three agents so that you can get a consensus. We've all seen the home makeover TV shows, where several estate agents walk around the freshly upgraded property after the work's been done, and give their opinion on its new value. And sometimes, the difference in views can be staggering, so make sure to ask more than one person. If you ask three and the results are disparate, go for a fourth and fifth.

Finally, face-to-face is always better with agents. And don't just turn up unannounced – make an appointment and be sure you get to see someone who knows what they're talking about. Bear in mind that you may want to take along an anonymised floor plan of what you're thinking of building along with the unit sizes etc. to show the agent. That sort of thing is much better done face to face for obvious reasons.

Some further estate agent considerations

Here are a few additional points that you may want to bear in mind.

1. As a developer, your target area could be any project within an hour or so's drive of home. There are likely to be hundreds of estate agents covering that area. Where you have a sweet spot (say, for example, in your local town), you should make a point of getting to know the agents. For the rest of your area, it won't be realistic to establish relationships with everyone, so you're bound to be meeting new agents for the first time when you have a project to consider. Always remember to ring to make an appointment to see an agent if you can, rather than simply turning up at their offices

2. Commercial finance companies welcome the input from estate agents as it provides them with a third-party evaluation of your project valuations. Without this, they would only have your assessment of the project GDV, which may be overly optimistic. By being able to show that local agents have confirmed the selling price of the finished units, you're giving the lender confidence that your sales numbers stack up

3. When you're considering properties where you plan to contact the owner speculatively, then we would recommend contacting the owners before you contact local estate agents. This is because it's a waste of your time and the agent's time discussing a property that isn't yet for sale. You first want to make sure you've got a viable proposition on your hands

So that's the ideal process you should go through to establish what would be the best types of unit to build, particularly when you are looking at properties that are on the open market.

How many units can I fit into the site?

This is the million-dollar question, since it can literally make the difference between a deal producing a healthy profit or being put into the 'too difficult' or 'doesn't quite stack' piles. Why? Because if you can squeeze just one more unit into your development by being a bit more creative in the layout, then you can dramatically increase your profit.

By way of a simplistic example, imagine you were building 6 flats and all your profit was in flats 5 and 6 (because in selling the first 4 flats you would simply be recouping your costs). If you could somehow squeeze in a seventh flat, then your profit would increase not by one seventh, but by 50%, as you now have three profitable flats instead of two. This is an oversimplification, but hopefully you get the principle.

So how do you work out how many units you can fit in to a development? The answer is to do something called block planning, and it's a highly valuable yet underutilised skill in the world of conversions.

Understanding block planning

The principle of block planning is very simple. You create a scale outline of the perimeter of your site and then inside that perimeter you draw in as many flats as you can reasonably fit, allowing for numerous factors, including:

1. Access – you must be able to get to the front door without crossing anyone else's property or climbing across the roof
2. Light – all your units must be able to have sufficient light coming into their living areas
3. Cycle and bin storage – you need to allow sufficient communal space for bikes and bins

4. Unit type – you'll need to know what mix of flats you're looking to build and the minimum size (floor area) of each type

We cover space, area, light, and access in later chapters, and you'll need to draw on that knowledge too, when you block plan.

So where do you start?

Firstly, you need to draw the outline of your site to scale. If there are some floorplans available (with dimensions) either on the agent's particulars or from a previous planning application on the council's planning portal, then this is great news. If not, you can use a little-known measuring tool on Google Maps, as follows:

1. Go to Google Maps and zoom in as close as you can to your target property in Satellite mode (i.e. aerial view and not street view)
2. Hover your mouse over the top left-hand corner of the building (as accurately as you can) and right click
3. Choose 'Measure Distance' from the drop-down menu that appears.
4. Now right click on the top right-hand corner of the building (or whatever the adjacent corner happens to be if it's an odd-shaped building)

You should find that Google has now drawn a line between the two points, and it will tell you the distance between them i.e. the length of that wall. How clever is that? Whilst this isn't going to be accurate to the nearest centimetre, it will be accurate enough to block plan, which is all we care about at this stage.

You can now make a note of that dimension on a piece of paper and measure all the other walls of the property in the same way until you have each one. You can then easily draw a scale outline of the property on a separate piece of A4 or A3 paper using your measurements and simply scaling them down proportionally. Since this is the document you'll be using to outline your flats on, you might want to run off a few virgin copies before you start experimenting, as you may not get the perfect layout first time.

The Google Maps magic doesn't end there. If you repeat the exercise but this time just right click on every corner of the building sequentially in one direction (e.g. clockwise) one after the other, Google will trace the outline. When you complete the 'circle' by clicking on the point you started with, Google will show you the area (square metreage) of the property. This is what is known in the development business as quite handy (we told you Google was your friend).

Ok, so you now have a scale outline of your building. How do you work out what flats to draw on it?

The basic rule of thumb here is to start by drawing one-bedroom flats since these are the sweet spot in terms of GDV per square metre. In other words, 1-bed flats are usually more valuable per square metre than 2-bed flats. That said, if your MAC analysis has already indicated that 2-bed flats are the only realistic option, then by all means start by drawing 2-bed flats in the block plan.

How big should these 1-bed flats be? Well, you'll remember in chapter 8 we said the minimum size of a flat should be $37m^2$ to comply with National Space Standards. So, your challenge, initially at least, is to see how many $37m^2$ 1-bed flat outlines you can fit into your floorplan. This in theory would maximise the GDV of the project.

Bear in mind that you're not trying work out the internal floorplans of each flat e.g. bathroom, bedroom, etc. You just want to mark in the external outline of each flat.

There is no right answer to block planning, which is both a blessing and a curse. You can't get it wrong, but it's easy to miss a layout that might be more profitable. Also, a practised eye is worth a lot, so you need to keep practising. Many's the time we've had students give us their best block planning efforts, only to be stunned when we show them how they can easily squeeze another one or more units in. They swear blind that it took them countless days to perfect their plan, only to have us pull it to pieces within a few seconds. Is this because we're brilliant at block planning? Well, in a word, yes; absolutely it is.

Actually, that's not entirely true – it's simply because we've done lots of it over the years, so we're more likely to see the most efficient layout than someone who's not had as much practice. And when that can add 50% to your profit, you'll understand why we say there's a benefit in getting good at it by practising QUITE A LOT.

Finally, here are a few tips when block planning:

1. Once you have your basic outline, commit to marking up your first $37m^2$ flat within 60 seconds of starting. Why? Well, most people take about four light years to draw their first line on the page, by which time the property has been sold/fallen into disrepair/crumbled to dust. Once you have the first flat drawn on, the second one comes more easily, just trust us on this ☺
2. Don't be afraid to try different layouts. For your second attempt try drawing your first flat in a different part of the floorplan or try varying the shape of your units.
3. Remember that a $37m^2$ flat doesn't have to be square (but it can't be 18.5 metres long by 2 metres wide either unless you're catering exclusively for ten-pin bowling fans).
4. Take on board all of the considerations of light, access, and space that we cover in the next few chapters. Some of the questions you should ask are:

a. Can I get access to each flat without going across neighbouring land?
b. Is there room for communal areas i.e. bikes and bins?
c. Do all the flats have enough light? This is not just a case of having windows, but making sure that the light from the windows is sufficient to reach all the living areas
d. Should I use roof windows in any part of the development to help get light in?
e. Can I create a second storey or duplex?
f. Are my internal courtyards (if I have any) wide enough to prevent overlooking or loss of light?
g. Do the units overlook each other or a neighbouring property?

You might be surprised that we include block planning on your task list given all this 'leveraging your team' stuff we've been banging on about. After all, surely an architect could do all this for you?

Well, that's certainly true, however they'll probably want to charge you a few hundred quid for the privilege, plus it may take them a few weeks to get back to you, by which time you may have missed the boat. Also, two heads are better than one when it comes to block planning – they won't necessarily have the same ideas as you, and vice versa.

Remember that you won't know whether your deal stacks up until you've crunched your high-level numbers, and you can only do that once you know how many units of each type you're likely to build. Being able to block plan won't guarantee you the perfect floorplan, but it will get you to a point where you can see roughly how many units you could fit in, and so get a good idea whether you're looking at a potentially profitable scheme.

What is the likely development cost of the conversion?

If you cast your mind back to the beginning of this chapter, we rattled off five pieces of information that you would need when working out what to build, and development cost was the fourth.

As we mentioned in the opening chapter, we're not going to dive into how exactly you calculate the cost of a development, as that sits outside the scope of this book. However, you clearly need to have a process and a model in place for working out the approximate costs for each aspect of any prospective project, which would include:

1. The asset cost (buying the site)
2. Acquisition costs (e.g. legal costs, sourcing fees, stamp duty)
3. The build/conversion cost, including professional fees
4. The cost of finance
5. The disposal costs (e.g. estate agent fees and legal costs)
6. Your profit

The key here is to build a generic model that includes all your costs rather than build one from scratch each time you look at a new deal, since you'll run the risk of forgetting something important.

Also, make sure that you are reasonably prudent in your estimates. It won't be possible for you to know the exact costs when you first analyse a deal, but that's not your aim. What you're trying to do initially is to understand whether the deal is worth spending any more time on i.e. should it stay in your sales funnel? So, put in some high-level assumptions initially, that you think are reasonable, as this will allow you to assess the deal without spending time trying to get quotes. If the deal stacks up, you'll be getting firm quotes further down the line, but for now, you're just looking to see if it's worthy of further analysis.

At the end of this exercise, you'll have a ball-park indication of the potential profit in the scheme. If it's greater than 20% it stays in the funnel, and you can do further work. If it's less than 20% it may still have scope so don't automatically dismiss it. It may just need more work either to refine the cost assumptions or the layout of the units. However, the exercise will very quickly flag up those opportunities that simply don't get close to an acceptable margin, and so can be discounted and removed from the funnel.

How much should you pay for the host building?

This is the fifth and final piece of the 'what should I build' jigsaw (ok, so a five-piece jigsaw puzzle isn't that challenging, but please just go with it as we can't think of a better analogy).

The maths is straightforward; you start with the amount you expect to sell your finished units for, then you deduct your (20% minimum) profit, your finance costs, your build/conversion costs and your acquisition costs. This then leaves you with the maximum amount that you can afford to pay for the asset itself. Note that we said 'maximum amount' – we're not suggesting that you offer your best price at the outset, for obvious reasons.

There's a very important point to note here, which is that the vendor's asking price for the asset does NOT play any part in your calculation. You DON'T start with the asking price, add on the costs and see how much profit you can make. Instead, you work it back from the GDV, assuming a 20%+ profit, then see what you can afford to pay for the site after you've deducted all costs.

That's because the price the vendor is hoping to get for their property or asset has no bearing on what it's actually worth to you. It simply represents a guide to their hopes or expectation, which may or may not be realistic. As we've mentioned, property does not have a pre-determined value – it's only worth what someone is prepared to pay for it, and this will vary from one developer to another.

That said, the asking price is still relevant because it frames the vendor's expectations. Clearly, if you run your numbers and can only afford to offer £100k on a site that's on the market at £500k, then you may want to pass. We would always encourage making cheeky offers, but there's a line where cheeky becomes insulting or laughable and you probably don't want to cross it if you want to be treated seriously by agents and vendors.

But you'd be surprised at how often cheeky offers are accepted, particularly when a property has been on the market a while. A good tactic can be to frame your initial offer verbally e.g. "At this stage I'm thinking we may be able to make an offer around the £xxx mark – does that sound like a good basis for further discussion?"

This approach enables you to gauge the vendor/agent's reaction to a low offer without making any formal representations. If their reaction is that the offer is too low, then you are immediately able to ask them how much further you'd need to stretch to get to an acceptable number, and once you have that, perhaps you may be able to meet them in the middle.

Of course, if they bite your hand off and shower you with effusive thanks, this can be a sign that you may have slightly over-egged your initial offer.

Following a system

So there we have it, a walk-through of the five steps you need to go through to determine what to build, for an industrial conversion opportunity.

There's no rocket science, but as you can see, there's a fair bit of work involved.

One thing you'll notice is that it's a system; you're simply doing the same process for every deal. Some will get rejected early on whilst others will make it through to the point where you can make an offer. The idea is to minimise the time you spend on the no-hopers and maximise the time you spend on the ones that have legs.

One word of warning – please make sure that you firm up your quotes and estimates before committing to a purchase. It can be easy to assume that an estimate is reasonable or shouldn't have changed since the last time you had a quote. The reality is that unless you've taken steps to nail down your numbers as far as possible, you're putting your profitability at risk, since you can't be sure the deal stacks up.

Now, we really need to be moving things on a bit. So why don't we leave deal analysis for a while, and instead take a look at the glamourous world of planning...

11. Understanding Permitted Development Rights

In this chapter, it's time to get your head around the planning system and the concept of Permitted Development Rights (PDRs) with Prior Approval. Like most regulation it's rather complex, but we'll do our best to steer you through it.

What is Permitted Development, and why does it exist?

Well, there's a question. As we mentioned earlier, you can't just go and build whatever you like on a piece of land that you happen to own. The government believes, rather cynically, that when developing property, you may have a tendency to prioritise factors such as your own profit over other factors such as green belt retention, population density, aesthetics, and environmental impact, to name but a few. As a result, we have a planning policy in place, which means that there is a set of rules determining what can and can't be built in any given part of the country. Any developer looking to build or convert property must have their plans assessed and ultimately approved by the local authority before work can commence. This is known as obtaining Full Planning Permission, and it is the default requirement for all property development in England and Wales.

In its wisdom, the government recognised that the planning process could be quite a lengthy, costly, and painful one. There were certain instances where it suited the government to make life easier for people to develop property, particularly if it meant addressing the current chronic housing shortage. These instances include building small residential extensions onto previously unextended properties, as well as converting certain types of non-residential buildings into residential accommodation.

So, for simple house extensions, certain PDRs exist which allow homeowners to extend without notifying the local planning authority – they can just get on with building it, albeit the usual requirements of building control, etc., must still be met. However, there is a requirement to seek and obtain what is known as' Prior Approval' for the change of use in certain circumstances where there is a change of use class (e.g., a 'conversion' from industrial to residential).

The Prior Approval process allows the local planning authority to check that the proposed change of use does not fall foul of certain 'showstopper' events. These can include:

1. The impact on transport and highways
2. Any contamination risks
3. Flood risk
4. Natural light provision
5. The design or external appearance of the building

and various others (each PDR has its own prescribed set of events that will be considered under Prior Approval).

Why does the government favour these sorts of conversions? Well, the primary reason is that property demand has changed. We currently have a desperate need for more residential housing in the UK. But we have a surplus of commercial, industrial, and retail buildings, with many lying derelict or out of use. The internet revolution succeeded the out-of-town shopping centre revolution, and both have left their mark on the demand for and location of commercial property. So by making it easier for people to convert these buildings from one use to the other, the government is encouraging the recycling of existing brownfield sites.

Note that the PDRs in England do not apply in Scotland, Wales, and Northern Ireland. These countries have devolved planning policies, and English PDRs do not apply there. How can you find out what planning rules exist in your part of the UK? There is an abundance of information available online, both at a national and regional level. We would also strongly advocate meeting with a local planning consultant to ensure your interpretation of the planning requirements is accurate and up to date.

Is the absence of PDRs a deal-breaker, irrespective of where in the UK you are based? Not really; it adds an element of risk and uncertainty since Full Planning Permission would be required, plus we'd also counsel against undertaking a non-PDR conversion for your first project for the reasons previously mentioned. But all the other benefits, including the lack of competition and ease of build, would still apply. For developers with one or more projects under their belts, it can be an excellent opportunity to play in a space where most other developers aren't even looking.

The process for obtaining PDRs with Prior Approval in England is not entirely free of bureaucracy. In most cases, you're required to apply for Prior Approval to the local planning authority, and in some instances (depending on the PDR), they have only 56 days to review it and respond. Compare this to the planning process where theoretically, the council has 8-13 weeks to reach a decision, but where projects can often take several years to come to fruition (or not), and you can see the attraction of Permitted Development.

Note that the government doesn't give carte blanche to developers when it comes to PDRs. There are still rules that have to be followed. Plus, there are various scenarios where PDRs aren't available and where Full Planning Permission is still required. But in general terms, these PDRs present an excellent opportunity for developers. They remove a considerable element of risk (will they or won't they get Full Planning Permission) as well as making things a lot quicker.

Historic Legislation

Like all things regulatory, the legislation surrounding PDRs doesn't stand still. You'll need to make sure that your team understands the current rules, and that's the job of your Planning Consultant, who should be fully up to speed.

Let's start with a little history lesson, as it's worth understanding how we've arrived at the current position.

Permitted Development Rights originally arose from The Town and Country Planning (General Permitted Development) (England) Order 2015. This is a statutory instrument, applying only in England, that grants planning permission for certain types of development (such development is then referred to as Permitted Development).

On 1st October 2017, the government temporarily granted a Permitted Development Right for the change of use from light industrial to residential. For a period of three years from that date, changing the use of a light industrial building (or part of a building used as light industrial) that is use class B1(c)[1], to residential, use class C3, benefits from a new Permitted Development Right, subject to a Prior Approval process and various limitations and conditions.

So, let's take a quick look at what those were...

Exemptions and Limitations

Various exemptions and limitations applied to the PDR for light Industrial Conversions. These include:

Light Industrial usage on 15th March 2014

The building must have been classified as light industrial on 15th March 2014 to qualify.

Prior Approval date must be before 1st October 2020.

The government did not grant PDRs indefinitely. The window for having a Permitted Development application approved ended on the 1st October 2020.

Gross floor space of the existing building cannot exceed 500m²

Anything bigger than 500m² (5,381 square feet) would need Full Planning Permission to convert.

Tenant and landlord consent needed if an agricultural tenancy

If you were converting an agricultural building, then the tenant's consent to the conversion was required in addition to the landlord's.

12-month delay if terminating agricultural tenancy to convert

If there was an agricultural tenant in situ, then they needed to be given 12 months' notice.

Certain types of building were excluded

The building being converted would require Full Planning Permission if it were any of the following:

1. An SSSI site (Site of Special Scientific Interest)
2. A safety hazard zone
3. A military storage building
4. A listed building
5. A monument (or a building which contains a monument)

An important point to remember is that just because a building is excluded from PDRs, it doesn't make conversion impossible. It merely means that Full Planning Permission would need to be sought and obtained.

The 2020 changes

2020 turned out to be quite an exciting year as far as planning law was concerned, as it saw the introduction of The Town And Country Planning (General Permitted Development) (England) (Amendment) Order 2020, which came into effect on 31st August 2020.

Unfortunately, the new order didn't extend the original light industrial PDR, and so this lapsed on 30th September 2020. However, it did introduce a raft of new PDRs, and one of these was called Class ZA.

In a nutshell, Class ZA provides for the demolition of certain types of building and the construction of new residential units (either flats or houses) in their place, all under Permitted Development and without Full Planning Permission being required.

What types of building can be demolished?

1. Single detached blocks of flats
2. A detached office building falling within class B1(a)
3. A detached research and development building falling within class B1(b)
4. A detached light industrial building falling within class B1(c)

For our purposes, item 4 is the most relevant as it introduces a brand new PDR for light industrial buildings. However, there are quite a few caveats attached to these rights (please note that the list below is not exhaustive – we've listed the main points but you will need to study the relevant Statutory Instrument 2020 No. 756 for the complete list of permissions and conditions).

Any building to be demolished under Class ZA must have been:

1. constructed before 31 December 1989
2. still in existence as at 12 March 2020
3. less than 1,000 square metres in area
4. vacant for at least 6 months prior to the date of the application for Prior Approval
5. less than 18m tall
6. not rendered unsafe or uninhabitable
7. unlisted, outside the site of a monument or a site of special scientific interest (SSSI), and not within 3km of an aerodrome

And any new building that replaces the demolished building must be:

1. built within the footprint of the original building
2. built with exterior walls no nearer to the public highway than the original building
3. no more than 18m high or 7m higher than the original building, whichever is lower
4. no more than two storeys taller than the original building, with the internal floor to ceiling height of these additional storeys not exceeding the lower of 3m or the lowest internal floor to ceiling height of the original building
5. built within 3 years of Prior Approval being granted

Local Authority application considerations

We mentioned earlier that Permitted Development is not a slam-dunk or a foregone conclusion. The local authority has several considerations that it must take into account when considering an application for Prior Approval. These areas are prescriptive, i.e., they can't reject an application just because they don't like it or because it wouldn't be acceptable under full planning. Here is the list of the specific areas in which an authority may decide NOT to grant approval for class ZA:

a) Transport and highways impact

Will the conversion have a detrimental effect on the local transport infrastructure? There could be circumstances where there is a lack of parking spaces in the immediate vicinity, or where the introduction of more traffic may be problematic as far as the council is concerned.

b) Contamination risk

Does the authority feel that there is a risk of contamination from the site? While many light industrial sites may have potential contamination issues, the existence of a robust and undisturbed base is often sufficient to satisfy the local authority that contamination will not be an issue. You would need to confirm in writing to the council that you will not be disturbing the existing concrete slab to install new drainage below ground. Your professional team will also need to report to the council that there are visual signs of any contamination within the building. We discuss this issue in more detail in chapter 17.

c) Flood risk

Is the building located in a high flood risk area?

d) Design

Good design has been a fundamental requirement of the new planning legislation, however clearly there is a degree of subjectivity here.

e) External appearance

Similarly, a not unreasonable consideration yet one that can only be judged by the eye of the beholder (if the local planning authority think it's ugly, it probably won't matter what YOU think).

f) Provision of adequate natural light

There must be adequate light in all habitable rooms (no more rabbit hutches without windows thank you very much)

g) Amenity impact

For example, considerations regarding overlooking, privacy, and light.

h) Noise from nearby commercial premises

The local planning authority clearly needs to avoid a situation where it grants Prior Approval only to have the new residents complain of the excessive noise from neighbouring commercial premises (who were there first).

i) Impact on local businesses

Will the introduction of your new residents have a negative impact on local businesses?

j) Impact on heritage and archaeology

Likewise, is there a detrimental impact on any historical assets?

k) Demolition methodology

Sounds straightforward in theory but, depending on the location and structure of the building, demolition can be a complex (and highly sensitive) subject.

l) Planned landscaping

This would include things like planting and the maintenance of shrubs etc.

m) Impact on air traffic, defence assets, and Protected Vistas

Which could quash any aspirations you might have to build a block of flats at the end of a runway, overlooking a top secret military base or in front of St. Paul's Cathedral.

In a nutshell, class ZA isn't quite as helpful as the original light industrial PDR, which allowed us to convert buildings rather than demolish them. Plus, you have to say there's a lot more subjectivity involved, particularly regarding aspects of design and appearance.

So, is there any way in which we could convert light industrial buildings under Class ZA without having to knock them down? After all, repurposing an existing building seems more environmentally sound, plus it would make for a much speedier project.

Luckily, there is one asset left in the toolbox you can bring into play, and that is the little-known strategy known as the planning fall-back position.

The Fall-back Position

The fall-back position relates to the development that COULD still take place under a PDR even if a Full Planning Permission application was REFUSED.

Let's imagine that you put in a planning application to convert a light industrial unit that would be eligible under Class ZA. The critical distinction here is that you want to convert the existing building, whereas Class ZA only allows you to knock it down and start again; hence you would need to apply for Full Planning Permission.

If planning was refused, you could still use the Class ZA PDR to demolish the building and rebuild a block of flats in its place. This is effectively your fall-back position, i.e., what you're allowed to build if you don't have Full Planning Permission. However, there may be a strong argument that the conversion route is a better option, specifically in terms of public betterment. On what grounds might it be considered 'better' for the public? Perhaps the new block of flats will be imposing and arguably out of character with the local street scene, have a far greater environmental impact, or require significant disruption to local residences and businesses during the demolition phase. Instead, you propose an alternative solution that involves repurposing and beautifying the existing building, thus avoiding any demolition, creating a better street scene, and with less environmental impact. The planning authority can then consider which of the two options is preferable from the public's point of view. Suppose they believe that your proposal, which would require Full Planning Permission, is preferable to the Class ZA Permitted Development option. In that case, the fall-back position allows them to grant you Full Planning Permission for your proposal.

A key point to note here is that the fall-back position is established by legal precedent, and so it is an accepted process within the planning system. It also has a refreshing pragmatism; after all, why wouldn't we want planners to approve better solutions, even though they technically fall outside Permitted Development Rights?

However, a word of warning; fall-back positions are by no means a slam-dunk, and they could take a considerable time to get across the line. We would also suggest that any approach regarding a fall-back position is made on the basis that you are looking for the planning department's input and guidance on the best possible solution since this is likely to he better received than a less 'collaborative' approach.

The position from 1st August 2021

Having enjoyed the ability to convert light industrial buildings up to 500m^2 from 1st October 2017 to 30th September 2020, when this ended, we were left with only the Class ZA PDR that could be applied to light industrial. And being honest, this didn't have a massive appeal for us. Not only did it have many subjective areas that planners could potentially push back on, but the fall-back position option was also likely to take time to get across the line and could not be guaranteed.

Luckily, we didn't have long to wait for some rather good news to come along. You will recall the 'super' use class, Class E, earlier, created in September 2020. This placed a whole raft of different building types into a single use class, which included (the artist formerly known as) B1(c) – light industrial.

Then, in December 2020, the government dropped an even bigger bombshell; it proposed a new PDR called class MA that would allow any building in Class E to be converted to residential use with effect from 1st August 2021.

For small-scale developers, this was huge news. It meant that we would now have Permitted Development Rights to convert the following Class E buildings to residential:

- Shops including post offices (formerly class A1)
- Financial services, including banks and building societies (formerly class A2)
- Non-medical professional services, e.g., estate and employment agencies (formerly class A2)
- Cafes and restaurants (formerly class A3)
- Offices (formerly class B1(a))
- Research and development buildings (formerly class B1(b))
- Light Industrial (formerly class B1(c))
- Doctors' surgeries and health centres (formerly class D1(a))

- Creches, day nurseries, and day centres
- Gyms and indoor sports centres

Having consulted on the proposal, the government confirmed that there would be several limitations that would apply to class MA, as follows:

- Any conversion must be for residential use only and not for houses of multiple occupancy (HMOs)
- The building must be vacant for at least three continuous months prior to the application for Prior Approval being submitted
- The building's current cumulative floor space cannot exceed 1,500 square metres
- Buildings to be converted must have been in Class E use for at least two years prior to the application
- You can't use class MA in an AONB, National Park, or World Heritage Site
- Class MA does not apply to listed buildings
- You CAN convert a building in a Conservation Area; however, an impact assessment may be required if converting the ground floor
- The planners have 56 days to respond to the application
- Works must be carried out within 3 years following Prior Approval

At face value, this is excellent news. But what about the small print? On what basis could the planning authority refuse your Prior Approval application? Again, there is more good news because the few criteria they can judge the application on are generally non-subjective. Here are the factors they will consider:

- Transport impact, including safe site access
- Contamination risk
- Flooding risk

- Impacts of noise from nearby commercial premises on occupiers of your development
- Where the ground floor being converted lies within a Conservation Area, does the impact of the change negatively affect the character or sustainability of the Conservation Area
- Provision of adequate natural light in all habitable rooms
- The impact on intended occupiers where the building introduces residential into an area important for general or heavy industry, waste management, storage and distribution, etc.
- The local impact where the development involves the loss of a registered nursery or health centre

So, despite the original light industrial PDR not being extended beyond 30th September 2020, we have now been given the ability to convert light industrial buildings up to 1,500m², far larger than the original PDR, which permitted up to 500m² only. While Class ZA remains viable, we would suggest that Class MA is a far more straightforward and less risky route to take for light industrial conversions.

Article 4 direction

When it comes to planning, the local authority has to deal with specific local planning issues that may not align with general government policy. They have at their disposal the ability to suspend any Permitted Development Rights and instead insist that any development requires full planning consent. The statute that gives them that power is Article 4 of the Housing Act. A council may apply what's known as an Article 4 direction to any part of the area within its jurisdiction should it so wish.

HMO landlords will be familiar with Article 4 since councils often use it to restrict the proliferation of HMOs or student lets where it is deemed the capacity for such accommodation has been reached in a particular area. Most city council websites will have a map indicating any areas under Article 4 direction, and so it's easy to check if your target building is in one.

External Envelope Alterations

Under Permitted Development, you're not allowed to alter the external envelope of the building. This means that you can't:

1. Alter or extend the building's footprint
2. Create new doorways, windows, or roof light openings, etc.

On the face of it, this would look like something of a deal-breaker. Most of these buildings will need some modification to make them suitable for residential use, not least to allow for light and access. So how can we do this if it's not permitted under PD?

The answer lies in the fact that these are relatively minor changes. The council can only object to a Permitted Development application on specific grounds, and those grounds do not include concerns relating to light and access. Once a building becomes residential, then Full Planning Permission would be applied for to insert the necessary windows, doorways, and roof lights required to make the project feasible. These changes would be subject to the usual planning considerations. However, your Planning Consultant will have already established that these changes should be non-contentious.

What would contentious look like? Well, if you were inserting a window that immediately overlooks a neighbouring property or garden, then this is unlikely to fly. By doing your homework (with your planning consultant) before acquiring the site, you should be able to ensure that all your proposed changes are non-contentious.

Local Authority position

We often get asked what local planners think about Permitted Development Rights. Do they welcome them or secretly detest them? The answer is it varies both from council to council, and from project to project. Just because the government thinks it's a 'good thing' as a blanket policy doesn't mean that local councils have to agree with them, although many do.

Is the council's view important? One of the strengths of the UK planning approval system is that it's designed to be non-subjective. In other words, the rules prescribe the outcome, and it's not down to the whim of an individual planning officer. This is in stark contrast to areas such as listed building consent, where the Conservation Officer has a much broader scope to use his or her own judgment.

Councils will always have scope to be awkward if they want to be, and as a rule they prefer to have total control over all things planning-related. But if your project adheres to the rules, then you'll be far less likely to encounter challenges.

How to get Full Planning Permission for essential changes

Please note a critical consideration with all Permitted Development opportunities; there will almost always be some changes you will need to make that will require Full Planning Permission.

We mentioned earlier that under Prior Approval, you wouldn't be able to change the footprint of the building or the external appearance. You may be able to visualise some nice flats going into the existing building quite comfortably. But unless they have doors and windows, you won't be able to sell them. Yet adding new doors and windows sits outside what is permitted under PD, so to change this, you will need to submit a full planning application.

Now, you might be thinking, 'Hold on a minute, I thought the whole benefit of this Permitted Development business was that I could avoid the vagaries of planning applications altogether, so what's all this about?'

Well, it's a fair point, so let us explain.

Ian Child & Ritchie Clapson

12. Planning Implications

Let's look in more detail at the various implications of planning on your potential project. Remember that Permitted Development Rights are an integral part of the planning process; they don't sit outside it. There are two scenarios you can encounter:

1. Full Planning Application only – for schemes that lie outside the Permitted Development criteria
2. Permitted Development Application + associated Full Planning Application – for schemes that take advantage of Permitted Development Rights, you will need to make both a Permitted Development application and a full planning application in respect of the associated modifications to the building, e.g., new window openings, internal courtyard, etc.

You could also have a scenario where you'd make a Permitted Development application without associated planning. But it's unlikely given that industrial buildings generally need some external modifications to make them viable. This may include simply adding or extending window openings.

Understanding Planning Risk

So why is planning risk such a major concern? Well, if you don't get permission to convert the building, your project won't get off the ground, full stop. What's the worst that can happen? You buy a site intending to convert it and then find out that you're not allowed to (generally because you haven't done your homework first). Expensive? Potentially. A waste of time and effort? Definitely. Avoidable? Almost certainly.

Full Planning Permission versus Permitted Development

Let's first get very clear on the difference between Full Planning Permission and Permitted Development. Full Planning Permission is the default requirement for all development activity. If you don't have Permitted Development Rights, then you will need to obtain Full Planning Permission before you can build or convert anything.

With Full Planning Permission, the local authority has a wide range of criteria against which your project will be judged. With PDRs, they can only assess your application against a much narrower set of criteria. Also, with the help of your Planning Consultant, you should be able to ensure that each of these criteria is met before you apply. This should give you a much higher degree of certainty.

Planning gain opportunity

There is a significant uplift in the value of land that has Full Planning Permission, and this is known as planning gain. Some people make a business out of creating planning gains. They acquire an option on a piece of land (or they buy the land itself) and then apply for Full Planning Permission. When permission is granted, they're then able to sell the project on to a developer who will now have certainty over what can be built. Sounds easier than building out a project, doesn't it? However, two risk variables come in to play. Firstly, there's no certainty that planning consent will ever be given. And secondly, even if consent is ultimately given, it may take months, years, or even decades to materialise. Many investors looking for planning gain are happy to buy properties or land parcels on a highly speculative basis, hoping that planning rules may change in time and thereby permit development in the years to come.

Can this model work for PDRs with Industrial Conversions? Well, it's a less obvious route to take. In theory, there's nothing to stop you from drawing up some conversion plans, making a Prior Approval application, and then selling the project as a package to a developer for a fee. This means you don't have to get involved in any of the development work itself nor the risks involved in selling the end units. But this comes at a price, as you won't be receiving any of the developer's profits either.

Planning Delays

When applying for Full Planning Permission delays can be commonplace, and they can have a significant impact on your business.

Finance implications

Your commercial funding will be available to you for a fixed duration, during which time you'll be paying interest on it. If your project overruns, then there are two potential implications:

1. If you have a planning delay that adds 3 extra months to your project, then you'll end up paying 3 month's additional interest on all your financing. It's worth noting that you're unlikely to get development funding without Full Planning Permission in place, and so will instead need to use private investment or bridging finance.
2. If the delay means you cannot sell the units before the end of the finance term, you'll need to negotiate a loan extension or refinance the project. This is not a great place to be since there's no guarantee that the lender will extend their terms.

Your Contractor and the rest of your professional team all need certainty to run their businesses. Let's assume they've scheduled their people to start work on your project this month. If they discover the work cannot begin because you've yet to secure Full Planning Permission, two things will happen:

1. They will need to deploy their teams on other jobs since they can't have them sitting around waiting on your job.

There is no guarantee they'll be available to start work immediately once you get Full Planning Permission
2. You'll look like you haven't got control of the project. You could lose the confidence of the Contractor and your professional team.

Other expenses you may incur

There are several other areas of extra cost that you can incur if you encounter planning delays:

1. The tender responses from contractors and professionals may expire. This means you may need to re-tender with no guarantee that they will hold the same prices
2. Some of your team will end up working on the job for longer, your Project Manager for example
3. Your administration overhead will be higher the longer you have to work on a project
4. You won't be able to go to the next project because your exit from the current project is delayed
5. You could lose the confidence of your private funders and may have to renegotiate their loans

The planning process

On paper, the planning application process for both Full Planning Permission and Permitted Development approval is very straightforward:

1. You'll prepare and submit an application to the planning department at your local council along with the relevant fee
2. They will assess it and if necessary, come back to you with questions or requests for further information
3. The application will then be either approved or rejected

4. If it's approved, then it will be subject to specific additional terms and conditions that you must fulfil. If it's rejected, their reasons for rejection will be given.

Local authority time limits

Your local authority assesses planning and Permitted Development applications. They have time limits set down by statute for providing a decision or response to these applications:

• For major developments, the time limit is 13 weeks

• For all other developments, the time limit is 8 weeks

This all sounds great, but can you guarantee that you'll get Full Planning Permission in those timescales?

Well, the short answer is no. There's no guarantee that planning will be granted even if you've submitted every scrap of available supporting evidence. There's always plenty of scope for the council to defer their decision. They can ask for further specialist reports to be provided, or some other information that they feel is required. When this happens, the clock stops and doesn't start again until you submit the requested information. Or the application can simply be refused, and the clock gets reset to zero since you'll have to make a new application.

It's also not unheard of for councils to issue last-minute requests for further reports as the deadline for making a decision approaches. This is presumably because they lack the resources to assess the application by the deadline. Frustrating and bureaucratic? Yup, but them's the rules and you have little choice but to play by them.

With a Permitted Development application, the scope for rejection is far less since the council only has a small number of criteria against which to assess your application. Plus, you will have already made sure that you've ticked those boxes before you submit the form.

What can go wrong?

Inexperienced developers can often fail to do enough preparation before submitting a planning application. Then they end up with a rejected application because it's deemed to be incomplete. This can be very frustrating since it may only be a minor piece of information that's missing. Yet it may have taken several weeks for the council to assess and then reject the application. However, don't expect the council to drop you a polite note asking for the information. Your application may just be rejected, and then you're back to square one. Can you resubmit it with the correct information included? Of course, but the clock starts from zero again, and you've now wasted several weeks.

So the key learning is this. Take the time at the outset to get your planning application thoroughly sorted, and don't rush it. Yes, it can be a frustrating time because it feels like nothing will be happening for the best part of two months. Of course you'll be keen to get the application in as soon as possible. But trust us, it's far better to get it right than spend another two months waiting because of a simple error or omission. In development, time is money.

Submitting an application

When you submit your application, we strongly advise against a do-it-yourself approach. Instead, you should use either your Architect or your Planning Consultant. They'll not only draw up the application (they will have done it many times before) but can also make the application on your behalf. Note that all the information involved with planning applications is in the public domain. If your name is shown as the applicant, you may find yourself receiving unsolicited offers from every tradesperson under the sun!

Your comprehensive planning package

If there's one word that we'd use to describe the ideal planning application, it would be 'comprehensive'. It should as a minimum comprise:

1. The plans of the site
2. The required supporting documentation
3. The required application forms, duly completed
4. The fee
5. Any extra specialist reports

Let's first look at the world from the view of the planning officer who's got to consider your application and apply a bit of human nature. If we were in their shoes, we'd be a bit hacked off if someone submitted an application that was poorly written, incomplete, or downright scruffy. If your job were to review these applications, you would at least expect people to make an effort to submit all the right information and to make the application logical and sensible. If they didn't, they're just wasting your time and making your task more difficult. If it were us, we'd have no compunction about rejecting the application out of hand and probably tutting quite loudly while we did it.

Now imagine a different scenario. An application is received which is totally complete and thoroughly comprehensive:

1. The fee is present and correct, and the application form signed
2. The developer has also thought to include some additional reports in case the planning office might find them useful
3. Photographs are in colour and very clear
4. The applications and statements are well written, logical, and concise
5. The package looks very professional

You can probably imagine the planning officer approaching that with a different mindset. Will it cause them to reach a different decision? No. But they'll view the application as one of the better efforts they've seen recently. They'll be able to access all the information they need quickly and easily. Will it reduce the chances of getting a request for further information? Will it get processed more quickly because all the information is there, and it's easy to read? Will it sit at the top of the inbox as opposed to being the one that gets looked at last? It's not possible to know the answer to any of these questions; one can only speculate.

However, we do know this; each deal you do is most likely going to be worth six figures to you. If you need Full Planning Permission, then <u>obtaining</u> Full Planning Permission is what makes each deal. If you don't have Full Planning Permission, you have no deal. So, make sure you give it the respect it deserves and put your best foot forward.

Plans of the site

These will be prescribed by the planning application form (both the type of plans and their scale/size) and will be provided by your Architect. They will include:

1. An overall site plan of the proposed development
2. A location plan showing where the development sits geographically and in relation to its neighbours
3. A plan of the existing building
4. Drawings of each elevation of the proposed development
5. Floor plans of each unit

Required supporting documentation

Your Architect or Planning Consultant will advise you on the additional documentation that should be supplied to support your application. One key document you will be submitting is your

Planning Statement. This gives the context for your development and describes what you're looking to achieve. The Planning Statement will be drafted by either your Architect or your Planning Consultant and will include:

1. An explanation of what the development is
2. Why it complies with the local plan
3. Why it falls under Permitted Development
4. The site context (the type of building, surrounding buildings, etc.)
5. History of the building
6. Previous planning history (including any refusals)
7. Compliance with both local and national planning policies
8. Sustainability considerations
9. Why the design is sympathetic to its surroundings
10. Accessibility
11. Appropriateness of the building
12. Justification of parking provision
13. Flood risk
14. Contamination
15. Bin and cycle store provision

For commercial and Industrial Conversions, you will also need to submit a Refurbishment & Demolition (R&D) Survey. A key aspect of this is to highlight the presence of any asbestos that may require removal and disposal.

Technical Corner: Asbestos

Asbestos is a collective name for a group of minerals that were used historically as roofing and insulation materials in many different types of property. When left undisturbed, asbestos represents no risk to health. However, when disturbed, the fibres become airborne and may be breathed into the lungs. This can cause a range of diseases that, over time, can be fatal, including lung cancer and asbestosis. While some asbestos can be readily spotted, many types are difficult to identify. This can make it difficult to assess the presence of asbestos from a cursory inspection.

A significant part of your R&D survey will involve an asbestos consultant (who will be part of your professional team). They will visit the property to make a non-intrusive inspection. This typically occurs before purchase and involves the examination of all visible aspects of the building.

An intrusive survey may be done once ownership is secured. This will involve drilling holes into walls floors and ceilings to identify any asbestos lying beneath the surface. Should the asbestos consultant recommend it, it may be appropriate to perform an intrusive survey before purchase with the vendor's permission. This would typically involve the cost of making good any damage caused by the inspection.

Once asbestos has been identified, it is graded into several levels of hazard. Your Contractor may remove the least dangerous forms of asbestos. The more hazardous varieties will need removing by specialist teams wearing suitable protective gear.

Be aware that asbestos can appear in all sorts of places, some apparently innocuous, such as artexed ceilings. It's seriously dangerous stuff, so don't take any chances. The asbestos dust that you could disturb when ripping out materials could stay on site and cause a hazard, not only to your workforce but also to the families who buy your flats. Get the professionals in and do the job properly and safely.

Required completed application forms

Your Architect or Planning Consultant will complete this.

Required fee

We've heard of developers submitting comprehensive planning applications but then forgetting to enclose the fee. Guess what happens 8 weeks later...

Additional reports that may be required

Each report that you provide will have a cost to you in both time and money, so you want to keep the number that you provide to a minimum. However, if you don't submit a report that is later requested by the planning department, you may encounter delays, since the application cannot progress until the report is received.

Your Planning Consultant will be able to give you a good steer on the reports that will be necessary. They will have an excellent working knowledge of how the planning department at the council operates. Many planning consultants have worked in their local planning teams before becoming consultants. They therefore have an intimate knowledge of the people and processes. Some additional reports will be reasonably obvious. For example, if your host building was previously used as a car garage, you know that the council will want to see a contamination report along with your application.

Here are some of the more common reports that may be required in support of planning applications:

Design and access statements

A DAS is a short report that explains how the proposed development is a suitable response to the site and its setting. It will also show that it can be adequately accessed by prospective users.

Contamination Assessment

A report provided following an onsite assessment of the current levels of contamination. It also assesses any contamination risk that could impact users of the property.

Flood Risk Assessment

Assesses the possible flood risk of the finished units. Is the building in a flood risk area, and if so, what measures can be taken to avoid flooding?

Traffic Assessment

How will the new site impact traffic in the immediate area? For example:

1. Can the roads in the vicinity cope with the influx of traffic that the development will bring?
2. Will road-users exiting the new development by car be able to access the public highway safely?
3. Do any proposed entrances to the development cause a hazard, e.g., are they near a junction or school?

This will be a more significant concern on larger scale development where the volume of vehicles will be greater.

Parking Assessment

Parking is a major concern, particularly in high-density residential areas. Each council will have a prescribed number of parking spaces that must be provided for each property type for new builds. That said, it's possible to take into account the on-street parking that may be available in the vicinity. You may need or opt to undertake a parking survey. This records the number of available parking places on the streets within a certain distance of the building at different times of the day.

One argument that can be useful with Industrial Conversions is that there will be (or will have been) a workforce that parks near the building. Unless you're building on the space used for employee parking, you can argue that the residential parking demand is no different from the current demand from employees.

Travel Plan

This short report describes how people will access the building by car, bike, on foot, and by each form of public transport. It also explains how close the building is to bus stops, railway stations, etc.

Tree Survey

Trees are not usually a significant issue with Industrial Conversions. Sites rarely contain a great deal of flora and fauna, plus you're not going to be chopping up any trees if you're only converting the existing building. But you may encounter trees that are protected by a TPO (tree preservation order) in the grounds. These are trees that the council deems should not be cut down or otherwise messed with. The council also has a mind to the visual impact of a site. They may be concerned if the development proposed the removal of trees that it deemed had a positive visual impact. A tree survey will identify any TPOs and will also show the other non-protected trees on site.

Archaeological Assessment

You're unlikely to encounter a request for one of these on an Industrial Conversion since you won't be doing much if any groundwork. Such assessments are more common in areas where there is a known archaeological interest. A team will typically visit the site to take a look once the foundation work has begun. This is one of the risks of going into the ground. If the team finds something of archaeological interest, they have wide-ranging powers and can halt works indefinitely.

Mitigating planning risk

Avoid schemes without Full Planning Permission or Permitted Development Rights initially

Planning is a risk and reward game from a developer's perspective. The difference in value between a piece of land that has Full Planning Permission and one that doesn't is significant. But Full Planning Permission not only takes time; the outcome cannot be guaranteed. Some organisations and investors maintain land banks. These are investments in land holdings where Full Planning Permission is not in place but where they one day hope to be able to build. Some of these holdings can be very significant, with the potential uplift running into the tens or even hundreds of millions. The uplift occurs once Full Planning Permission is granted – and without a single blade of grass being touched.

When you start as a developer, we strongly suggest that you only consider schemes that have Full Planning Permission in place or they have Permitted Development Rights (even though they may need subsequent permission to alter the external appearance, door and window openings, etc.). That's because you want to get your first project completed as soon as possible. You've spent all that effort in creating your property brand and building your professional team. Now they may have to wait for several months (if not longer) for you to get started. And what if you don't get permission? Do you have the financial resources to wait for planning to be granted?

You're already learning the ropes as a developer without needing to make the task in hand any more complicated or demanding. So we suggest that even though the profit may be smaller, a simple Permitted Development scheme or one with Full Planning Permission already secured is what you need to get the team working together. You can also identify your strengths and weaknesses and get to know and understand the entire end-to-end development process.

Planning risk for more experienced developers

When you have more experience behind you (and deeper pockets), you may consider taking on a project without Full Planning Permission. These deals tend to offer limited security at the outset but can have a massive upside if planning is approved. Here are a few considerations that you should think about when tackling a project without planning or Permitted Development:

1. Always get advice from a Planning Consultant. They can be worth their weight in gold when it comes to taking on planning risk
2. Make sure you have at least two exit strategies. You don't want to be left with no option to rescue things if planning is refused
3. You may need to beef up your professional team, since more specialist advice may be needed
4. Since there is no Full Planning Permission in place or Permitted Development Rights, commercial funding is unlikely to be available to you. This means that you'll need private funds to acquire the site (if that's the route you're taking). You'll also need to have funds available to pay for your professional fees upfront
5. You don't always need to acquire the land upfront; you can secure it on an option and then only buy it once Full Planning Permission is in place

Planning considerations

Aside from those we've mentioned so far, here are some of the additional factors that the council will take into account when considering a planning application. Each one needs to be a commercial consideration for you as the developer since they each impact the appeal of your project to potential buyers:

Location, location, location

An obvious point, but if the building is located slap-bang in the middle of an industrial estate, then it's unlikely to be viable. There are no amenities nearby, the nightlife is non-existent, the neighbours are noisy during the day but silent at night, and so on. That doesn't mean to say that a building on the fringes of an industrial estate wouldn't be viable. It's likely to be close to other residential housing, and so will enjoy the same level of amenity. Wherever the building is located, common sense will usually tell you whether it's a good place for people to live or if it's a compromise.

Design style

Industrial buildings tend to suit a more urban style that appeals to young professionals more than downsizers. A gross generalisation, but you need to understand how the design of your end product will relate and appeal to the target market.

External alterations

Any new or alterations to existing external openings (doors, windows, roof lights, courtyards, etc.) require due consideration to neighbouring properties, in particular, the issue of overlooking. Be aware that overlooking can be an issue not just for neighbouring properties but also for the flats within your development.

Amenity space

This refers to outside space that can be enjoyed by the users of the property. Gardens are such an element (whether private or communal). It's also valid to consider what parks and outdoor recreational spaces are available nearby.

Living environment, e.g., placement of bins, cycle stores, 'nice place to live'

The planners want to make sure that residential accommodation is a 'nice place to live'. They have an increasing ability to influence this under the Prior Approval process. While this can be a somewhat subjective assessment, there are some obvious candidates you can address, such as ensuring that:

1. The placement of bins and cycle storage is done sensitively
2. There is adequate natural light
3. The outlook for each unit is suitable (e.g. they don't overlook the bin-store or a brick wall, etc.)
4. Each unit can be accessed safely and securely (e.g. no dark alleyways, etc.)

Section 106 and the Community Infrastructure Levy

It's worth mentioning a couple of potential costs linked to the planning process that you may encounter, which could be significant depending on several factors.

Section 106 agreements are where the developer is required to fund an aspect relating to the proposed site that the planning authority deems necessary before granting permission. This could be to undertake works to make access to the site better or safer or to include affordable housing. S106 agreements are specific to the site being developed and relate to significant items that can't otherwise be dealt with by adding conditions to a planning decision.

It's also worth noting that S106 is not prescriptive and that the agreement of the amount payable involves a negotiation with the local authority (specialist S106 consultants are available for hire).

Community Infrastructure Levy (CIL) is a general levy that applies to all developments and is designed to contribute to the local infrastructure costs resulting from increased development. CIL does not apply in Scotland or Northern Ireland, and not all local authorities in England and Wales have adopted it (you can check on your local council's website).

Permitted Developments are liable for CIL in the same way that developments permitted by planning permission are. However, no new buildings are being created when an existing building is converted to residential, so a CIL payment will not usually be triggered. There are several caveats to this, and you should confirm with your planning consultant and the local council whether your project is exempt. Where payable, CIL can be a hefty bill, particularly on larger schemes, plus it is payable when work starts on-site rather than after all units are sold.

The 2020 Planning White Paper

The current planning system in England & Wales was created in the 1950s, and frankly, not much has changed since. The system is underfunded, bureaucratic, subject to politically motivated decision-making, and is generally time-consuming and exasperating for everyone involved.

In 2020, the UK government published a White Paper which reflected its vision of dragging the planning system, kicking and screaming, into the 21st Century. At the time of writing, there's certainly been a lot of screaming, with many believing the proposed changes take too much control away from local planners. Equally, there is an argument that draconian action is what's required and that pandering to the naysayers will simply dilute the impact. After all, the local planning authorities have control today and look where that's got us.

Whatever your opinion, there are legal changes afoot over the next two years or so that will have profound ramifications for the planning process. Here are the highlights of what you can expect to look forward to:

- Binding new build targets for local authorities
- Identification and delineation of land into Growth, Renewal, and Protected areas
- Greater engagement with the public on planning applications
- A digital-first approach (as opposed to the current 'what's digital?' one)
- A greater focus on design and a 'fast-track process for beauty,' with a Chief Design Officer appointed in each local authority
- A new fixed-rate Infrastructure Levy to replace both the S106 and Community Infrastructure Levy (CIL), which could also extend to PDR schemes
- A new resources and skills strategy for the planning sector
- Planning system operational costs to be funded by planning beneficiaries (landowners and developers) instead of the taxpayer
- A new performance framework for local planning authorities

So, lots of exciting things in store, but it will take some time for these to be implemented and enacted. We're not at this early stage going to speculate on what these measures could ultimately mean for the conversion of industrial buildings; however, we wanted to make you aware that there were some significant changes in the pipeline. As ever, your friendly local Planning Consultant will be up to speed, and of course, the media will sporadically vent forth on the subject as and when someone starts screaming again.

13. Space Planning

It's worth us looking at the issue of space planning as it's key to understanding how to make Industrial Conversion projects work. There's an overlap with some of the aspects we've covered previously, particularly the block planning section in Chapter 10. However, these key elements should form a go-to checklist for any development plans you work on, so it makes sense to group them here in one place.

But won't your Architect do all this? Well, you'd like to think so. That said, Industrial Conversions are somewhat niche for many architects. In our experience, there's no harm in you as the developer knowing your stuff, at least conceptually. Also, your Architect's time costs money. So, you won't want to be passing him or her every deal that comes across your desk without first checking it yourself to see if it's workable, space-wise.

Thinking laterally: the internal courtyard

Since many industrial buildings are built out to the limit of their boundaries, access and light can both be a real issue. Take the building in Figure 13.1. It's a prime conversion opportunity, a single-storey light industrial unit sitting in a residential area with scope to convert into 5 or even 6 flats. If access was straightforward and the unit sat in the middle of a bigger plot, the logical approach would be to divide the building up into the 5 flats shown in Figure 13.2. Flats 2 and 3 would have light and access from the north elevation, and units 4 and 5 would have the same but from the south.

Figure 13.1: A prime conversion opportunity

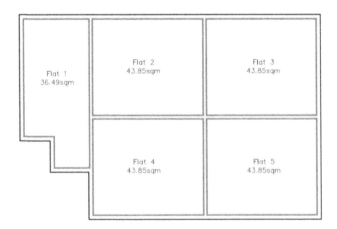

Figure 13.2: The logical way to form 5 units if access or light were not a problem

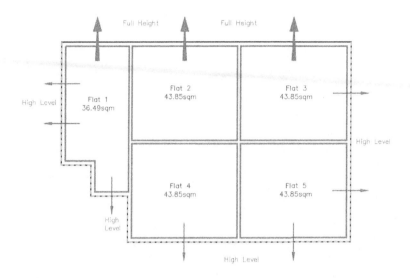

Figure 13.3: The reality: no access to the sides or rear of the building

However, this unit, like so many others, has been built right up to the boundary on three sides. Only the north side has access and can, therefore, have large windows. As can be seen in Figure 13.3 where the dotted line marks the property's boundary, there is no way of gaining access to flats 4 and 5 as there is no right of access to the rear or side of the building at all. We wouldn't get Full Planning Permission to add full-sized window openings in the East, South, or West elevations because the building abuts the rear gardens of neighbouring residential properties. We would have to make do with high-level windows (denoted by the smaller arrows).

The solution to this problem reminds us of a famous puzzle that demonstrates outside-the-box thinking. Here it is:

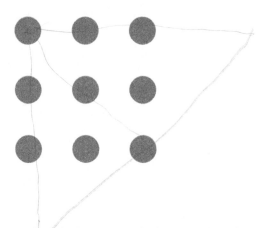

"Join all the dots with only four straight lines and without your pencil once leaving the paper."

We've known students who haven't seen this before, agonize over the answer, many insisting that it cannot be done. If you don't know the answer, please feel free to give it a try; it's certainly not a trick question. If you give up, can't be bothered, or just need to double-check that you were right (we believe you), the answer is at the back of the book.

Many people find themselves in a similar predicament when it comes to creating a solution to getting access and light to flats 4 and 5 in our example. How can you resolve the issue entirely, make both units light and accessible? But then not be reliant on permissions or rights of way over neighbouring properties?

The answer lies in creating what we call an internal courtyard. Figure 13.4 gives you a high-level overview of the solution. Note that this example pre-dated the introduction of National Space Standards for Permitted Development schemes that came into effect on 6th April 2021, hence the flat sizes are less than 37m^2. What we're doing here is carving out the central part of the building to form a courtyard. The courtyard provides two critical things:

1. A means of accessing the rear flats without going across neighbouring land
2. The means to get light into the building through standard height windows without overlooking existing neighbouring buildings

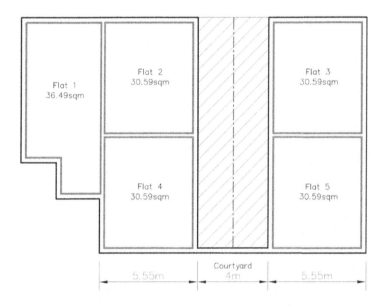

Figure 13.4: Using an internal courtyard to create light and access

Note that the courtyard is large to let enough light in, while also creating a degree of privacy between the flats that are opposite each other. If your courtyard were to be much narrower, then while this may result in larger flats, the windows of each apartment would be too close to each other. Also, you may not get enough light in.

You'll see that we've marked on the revised unit floor areas in Figure 13.5 now that the courtyard has been formed. The flats are now much smaller, yet each is over the minimum mortgageable size of 30m². We've also indicated where we can have standard windows and where there are existing high-level windows that can also be utilised.

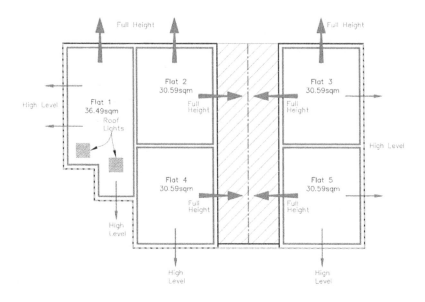

Figure 13.5: Light and access impact of the courtyard scheme

Congratulations if this solution was obvious to you from the outset. Most people don't see it right off the bat; they need some prompting before the penny drops. Those looking at it without the benefit of that experience often fail to see the solution at all, and write the scheme off as unworkable. Which is fantastic news for you because it further depletes the competition. Few developers are looking to convert these types of building in the first place. And the few that do may well fail to see how they can make the scheme work due to the poor access and light issues.

Finally, in Figure 13.6, you can see a 3D sketch of the finished article. We need to add some proper rendering to the external walls and landscaping to the courtyard and front. But we now have a unique and attractive development of five new apartments.

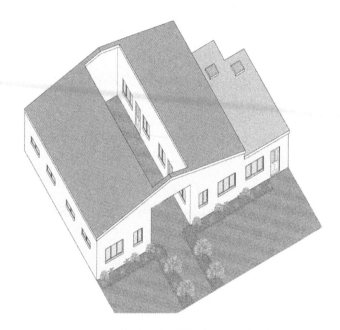

Figure 13.6: 3D sketch of the proposed scheme

Different courtyard types

There are several different options available to you when creating an internal courtyard:

1. Remove the roof entirely
2. Remove the roofing material itself but leave the roof trusses exposed. This can create an interesting effect, the area having a half inside/half outside feel
3. Use a glazed roof. This is similar to the solution used in many shopping centres and arcades. The Architect wants to admit natural light, but the area cannot be exposed to the elements. This is a costlier option but still workable

Note that creating an internal courtyard will need Full Planning Permission. See chapter 12 for how best to approach this.

259

So, what aspects should you consider when building an internal courtyard?

The first thing is to ensure that your courtyard has enough width so that the flats on opposite sides are not too close to each other. On some properties, it can be challenging to keep the courtyard wide enough while still maintaining unit sizes greater than $37m^2$. Make sure you don't end up with a courtyard that's little more than an alleyway.

You have a few options with internal courtyards in terms of their shape:

End-to-end: The courtyard runs right to the rear wall of the property as in Figure 13.7.

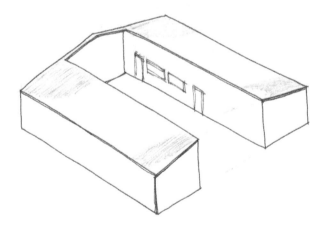

Figure 13.7: An 'end-to-end' courtyard

U-shaped: See Figure 13.8. The courtyard doesn't run all the way to the rear wall, allowing for accommodation at the rear end. This is usually only achievable where window openings are possible on the rear wall, as light will otherwise be compromised.

This can be a good alternative to an end-to-end courtyard if you're struggling to get enough units in.

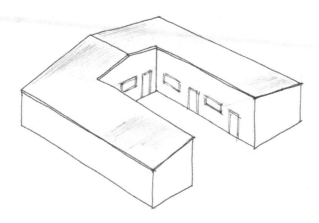

Figure 13.8: A U-shaped courtyard

Irregular shaped courtyard: This may be relatively simple as in Figure 13.9 or more complex in larger, more difficult sites.

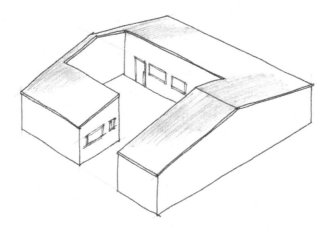

Figure 13.9: An irregular shaped courtyard

261

Collared courtyard: the courtyard is accessed via a short passageway or 'collar' before opening out. This creates more accommodation space at the courtyard entrance. It also makes it more practical to have gated access. Make sure that the collar isn't too long and that there are no overlooking issues.

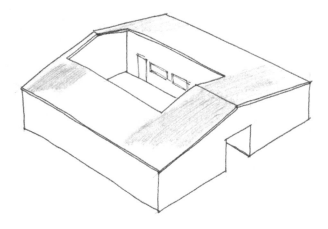

Figure 13.10: A collared courtyard

You can make an amenity feature of larger courtyards, particularly if you turn it into a garden rather than leaving it as paved access. Laying turf is an option, but it's not always the most practical consideration. That said, the industrial nature of these buildings can lend itself to a 'city garden' design, with low walls, planters, and even water features. One attractive aspect of internal courtyards is that they can be quiet spaces, even where the building is in a busy city centre.

You can also add a gate at the entrance to the courtyard that creates a 'gated community' and extra security – a feature that could add value to your finished units.

Importance of outward aspects

Try always to have your apartments face the best possible view. The planning authority will deem it necessary that your building faces the most attractive outward aspect.

Not every development will have a good side and a bad side, plus of course, many developments have flats pointing in more than one direction. A key trick is to site the living areas to the front of the building where the view is generally better. You can then put bedrooms, bathrooms, and kitchens towards the rear where the aspect is less important. The planners will expect you to do this, and of course, your end customers will have a strong preference for it too.

Access to flats

Always think about how residents are going to be able to gain access to their flats. It may seem an obvious point, but you'd be surprised how many developers don't think this through. That's not to say they end up building a flat that has no front door (change your Architect if this happens), rather that the routes of access are not ideal. For example, you should try and avoid the access to one flat being too close to the living room windows of another. You may also need to consider disabled level access and potentially ramps. Finally, have a thought about security (as mentioned previously) e.g. make sure front doors are not tucked away in a dark corner.

Overlooking

Make sure that your flats do not overlook existing neighbouring properties and also that they don't directly overlook each other. Many local authorities have a quality space standards document which gives suggestions and advice on how best to work out your scheme's amenity and layout. Your Architect and Planning Consultant will be able to advise you in this regard. It's also worth noting that even where you have Permitted Development Rights it can still be beneficial to follow the council's quality space guidelines where possible, even if they do not formally influence a planning outcome.

Bin and Cycle Stores

Be sensitive to where these are sited; just because you have a bin and bike storage allocated on your plan doesn't mean you've ticked a box. No one will want the communal bin storage right outside their window or front door. Nor will they want to be woken up by the night shift worker from flat 3 unlocking his bike at some unearthly hour. If you can locate these in a place where they're not likely to be a nuisance for any of your residents, only then should your box be ticked.

14. Natural Light

Why natural light is needed

We take having access to natural light in our homes for granted, and it's a desirable feature of any living accommodation. Most people prefer homes that have a great deal of natural light. They're turned off by those houses and flats that don't, as the spaces often feel smaller and more claustrophobic. Unsurprising then that planning authorities have always considered natural light when reviewing planning applications, and it has recently become a key driver for recent planning regulation changes (you may recall that the council can reject your class MA Prior Approval application if there is inadequate natural light).

Natural light is more critical in some rooms than others. It would be challenging to sell a home that only had high-level windows in the living areas; people want to be able to see out. However, natural light is not such an issue for bathrooms, WCs, and utility areas. So, siting these rooms in areas where window openings aren't possible can work in your favour.

The message is clear. The more natural light you can get in, the quicker you'll be able to sell your units, and potentially the more money you will command for them. Is it up to you as the developer to work out how much light comes into your project? This is a job for your Architect, who will have light in mind when designing your scheme. But as the property CEO, it pays to understand both the challenges and the solutions available.

Common natural light challenges

So, what are the common challenges you're likely to face with light in industrial buildings? Well, there are five main ones:

A large central volume of space

Many industrial buildings were constructed to create a large volume of internal space, i.e., a sizeable open-plan factory floor. As a result, these units have a deep floorplan. They also have a large amount of interior space with no partition walls, electrical trunking, and pipework. This is a significant positive since it provides us with a blank canvas in which to put up new partition walls. The downside is that there's often not a great deal of natural light available in these spaces, particularly in the central area. There may be windows around the perimeter, but it's unlikely that enough light will reach the centre. Some industrial buildings have north lights in the roof (see later section). It may be possible to retain these to get natural light into some of the rooms in your floorplan.

A lack of windows

Industrial units often have fewer windows than would be ideal in residential buildings. Also, what windows there are may not be ideally located.

The wrong window type or size

Often the window openings are functional rather than practical. For example, high narrow windows may be practical in an industrial environment. But windows you can't look out of in residential units are far from ideal. There may be a need to increase the depth or the height of existing window openings to make them more suited to a residential dwelling. There may also be a requirement to insert new openings.

Overlooking prevents new windows being added

You can't punch a couple of new window openings into a wall with abandon. This may often breach restrictions that protect neighbouring properties from being overlooked. All residential properties are entitled to a degree of privacy. Where your wall overlooks an adjacent property, it's unlikely that the planning authority will allow a new window opening. Sometimes it may be possible to reach a compromise. For example, smaller windows, windows positioned higher up the wall above eye-level or windows with obscured glass. But this is not guaranteed and, in any event, may not suit the needs of your project.

Overshadowing

Overshadowing occurs where one building casts a shadow over another, impacting on the latter's enjoyment of natural light. Typically this can happen when a building is taller than its neighbour (either in size or because it's sited above it on a slope), and it's built in close proximity. The planning authority wouldn't let you build a new property that overshadows someone's home. But historically, this wasn't an important consideration for industrial buildings. You shouldn't need to worry about overshadowing someone else's property unless you're planning to increase the size of your building. But you do need to make sure your host building isn't already overshadowed since this will make your units more difficult to sell.

Be aware that overshadowing can potentially be an issue within your new development itself. For example, you may have created an internal courtyard, but will need to ensure that the width of the courtyard is sufficient for light to reach the ground floor windows on either side. Again, your Architect and Planning Consultant will be able to advise you on this.

Light solutions

Are all these light challenges a pain in the backside? Well, put it this way, they immediately put a lot of developers off doing Industrial Conversions. It's far easier to convert a commercial building like an office block. Here the window openings are already in place, and natural lighting is not a problem. But if you're traveling against the herd AND you have a solution to these light challenges, we think you're in quite a good place. So, let's look at the range of solutions that are at your disposal.

Internal Courtyards

We've covered these in the last chapter. They're not the most subtle or inexpensive solution, but they may often be the only solution to get both light and access into your project.

Roof light options

Roof lights come in various guises and can be a great way of getting natural light into your building. The big advantage roof lights have over windows is that they don't usually overlook anyone. As a result, there are a greater number of opportunities to use them. The big disadvantage is that you can't see out. The view from a roof light tends to be the same in every building wherever it is in the world! Cleaning roof lights can also be trickier than cleaning windows due to access restrictions. This won't be a primary concern for you (you won't be cleaning them), although it could potentially be a concern for prospective buyers.

Let's take a look at the different types of roof lights that are available.

North light roofs

You may be familiar with the typical 'saw-tooth' roof found on many industrial buildings. This is where the roof comprises a series of ridges with dual pitches on either side. The steeper surfaces are glazed and typically face northwards. This shields workers and machinery from direct sunlight while still admitting natural light. This is useful in buildings that may have a deep floorplan since light can now reach the interior.

Pitched roof windows

These are more familiar in residential settings and are often found in loft conversions. Many people refer to them as Velux windows, named after the preeminent manufacturer. Since they are usually tilted skyward due to being on a pitched roof, the issue of overlooking is not often an issue. This is not always a given – it will depend on your specific location and the sensitivity of your neighbours.

A key attraction of this type of glazing is that it feels very familiar and doesn't look at all out of place in a residential setting. Also, it doesn't feel like a compromise, unlike many other types of roof light.

There is an essential requirement for pitched roof windows that you'll need to bear in mind, namely that you'll need to have a pitched roof on your building in the first place on which to put them! It can be a pitched roof that is already present, or you may even decide to create one (this would require Full Planning Permission). This would have the added advantage of creating a vaulted ceiling, which increases the cubic capacity of your units.

Skylights

These are windows that are inset into a flat roof and sit parallel to the ground, i.e., they face directly upwards. These can be very useful in hallways, communal areas, and bathrooms. In fact, any room where natural light is desirable but where there is no option to create a window.

You may remember the case study we used in Chapter 13 when we talked about internal courtyards. Flat 1 in that development was on the left-hand side of the plan. It was a large but quite deep unit with light available at the front but not to the right or the rear (see Figure 14.1).

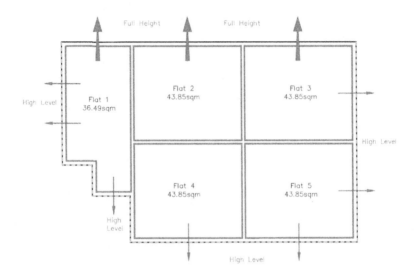

Figure 14.1: Flat 1 on the left lacks light at the rear

In this situation, it's not possible to create a further internal courtyard since the area is not large enough. However, we would not be able to put new windows in the three walls highlighted in Figure 14.2, since it would overlook neighbouring properties.

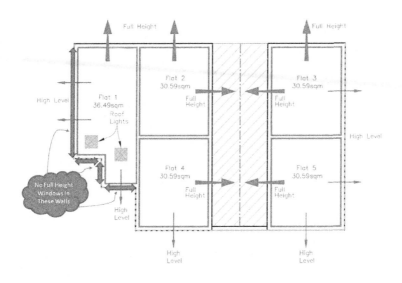

Figure 14.2: Planners will not allow new windows due to overlooking

So, what do we do? This part of the building has a flat roof, and so the solution is to use roof lights (see Figure 14.3). By siting these towards the rear of the unit, we ensure we're getting natural light into that area. We then make sure that rooms in which window openings are not essential are at the rear of the floorplan. The living areas are then moved to the front, and so take advantage of the windows on the front elevation.

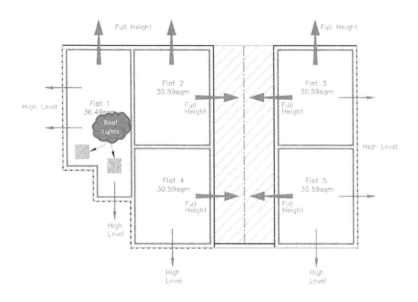

Figure 14.3: Roof lights are the answer

Light tubes

Light tubes have a variety of different names. These include tubular daylighting devices, sun pipes, sun scopes, sun tunnels, light pipes, daylight pipes, and tubular skylights. Whatever you call them, they all work in a similar way. You first create a hole in the ceiling of the area you want to allow light into. Next, you run a tube (which can either be rigid or flexible) from the hole to a glass or Perspex mini dome that sits on the roof. The dome (or alternatively a flat piece of glass) maximises the amount of light, and this then flows down the tube and through the ceiling opening. There's absolutely no rocket science involved. The ceiling opening usually has a glass cover and looks like a large downlighter (see Figure 14.4).

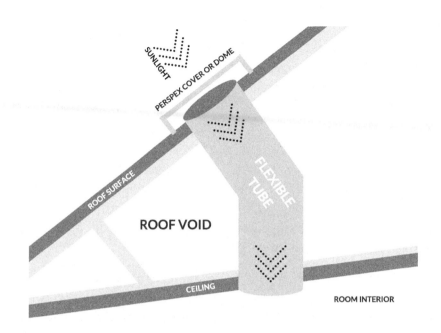

Figure 14.4: Anatomy of a light tube

Light tubes can be cost-effective ways of getting natural light into a space. However, you will also need electrical lighting since, despite looking like downlighters, they (obviously) only admit light if it is light outside. Clearly, they don't work at night, and the light quality is likely to be poor on overcast days.

Light tubes come as complete units rather than your contractor having to create one from scratch. They're available in a range of diameters, plus it's also possible to get tubes that are positioned on walls rather than the ceiling. This can be useful when getting light into rooms such as basements. Rigid tubes are preferable to flexible tubes since they admit more light. That said, flexible tubes may be a good solution where there are obstacles in the roof that prevent the installation of a rigid tube.

Roof glazing

Glazed roofs tend to cover a larger area than traditional skylights and can, as a result, be very expensive. They do maximise the amount of natural light available and can often be impressive architectural features in their own right.

Window options

South-facing windows let in the most direct sunlight. Of course, the scope for south-facing windows will be determined by the orientation of the existing building. However, it's always a good idea to raise this question with your Architect at the design stage.

Where you have restricted light at one end of a unit, you may have options to increase the light coming into the unit from the front. For example, it may be possible to have large floor to ceiling windows on the front aspect. These allow light to reach further into the unit, although it won't help you much if you have closed rooms at the rear.

A further option is to place high-level windows on walls where standard window openings are not permitted due to overlooking. This is more likely to be acceptable to planners (and neighbours), albeit it's a compromise. You would only want to have this in non-living rooms such as bathrooms, bedrooms, and kitchens.

One final option is to use opaque glass (like the modesty glass found in bathroom windows). Again, it's a compromise, but it may allow you to have full-sized windows, which will allow in much more light than high-level windows. Also, the level of opacity need not significantly restrict the amount of light that's let through.

You'll be getting the input of your Planning Consultant and Architect in determining your window options. They'll advise you on both the siting of new window openings and the range of compromise solutions that may be acceptable. You may also get the input of the local authority as well if your Planning Consultant suggests approaching them.

Getting the décor right

The internal décor that you utilise on a scheme can have a significant impact on how much natural light there is in each of your units. Dark colours absorb light while light colours reflect it. A wall painted with white emulsion will bounce more light around the space than a wall painted a darker tone.

Having an all-white apartment won't be to everyone's taste since it could feel like you were living in a science lab, so you need to strike a balance. We often use white walls to contrast with specific features. For example, we may have silver or black appliances in a kitchen, or a contrasting worktop, splashback tiling, or floor covering. In bathrooms, tiling and shower cubicles can provide contrast. In bedrooms and living rooms, we may have contrasting wardrobes and furniture. We may also opt to create a single feature wall in a different colour or expose brickwork if it's of a good enough quality.

The idea here is a simple one. When we observe a space aesthetically, we like to see areas of contrast rather than a uniform colour throughout. These contrast areas may account for only 20% or so of the space, but as long as they are there, sufficient appeal is created. So, use white (or an off-white if you prefer) as your 80% colour, then choose darker contrasting colours for the rest. In this way, you're maximising your use of natural light without compromising the visual appeal of your units. Try also to use more than one contrasting colour if you can. Blacks, greys, and browns tend to work well since they are less 'Marmite' and will appeal to most. Using a very strident colour, even in small doses, may alienate some of your potential buyers, so you should avoid it

Figure 14.5: Examples of some finished, basic flats

Make sure that you ask for design advice from your estate agent, since they'll have a good idea of the sort of fit and finish that appeals to your target demographic. You should also consider employing the services of an interior designer as this really can pay dividends, however it's best to get them involved at the start of the project rather than at the end.

Figure 14.5 shows images from some of our own projects that give examples of the type of look you could opt for, which would maximise light. White walls and units, light grey carpets and dark grey worksurfaces and hard flooring makes everything appear very clean and fresh without making them seem too sterile. This look can work very well with Industrial Conversions since there may be industrial themes or cues elsewhere.

It's also worth remembering that shiny surfaces also reflect light better than matt finishes. Care needs to be taken when using a lot of reflective surfaces, as it can be a tad overwhelming. A gloss kitchen finish is one area where you can take advantage without being too controversial.

Wall mirrors can be another great way to bounce light around an apartment, plus they also create a greater sense of depth and space. Use mirrors sparingly as an abundance of them can look rather odd. Also, people can get distracted on viewings when they see their reflection in every room!

If you have a bathroom that's on the small side, one trick is to have one entire wall covered by a mirror. This can either be a sheet of mirrored glass that is stuck on to the wall, or mirrored tiles. People expect to find mirrors in bathrooms, and by having an entire wall mirrored, you're able to create the illusion of greater space. It also makes good use of the available light. One word of warning - we wouldn't recommend having more than one mirrored wall, as the effect can be very distracting!

Another bathroom solution can be the use of textured wall tiles known as 'bumpy whites'. These not only throw light around the room, they can also help disguise walls that are less than straight.

.

15. Thermal Insulation

Modern residential buildings need to have a high degree of thermal insulation. It won't be a surprise to learn that most industrial buildings don't come up to scratch, often by quite a long way. Like most other aspects of modern construction, thermal capacity is dictated by regulation. It's not a case of choosing how much insulation you want to install. Many older buildings have little or no thermal insulation in place at all, while newer buildings may have some. But even these are unlikely to have the thermal capacity demanded by residential buildings. So what are the options?

There are four ways in which heat can escape a building:

1. the walls
2. the roof
3. the floor
4. the external openings (windows and doors)

You'll recall the 'building-within-a-building' concept we mentioned earlier. Let's take a look at how this can help us.

Walls

Around a third of all heat from a building is lost through its walls. Most industrial buildings will be built from either metal sheeting or single-skin brickwork, with no additional thermal insulation involved. Occasionally you'll come across industrial buildings that have a skin of plasterboard on the internal walls. This is where sheets of plasterboard have been tacked on to the solid brickwork or metal sheeting internally, and a plaster skim applied and then painted. None of these types of construction is of a standard suitable for residential accommodation, so you will need to address it.

The arrival of the twentieth century saw the introduction of cavity walls. This remains the preferred method of construction today. So what is a cavity wall? In simple terms, you have an outer brick or stone exterior wall, with a second wall built inside it and a small gap between the two (the cavity). The cavity stops the cold and damp transferring from the outer wall to the inner wall.

In modern times it's common to have the cavity filled with an insulating material to increase the thermal rating of the walls further. This insulation can take several forms. These include lagging (akin to loft insulation) and solid sheets of insulation material. Another common solution is to pump liquid foam into the cavity through small holes in the outer wall. This then sets, creating a honeycomb-like layer between the inner and outer walls that is very effective.

Technical Corner: Insulation

Walls are given U values to denote their thermal insulation qualities; this is the rate at which heat (in watts) escapes one square metre of wall space (W/m^2). The lower the W/m^2 number, the better the insulation qualities a wall has. A standard brick wall with no insulation will have a rating of around 1.9W/m2, which compares to about 1.7W/m^2 for a stone wall. A cavity wall without any insulation is around 1.5W/m^2. The current minimum standard for residential accommodation is effectively 0.2W/m^2. This is significantly better than that of a standard cavity wall. As a result, there is a need to include some form of further insulation within the cavity.

The inner and outer walls are held together with metal 'ties'. These are strips of metal bedded into each wall as it's built, which hold the walls together. A common problem with these ties is that they create a 'cold bridge' from the outer wall. This allows coldness to pass to the inner wall, thereby reducing the temperature inside the building. This reduces the thermal rating of the wall as a result.

It's common for modern cavity walls to have a vapour control layer within the cavity. This is usually a metal foil that prevents moisture bridging the gap between the two walls through the insulation material. The better insulated the internal wall is, the closer the dew point is to the inner wall. The dew point is the point at which air reaches a temperature where it turns into condensation. The vapour control layer prevents this condensation from reaching the inner wall. This would appear as damp patches on the inside wall.

The 'building-within-a-building' concept involves constructing a new building inside the existing one. With a single skin industrial building, we have the outer half of a cavity wall already built. If we were to build a second inner wall next to the existing outer wall and then insulate the cavity between the two, we've now created a cavity wall. Not only will this meet the required thermal capacity, but we can also apply new render to the external wall (subject to Full Planning Permission) to enhance its appearance. As a result, we have created a 'new' wall that has the same qualities as one built from scratch, but with the following advantages:

1. *We haven't had to dig any foundations*
2. *We've not demolished anything*
3. *We haven't had to build the external wall (it's already there)*
4. *We've done most of the job working inside, unaffected by the weather*
5. *The cost was a lot less than building a new wall*

Roofs

The roofs of industrial buildings present a similar problem to the walls. They're unlikely to be built to residential insulation standards. They may also contain asbestos, and your asbestos specialist will be able to identify this. But from an insulation perspective, the solution is broadly similar to that of the walls.

Roofs usually come in two different flavours; pitched roofs and flat roofs. Let's look at each in turn.

Pitched Roofs

The most common approach is to attach a form of insulating material to the underside of the roofing material. This acts as an insulation barrier between the roof tiles and the internal plasterboard ceiling. There are several different types of insulating material you can use. Traditionally mineral wool and fibreglass wool were used to insulate roofs. These are not as effective as more modern solutions such as spray foam (a sprayable insulation material) and rigid foam insulation (ready-made insulation boards that can be sawn to fit between the rafters). You will also need to have some form of waterproof membrane to stop water coming through to the inside from the exterior.

Flat Roofs

These are best dealt with by applying insulation on top of the existing roof rather than underneath. The latter approach can often lead to condensation problems later. A rigid foam insulation board sits on top of the existing roof, with a waterproof membrane applied on top of that. Finally, you would apply a weatherproof layer to the exterior.

You'll need to consider whether there is an option to retain the existing outer roof covering. This is a discussion to have with your Architect, Project Manager and possibly your Contractor. Aesthetics play a part here. We often change the roof coverings on our conversion projects just because it makes the building look more 'residential'. Plus, it can make the building look newly built since you'll also have new rendering, windows, and doors. Externally every aspect will be brand new, and that makes the whole building look new. Clearly, new roofing tiles come at a cost that you'll need to factor into your deal assessment and make sure that you budget accordingly. You'll also need to talk to your Structural Engineer regarding any potential roof strengthening that may be required with your choice of tile, due to the additional weight.

Floors

Although your building will most likely be sitting on a solid concrete slab, insulation is still required and must sit over the top of the slab. We also discuss in the next chapter creating a void between the slab and a newly created suspended floor immediately above it. Why would you do this? Well, you'll need to run services from the kitchens and bathrooms to the mains drainage. This requires gravity, i.e., the waste pipes must run downhill. Unfortunately, if you have a big flat concrete base in the way, then it's going to be difficult to get enough gradient for gravity to do its job. You don't want to dig up the base for all sorts of reasons, not least of which is disturbing any contamination that may lay underneath. Since industrial buildings often have a lot of headroom, one solution is to raise the ground floor height by creating a suspended floor. This then allows you to run the pipework under the floor with enough gradient and without going into the slab.

If you've gone down that route, then you now have a void under the suspended floor that you will need to insulate. The insulation approach is very similar, whether you're insulating a slab or a suspended floor. The insulation material will sit either on top of the slab or directly beneath the suspended floor.

External openings

In many respects, these are the easiest to find a solution for, since, in most cases, you're unlikely to be keeping the original windows, frames, or doorways. For mainstream products, your replacement units should have an appropriate thermal rating. The plans drawn up by your Architect will specify this.

An exception to this can be where you're looking to keep the original windows or doors as an architectural feature. Your Architect will be able to advise on the best solution that will meet the applicable thermal capacity requirements. Be wary of the extra cost involved in this approach. You may be creating a wow feature but be sure that the additional investment pays dividends. It will either need to make the units easier to sell or must allow you to command a higher price.

Final considerations on thermal insulation

The thermal insulation requirement for a project is based on each unit as a whole. It's not assessed on each room or apartment in isolation.

Why is this important? Well, we recently had a project with restricted headroom in one of the bedrooms. The council was insisting we needed to add insulation to the floor. Unfortunately, the insulation couldn't be added without making the room height untenable. As a result, this would have meant digging up the concrete floor. Not only would this have been an extra cost, it could also expose us to contamination issues.

We agreed the room did not meet the required insulation standard. But we pointed out to the council that we'd added extra insulation to other parts of the same apartment, and this more than compensated for the shortfall. Since the apartment as a whole now had the required level of thermal insulation, it didn't matter that one of the rooms in isolation did not. The council concurred, and we were not then required to insulate the floor of that room.

16. Services Implications

Let's now move on to the provision of services. So what exactly do we mean by services? Well, here we're going to be covering each of the utilities, namely water, gas, and electricity, plus the drainage i.e., waste pipes for toilets, baths, and sinks.

There is a common challenge when converting commercial or industrial buildings. These services are often present, but they're either in the wrong place, or there's not enough of them. On a typical conversion project, we'll be taking a unit that has one set of services (the host building) and converting it into multiple units (the flats). Each flat will need its own services, located in a particular place. Let's look at each element in turn.

Drainage

Industrial buildings often have a concentration of toilet facilities in one place. For example, there will be a toilet 'block' with several cubicles/urinals and basins at one end of the building and nothing at all at the other. The waste pipes from these blocks usually lead to the mains drainage system without disturbing the concrete slab. The presence of a toilet block is good news in as much as there is mains drainage on site. But each flat is going to need its own toilet, and they won't all be situated next to each other! The challenge is how to extend the drainage network throughout the entire building so that this is achieved.

Drainage relics on gravity to take waste from each flat to the sewer. But with each new toilet sitting right on top of the slab, there's very little opportunity to get the waste to run downhill unless you cut into the slab. Even if there were enough gradient, you wouldn't want to run your soil pipes through the living space. Even running them outside is far from ideal. Also, you don't want to cut into the slab to run the pipes underneath if you can avoid it. This is because you may then have to deal with any contamination issues, as well as incur extra cost.

So a catch-22 then? Well, this is where the suspended floors mentioned in the previous chapter can come to your rescue. Many industrial buildings have a much higher headroom space than you need in residential dwellings. This means we may have room to insert a suspended floor. This would sit around 1 foot/30cm above the existing slab and still leave enough headroom for the living space. It would create a void underneath the new floor along which we could run not only the waste pipes but also any new water pipes that we'd need. In this way, we create a downhill gradient, we avoid disturbing the slab, and at the same time, all the service pipes are out of sight.

One further complication may occur where the host building isn't connected to mains drainage at all. Here the building would rely instead on a septic tank to dispose of all waste. While this solution is acceptable for houses, it isn't desirable for flats to have a communal septic tank. You should investigate the cost and feasibility of getting the units attached to the mains drainage system before you buy the site.

Water

A mains water supply will likely be present in at least one location on the host site. Like the drainage, you'll need to be able to run pipework to each of the flats. If you're creating a suspended floor, then the pipework can run underneath. But since water pipes are far less obtrusive than drainage pipes, it may also be possible to run the pipework across walls or in ceiling voids.

Electrical

The capacity of the electrical supply coming into an industrial building is usually dependent on the building's historical usage. Where heavy, electric-powered machinery has been used, you may already find you have a high-capacity supply. This will usually be in one location, and as a result, you'll need to split the supply so that each unit has its own.

Some buildings may not have needed much in the way of electrical power historically. For example, a barn or a storage building may only have a set of lights and no mains powered equipment. The challenge here is to get more electricity into the building. There may be a sufficient electrical supply in the vicinity, in which case it's a straightforward job of running cables to each unit to extend the supply reach. However, the mains supply to a property doesn't involve an unlimited amount of electricity that can just be drawn on as required. It may be that the electrical supply is insufficient to support the residential units you're building. In this case, the electricity board will need to upgrade the supply to your property, which will be at a cost to you.

Gas

Your host building may or may not have an existing gas supply. Either way, you should still consider whether it's desirable for your flats to have gas for heating or cooking. You may be better off having everything electric. Many industrial buildings have a gas supply for heating offices where the demand is minimal. The demand from multiple flats that have both gas heating and hot water would be far higher. You'd need to establish whether the supply would need upgrading if you were to have gas throughout. Talk to your professional services consultant about this. If your host building runs an oil-fired boiler, then you may want to replace it since oil-fired heating in flats isn't practical. There are strict and complex rules governing the placement of gas pipes, so going electric-only could avoid a number of complications.

Avoiding delays

Utility companies are a law unto themselves when it comes to timetabling the work needed to get utilities into new units. They can be a source of constant frustration due to their failure to get their work done in a timely fashion.

The challenge is that your contractor (or anyone else, no matter how well qualified they are) is not allowed to touch the utility supply cables/pipes/infrastructure that come into the building. Only the utility companies themselves can do this. And of course, they have no vested interest in helping you achieve your deadlines as a developer. So they'll turn up and do the work when it suits them, rather than when it suits you.

The impact of this can be significant since it can stop work progressing on site. This, in turn, delays completion, which means your finance costs are higher and your profits delayed. Ultimately this could impact the financing of your next project.

So what can you do about it? Here are our top tips for dealing with utility companies:

1. Make sure that you get your services applications in as soon as possible after you've secured the development site
2. Some utility companies will only deal with the building owner (you); however, this isn't going to be ideal. The best approach can be to give authority to your M&E Consultant, Architect, or PM at the outset. They can then be responsible for liaising with the utility companies on your behalf. You can then transfer this delegated authority to your Contractor once they are on site

3. Have a system for keeping in touch with the utility companies. Don't just chase when you remember or when you're desperate – make sure you have someone chasing them every week

4. Chasing utility companies isn't a difficult task, but it can involve spending hours on the phone. Be aware of this and give the job to someone who is both patient and tenacious!

5. Most utility companies operate a hub system where all requests go to a head office that then schedules a local team to do the work. The challenge is that the head office may be miles away, and they have very little clue what's going on, at least from a technical point of view. Your request is only an admin issue to them – it simply needs to be added to the local teams' task list and the work scheduled in

6. We have often found that the utility companies' local teams can be extremely helpful. They often know exactly what's going on since they are technicians who have local knowledge, whereas head office staff are administrators based elsewhere. Better still, they are often happy to give you their direct contact details so that you can get hold of them when you need them. This can be a godsend; if you get a chance to foster a good relationship with the local team(s), it can serve you well

Registering the new addresses

You should also be aware that utility companies will need to know the address of each flat since each will, in due course, have its own billable supply. When you acquire the site, there will only be one address, namely the address of the host building. You will then need to apply to the local council to create the new addresses. You want to do this at an early stage so that you can then pass this information on to the utility companies. The process is not a difficult one; however, there will be a fee to pay, plus there will be no guarantee how long the council will take to process your request.

17. Building Without Foundations

Typical problems with groundworks

Previously we've touched briefly on the benefits of not having to go into the ground to dig foundations. In this chapter, we want to explore this area in a little more detail.

The problem with groundwork is that you can't see what's under the soil. There could be all manner of nasty things lurking there that could alter, delay, or even halt your development plans altogether. Or there could be absolutely no problems whatsoever, and everything is just tickety-boo. The problem is you won't know until you've started digging, by which time you're already committed.

To recap, the sort of problems you could encounter when you start digging the foundations are:

Contamination

Particularly if the site has been used by businesses where chemicals or fuels were stored or used, e.g., garages and workshops.

Underground services

There may already be services located in the ground that are connected to neighbouring properties. There may be drainage, gas, or electrical pipes that you could disrupt or uncover as you dig your foundations.

Poor ground conditions

Your foundations need to be dug into solid ground. When digging foundations, you may encounter unstable ground such as backfill.

This will then need to be removed, and the foundations dug deeper until solid ground is reached.

Wells

These may have been capped below surface level, but the well itself remains and will need to be filled.

Archaeological remains

You may find something of archaeological importance while digging the foundations. This may merit an archaeological survey. At best, this will incur cost and delay, but if the survey discovers something worth preserving, your development may not be able to progress.

Now, every building needs foundations, since, without them, they have a tendency to topple over (this hopefully isn't news to you). Foundations aren't generally very complicated things. In fact, the most common type of foundation, a strip foundation, is merely a trench filled with concrete on which you build the load-bearing walls. All foundations must be built on solid ground. If your Structural Engineer has established that the land is too soft or unstable, then you'll need a deeper foundation, known as a trench fill. This extra depth means more concrete, and this will come at an additional cost.

Beyond trench fill there are piled foundations. These are used where there are areas where no solid ground can be found on which to lay foundations, and so a specialist installation team is needed to force piles deep into the ground. Not surprisingly this is likely to add a significant additional cost to the development (but will not automatically be prohibitive).

You may find soft spots in the foundations, e.g., where there is a short length of the strip foundation that is unstable. Here the Structural Engineer may decide to put in some steelwork to reinforce that part of the foundations. This is a steel mesh that will be set into the concrete that will bridge the soft spot within the strip.

The technical part involves knowing how deep your foundations need to be. If you were building a garden wall, you wouldn't need very deep foundations. If you were building a skyscraper, the foundations would need to be a lot more extensive (nothing you don't know already, we're sure).

Now, you won't be surprised to learn that the depth of foundations you have to build isn't arbitrary. It's not left to guesswork or dependent on how much concrete your Contractor happens to have left in the mixer. There are calculations that determine precisely how robust your footings need to be to support the building above. These are called load-bearing capacities, and if you're a Structural Engineer, they can be really quite exciting.

Luckily as the developer, you don't need to know about this in any great detail. Just accept this as something with which your Structural Engineer will be intimately familiar, and you can just nod knowingly when he or she mentions it ☺. However, it won't hurt you to understand the principle of what's involved at a high level, so if you're interested here goes.

Technical Corner: Foundations

The demand placed on a building's foundations consists of two elements:

Dead Load (a.k.a. stuff that's permanently there): This is the mass (weight) of the building's physical structure that the foundations have to support. For example, a skyscraper is more massive than a house, so the demand placed on the footings is greater.

Live Load (a.k.a. stuff that could move in or out of the building): This is the mass of any items, equipment, or people that are housed in or which use the building. In the case of commercial buildings and houses, this would include furniture, appliances, and employees. For industrial buildings, this could also include heavy machinery and vehicles. These items tend to be a lot heavier in industrial buildings than anything found in commercial or residential buildings.

Now for the really exciting bit. As a non-technical property CEO, you will <u>never</u> need to know that the unit of measurement for the load bearing capacity of foundations is a thing called "kilonewtons per square metre (kN/m^2)". So, you can now instantly forget this. If you've just glazed over like a donut as you've read this paragraph then don't worry, this is completely normal. If you prefer you can think of them as Killer Neutrons per Square Pizza; much more memorable and almost certainly a lot tastier.

So, one kN/m^2 is simply the amount of force exerted on one square metre of ground.

The more mass a building has (dead load) or the heavier the things that go in it (live load), then the stronger the foundations need to be. And since most industrial buildings typically carry a heavier load than other types of building, their concrete base must be built to withstand more kilonewtons per square metre. All very straightforward.

So what sort of quantum are we talking about here? How much more weight does the base of an industrial building have to support compared to a block of flats, for example?

A single-storey residential property typically has to support a dead load of 2.5 kN/m^2 and a live load of 1.5 kN/m^2 (per storey). This makes 4.0 kN/m^2 in total.

A light industrial building will typically have to support a weight of 2.5 kN/m^2 for each metre of building height. So if the building is 3 metres tall, then the base would be designed to support 7.5 kN/m^2.

Since we could fit a single storey residential unit in a 3-metre-high building, you can see that the existing base at 7.5 kN/m² is more than the 4.0 kN/m² we'd need for residential, therefore we can build straight off the base.

Now, a lot of light industrial buildings will be significantly taller than 3 metres – so now let's assume that our target building is 6 metres tall.

So, if we were to convert our 6-metre-tall light industrial building into a single storey residential building, then we already know that the existing base is already going to be strong enough. It has a load-bearing capacity of 6 x 2.5 kN/m² which equals 15 kN/m² whereas a single-storey residential building only requires 4.0 kN/m².

But given that we have such a tall host building, why don't we create two floors of residential units instead of one?

Adding another residential storey would add a further 4 kN/m² to the load capacity requirement, which means we'd now need 8 kN/m² in total. But in our 6m high building we already have 15 kN/m², which means we can add another storey using the existing base.

Now the mathematical geniuses among you will be thinking, hold on a sec, if the base supports 15 kN/m², and we've only used 8 kN/m², couldn't we add a third storey as well? That would take us up to 12 kN/m², and we'd still have 3 kN/m²to spare.

Well, you'd be absolutely correct, however you need to remember that your host building is only 6m high. Consequently, the chances of squeezing in 3 storeys are pretty remote, unless you're thinking about some sort of rehousing programme for short people, albeit this would rather limit your market. As a result, if you wanted an extra storey you would need to get Full Planning Permission to raise the height of the existing building, and of course this then introduces an element of a risk, additional cost, and uncertainty.

Finally, please note that the figures we've used above are all 'typical' – there's no guarantee that any individual base will have a sufficient load bearing capacity, so your team would need to check.

Hopefully that gives you a useful overview of load bearing capacities, and you can now de-glaze in time for the next section. Just remember that you won't be the one deciding whether the load capacity of your building is sufficient. That sits firmly within the remit of your Structural Engineer, the lucky devil.

The advantages of using the existing slab

There are several very significant advantages in building off the existing slab:

Coverage

The concrete base covers the entire site. No matter where you need to put load-bearing walls, you are guaranteed to have the slab underneath you. This gives you a lot of flexibility. You're not trying to re-use existing footings that only exist in certain areas. You know the base covers the entire site, and subject to your Structural Engineer's analysis and confirmation, you can build on any of it (it's worth noting here that he or she may want to drill core holes through the existing slab first, to determine its thickness and therefore its actual load-bearing capacity).

Cost savings

The cost of laying foundations is not cheap, and it becomes even more expensive if you first have to dig up an existing base. By using the existing slab, you avoid this cost altogether.

Time savings

Time is money on a development project. The sooner you can get your units finished, the earlier you can take your profit, plus your finance costs will be less. Digging up an existing slab and laying new foundations takes a fair amount of time. And of course, that's before you find out whether any issues in the ground could increase both your costs and timescales.

Avoiding contamination issues

As we've mentioned before, contamination can be a problem with industrial buildings. This is usually as a result of chemical or oil spillage that has taken place historically. However, there's a strong likelihood that any historical contamination will not be affecting the slab itself. Any residue will have been cleaned up for obvious reasons to enable the building to function. But it's still possible there could be contamination under the slab. However, if you're not disturbing the slab, then you won't be disturbing the contaminated soil underneath. The slab effectively acts as a cap, keeping the contamination in place.

A word about contamination

It's worth remembering that, just because there's contamination on your site, it doesn't mean that as the building's new owner, you will have to address it. Contamination doesn't always affect anything unless it's disturbed (in which case you probably will have to deal with it). The presence of contamination itself may not, therefore, be a problem. If the contamination has lain under the slab for 50 years, then another 50 years is unlikely to cause an issue. Also, contamination is largely incurable. If you were to dig up the contaminated soil, it has to go somewhere – you can't just give it a quick jet wash and put it back.

The government's view is that removing contamination from a site simply shifts the problem somewhere else; it doesn't solve it. Historically, contaminated soil was taken to specific regional sites and disposed of in landfill which had the impact of concentrating the contamination in that area; in hindsight not a particularly great idea. Not surprisingly this didn't go down too well locally, plus it actually caused more problems due to its concentration. As a result, more modern thinking is to leave contamination where it is, providing it's not problematic.

Talking of which, you do need to be mindful of contamination migration. This is where existing contamination can move from your site on to an adjacent location over time. Where this happens, you would be liable as the owner of the building even if you didn't cause the contamination in the first place.

18. Creating A Design Advantage

Over the years, we've come across numerous developers who place good design way down their priority list. After all, if they're not creating designer apartments, why bother going the extra mile thinking about good design? Surely it just adds to the cost and therefore depletes the developer's profits?

The reality is that design is one of the most important things to get right in any development, no matter what type of unit you're building. People buy with their eyes, and when they visit your new flats for the first time, you need to make sure that they can see themselves living there. You need as much 'wow-factor' as you can get. Plus, you also want to make sure that your product is a more attractive proposition than the one for sale down the road.

One key point to reinforce in this section is that all-too-common beginner's error of designing for yourself. If you're personally not going to live in one of the units, you should never add a design feature just because you like it. Every element of the design has to have both your end customer in mind AND your bottom-line. We've lost count of the number of new-builds, conversions, flips and rentals we've seen where the owner has a passion for a particular colour, or just HAD to have the granite worktops with the fancy taps. There are two cardinal sins rolled into one here:

1. People don't dislike neutral – if you go bold on your design, you'll alienate many of your potential buyers. Trust us; this Is a bad thing. Some may love it, but what's the point of narrowing your target market before you've started?

2. Overkill kills your profit – buying expensive items because they're what YOU would have in your own home is throwing money away. You may as well hand a wad of banknotes to your new buyers. In the next section, we'll talk about the little things that make a big difference. But you definitely want to avoid buying big (expensive) things that make very little difference

Now you're likely to have already considered 'dressing' the interior. You might bring in some nice furniture and soft furnishings during the sales stage. This will make the photos look great and get the place looking as spectacular as possible. We talk about this in the next chapter, but design starts way before then. In fact, it starts right at the very beginning of the project.

Let's take a look at each of the design elements in detail, so you get to see the whole picture.

Exploiting architectural advantages

One of the great things about industrial buildings is that their features can be very different from those of residential dwellings. Standard small residential units like 1-bed flats are often little more than shoeboxes. Each is identical and all encased within the shell of an equally uninspiring outer building. But industrial buildings have a lot of architectural advantages that you can make great use of at minimal cost if you know how.

Vaulted ceilings

These are one of our favourites because they can dramatically increase the sense of space in a room. Instead of having a standard ceiling running parallel to the floor, the headroom of a vaulted ceiling extends all the way to the roof. Often a vaulted ceiling could have the roof beams and trusses exposed.

Vaulted ceilings can be a key advantage when you're building smaller units, as these flats could appear small, on paper at least, when compared to other flats on the market. But industrial buildings usually have much greater headroom than residential buildings. This means you can use vaulted ceilings to increase the capacity of each unit, even if you're not changing the floor area. This is a crucial area to discuss with your Architect at the outset since it is integral to the whole project.

Vaulted ceilings can cause a compromise, and you'll need to weigh it all up. Could you get duplexes in there? What about an entire second storey? Or some storage space? If the area that's occupied by your vaulted ceiling could be repurposed, then it might not be the best option. You'll need to think this through at the start and discuss it with your Architect. There's also a cost to them.

However, as a rule, we'd recommend you ask yourself the following questions when assessing the headroom in any industrial building:

1. Can we get an entire additional storey in there? This will almost certainly give us a greater return, whether this is a second floor of flats or one floor of two-storey units
2. Could we create duplexes, i.e., where each apartment has a second storey element, albeit the first-floor floor area may be smaller than the ground floor?
3. Could we create raised floor areas? These are effectively a second storey where the reduced headroom or access prevents the area from being used as living space (under building regulations), but it may be used for storage. It may be accessed via a 'ladder', and whilst it can't be marketed as accommodation space, your prospective buyers might look at it and think what a great place for a home office, etc. (but you couldn't possibly comment ..)
4. Could we create storage/loft space? This is always a premium in smaller flats

5. Could we create vaulted ceilings?

6. Do we need to use some of the headroom to raise the floor levels at ground level, to install new drainage runs and therefore avoid digging up the slab?

Interesting Features

Industrial buildings can often have unique features that you can incorporate into the finished design. Industrial design cues are very much in demand by some buyers, particularly younger ones. You'll be familiar with the wharf buildings converted into luxury flats on the Thames in London, and the stylish loft apartments in New York. The original purpose of these buildings adds interest, and that in turn adds a lot of value and appeal.

Now, if we were converting a run-down old MOT centre, you might be thinking that it would be a far cry from the loft-living dream. Yet actually, the same rules apply but on a smaller scale. Wooden beams, exposed steels and brickwork, old signage; these can all add character and desirability, at worst making your units sell faster and at best, increasing their value.

A significant advantage of Industrial Conversions is that you often find that your finished units all differ in some way. You may be selling five 1-bed apartments, but they're not carbon copies of each other. This can be a great attraction, particularly if you have an open-day event. If there are five flats all the same, then no one will have a favourite. If one sells, there are still another four left to buy, so what's the rush? But if all the flats are unique, then they will <u>definitely</u> have a favourite. And they may be tempted to get in quick to make sure they secure their first choice. An open day can create this demand.

A word of caution. Make sure your plans for keeping an industrial theme are aligned with your target market. If you're going to be selling to an older demographic, then they may think less is more when it comes to industrial design or urban cues.

Exposed brickwork

This can create some of that vaunted wow-factor; however, unfortunately, not all bricks are created equal. One of the common challenges with industrial buildings is that they are often of poor construction. They are usually put up at minimal cost to perform a very basic function. As a result, you may find that the brickwork is not suitable (because it looks terrible). Another issue is insulation; the walls may have decent bricks, but they'll still need to be insulated to meet building regulations.

One idea that can work well is the use of faux bricks. These artificial stick-on brick facings come in various types and styles (and they look a lot less tacky than they sound). You would apply them to your feature wall, and they do an excellent job of resembling exposed brick. Less is usually more with this type of effect, and of course, it comes at a premium. It's a lot more expensive than a coat of emulsion, plus it also soaks up light. But where you have a limited number of industrial design cues and are looking to maximise the loft style, these can be a great way of adding character.

Urban/Industrial look

Retaining the industrial features of a building can be extended to some of the other aspects of your design. Kitchens are a particularly good area to work on. A modern, functional-looking kitchen with plenty of exposed metal can complement the industrial theme. Plus, it can often cost less than its less urban-looking equivalent. Long pendant lights hanging from vaulted ceilings are another great feature, as are metal light fixtures and fittings. When dressing the finished units, you can add urban-themed artwork, while large wall clocks can also add 'wow'.

As ever, the Internet is an excellent resource for design cues for your project – there are too many possibilities to list them all here. There are countless sources of interior design images. Pinterest and Google Images are two of our favourite starting points. When assessing an image, the important thing is first to decide whether you like the overall look of the room. You can then zoom in closer and try and identify the individual elements that make you feel that way.

Hiring an Interior Designer

Interior Designers suffer from one particular malaise that persistently blights their profession, and that is this; we all think we're quite passable (if not downright brilliant) at interior design ourselves, and so why on earth should we bother hiring a designer?

However, this is a similar situation to people who whistle in public, thinking that everyone else can immediately catch the tune in their head and marvel at their incredible pitch, tone, and musicality. The reality is of course rather different, where everyone else in earshot tries to resist a strong urge to hit the tuneless so-and-sos with something to make them shut up.

Other members of the design team are at least protected by regulation. You can't for example decide to be the architect on your project or the structural engineer, as there is a strong likelihood that what you've built won't stay up very long. So, regulations require that your plans are drawn up by suitably qualified people. But the poor old Interior Designer has no such protection. Anyone can do interior design, and some people can be shockingly delusional in their abilities in this area.

So, should you hire one? To be honest, the answer is 'it depends'. If you've been given a strong steer by local estate agents in terms of the look, fit and finish to go for and your budget is tight, then you could certainly save a few bob by skipping on a designer. The problem is that you don't know what you don't know. If you involve an interior designer at the start, they can offer a lot more input into the design process, so it's not just about colour charts and show flat furnishings. Our advice would be to get a discussion going with a reputable interior designer before the start of your project, and then take a view on what you believe they can offer versus the additional cost. You may be genuinely surprised at the value they can add, plus the benefits can go way beyond your first project, since you'll be able to use their initial advice on subsequent projects.

If you're still not convinced, check out our podcast episode where we interview a leading interior designer and ask her about the benefits of hiring in some interior design expertise.

The
propertyCEO
Podcast

Season 3; Ep 5

The advantage of light

Nothing sells a property better than good natural lighting. We've talked at length about natural light being a priority for your project throughout. It's often a significant challenge as far as larger industrial buildings are concerned, but don't think of it only as a utility. The idea is not just to get 'some' light in or 'sufficient' light. You want to think about how you could dramatically enhance the light levels in each unit.

In the same way that vaulted ceilings create extra capacity, good natural lighting can make the space sing. It's easy to think that poor light in a bedroom is less critical. After all, it's typically used at night when it has cosy electric lighting on. Unfortunately, your customers won't be able to appreciate this on their 10am viewing. So, make

ِ out with your Architect to discuss light at the
ِt. Focus not only on getting enough light into each
ıg it a real priority.

ıl lighting configuration is equally critical, and you
certa.   ıant to avoid having any gloomy rooms. However,
remember that your sales viewings and brochure images will show
the building in daylight, so there's not much point installing
sophisticated mood lighting if no one gets to see it. It's not likely to
influence the selling price or the saleability, your two key areas of
focus.

You may also wish to consider using the services of a specialist
lighting consultant who could add value to your scheme by devising
creative lighting designs, without necessarily adding significant cost
to the project.

The wow-factor list

This is one of the biggest secrets to getting any property sold quickly
(and often at a premium), so pay close attention!

If you were building a suite of luxury apartments, then the gold taps
(and all the other high-end features) are essential. You wouldn't nip
down to the local hardware store to pick up some cheap door
furniture, nor would you install a cheap and cheerful kitchen.
People will be paying a premium for the property, so they'll expect
to have premium fixtures and fittings.

But many developers make the mistake of assuming that the
opposite is also true. They think that if you're selling smaller, entry-
level flats, then all the fixtures and fittings should be very cheap and
basic. This is a big mistake, and it's a case of a little investment in
the detail taking you a long way.

There's a simple marketing tool at work here, and it's impossible not to be affected by it. By installing a small number of premium items or features, you achieve several things:

1. Buyers assume that the whole unit is of a similar premium quality
2. They get to imagine using/enjoying these premium features
3. They will note that the other properties that they've viewed didn't have these things

Remember, people buy with their eyes. If they like what they see enough, then they'll see themselves living there. And once they want to live there, you're in exactly the right place to get a sale.

Now the idea here is not to go mad. You could install premium fittings that cost more than the entire flat if you wanted to, and that's definitely not the plan. Instead, you need to strike a balance between cost and effectiveness. You want to minimise your expenditure and yet get the most bang for your buck in the 'wow-factor' stakes.

So, would you like to know what items make the most cost-effective wow-factor additions? Here are some of our favourites. View this as a list of potential options rather than a shopping list. You don't need to tick every box, but you will need more than one of them to get the reaction you're looking for.

Multi-room Bluetooth integrated speaker system

You can't beat a bit of tech to create an impression. What about installing speakers in every room that sync to your phone, tablet, or computer? This allows your new owners' favourite music to be piped all around the flat. You need to factor this in at the design stage as the speaker units themselves fit directly into the ceiling. But the cost is not prohibitive, even in cheaper flats This is something that may appeal to a younger audience, so make sure you keep your target market in mind.

Premium doors

Cheap doors are a pet hate. You know the kind; budget four-panel jobs from the local builders' merchants. Or worse still, a completely featureless door that looks like it came from an institution. Doors can get expensive if you go for a premium finish, but there's a sensible mid-point that gets you decent looking doors at a reasonable price. Remember that you're likely to be building smaller units with not too many rooms, so your door count shouldn't be excessive. And don't forget the front door; the same rules apply.

Premium door furniture

You only need to take one or two steps up in quality to get some very nice-looking door furniture. What about brushed steel fittings on your premium door? There are lots of options, and people notice these things even if they don't register them individually. They can add a real feeling of quality to the entire flat.

Storage space

Storage is something that no one has enough of, but in small flats, it comes at a real premium. When you live in a house or larger apartment, having somewhere to store something like a suitcase isn't a problem. But in a small flat, there's often nowhere to store a suitcase, so you're left leaving it in the bedroom or not keeping it in the flat at all. If you have the extra ceiling height, it can give you scope to get creative with storage space, even if it's not throughout the entire flat. National Space Standards specify a minimum storage space volume for new builds, and from 6th April 2021 this applies to Permitted Development conversions as well. Appreciate that storage space will be right up near the top of many people's buying checklists. You may be competing with lots of other properties that have more storage space than your units. You need to be aware of this right from the outset, as this can be a deal-breaker for many buyers.

Figure 18.1 shows how we managed to create a high-level enclosed storage area in the void above the bathroom whilst keeping the rest of the flat ceilings vaulted. We also created a deep but narrow cupboard to the left of the bathroom door which could hold a vacuum cleaner and potentially coats, etc.

Figure 18.1: Storage space provides valuable benefits in smaller flats

Switches and sockets

Quality white fittings are perfectly acceptable for cheaper flats. Brushed chrome light and power socket fittings could also be considered, although they can be costly, ask your estate agent's advice on whether they're worth it. The basic white plastic affairs are cheap and cheerful – so ramping up the quality again speaks volumes about the perceived quality of the overall build.

LED downlighters

Back to our light theme again, LED lighting is effective and efficient, plus the bulbs tend to last a lot longer. On the downside, the lighting units themselves are more expensive. However, prices have reduced dramatically, and LED is very much mainstream these days.

Feature lighting

The world's your oyster with lighting, but a well-placed feature light can really add something to a room. We often use long pendant lights suspended from vaulted ceilings to create some extra wow. But a spot of online research will reveal hundreds of potential ideas. You could also consider putting touch sensitive LED mirrors in bathrooms for added impact. The trick is to make sure you keep an eye on your budget, as lighting can get expensive if you're not careful.

Large shower cubicles

This is a big selling point because so often, shower space is at a premium in a small flat. Remember that often you may not have room for a bath, so the shower could be the only game in town. We've all endured cramped apartments or hotel rooms where the shower cubicle was barely wide enough to fit into, let alone wash once you're in there. If people can see that they'll be having a luxurious shower with plenty of space to move around in, it can be a significant influence on their inclination to buy.

Wall to floor tiling behind basins

The cheapest way of tiling around a basin is not to tile under it. Yet the cost-saving is minimal in the scheme of things. Plus, the area under the basin can get grubby, yet it can't easily be wiped down because it's not tiled. If you tile to the floor, you avoid the problem, plus it adds to the perception of quality for an insignificant increase in price.

Chrome shaver sockets

Don't just go for the standard white plastic fittings – invest in a chrome or brushed steel finish to enhance the feeling of quality.

Premium kitchen appliances

The kitchen is a crucial area of influence for prospective purchasers, and it can pay to feature an upgrade or two. Putting in some premium appliances is a great start. Going for the Bosch/Neff/Siemens brands sends a strong message of quality. There's no need to go for the all-singing-all-dancing models. A base-level model will do all the basics well and still has the brand cachet at half the price of its top-end siblings. You could also consider including a glass extractor hood above the hob or oven.

Premium work surfaces

These days there is a wide range of worktops available. These range from basic laminate right through to granite and marble. At the lower end of the market, upgrading from the basic laminate to wood or a Corian-type finish can look good, but can be prohibitively expensive, even in a smaller kitchen. Instead, you may be better off upping the thickness of the laminate and being careful with your design choice.

Quality splashbacks

We like to install deeper-than-usual splashbacks in our kitchens as this improves the aesthetics and is also more practical. We would also install glass splashbacks in the hob area as this adds a quality touch without breaking the bank.

Premium mixer taps

You can spend serious money on taps, but you don't need to. Just make sure you avoid the cheap and nasty looking units and make sure you choose mixer taps in the kitchen. Keep the design in keeping with the rest of the kitchen; if you've gone urban chic, get the taps to match.

Boiling water tap

These can be pricey, but they do pack a punch in terms of wow factor. They're a luxury item and not something that your non-premium flat buyer would usually consider. On the downside, the taps use filters that can be costly to replace, and people may feel they're paying for something they can live without. Think about your target market – if you're aiming at a premium finish, then adding a high-end item like this may pay dividends.

Fitted wardrobes

These can be a mixed blessing and you should discuss them with your estate agent. Returning to our storage-space-is-at-a-premium theme, having built-in wardrobes can be very desirable in flats, but in smaller units they can really close in the space and make them feel cramped. Try to make use of recesses if you have them. Also, consider a wider, shallower wardrobe with clothes hung facing you, as this reduces the extent to which it extends into the room.

USB charging points

These are wall sockets that take a USB connector for charging mobile phones in addition to a standard 3-pin socket. Add at least one into each kitchen and two into each bedroom.

Fusebox cupboards

Each unit you build will have an electrical fuse box. Rather than leave it open to the room, get your Contractor to box it inside a cupboard, and then paint it to match the walls. It only costs a few hundred pounds but makes a big difference aesthetically.

So there we have it; a shortlist of the most common elements that we add to our units to get them to sell more quickly. And, if we're lucky, to get a better price.

Don't underestimate the benefits of a quick sale. Your financing will still be attracting interest until the final unit sells, plus it's the last units that contain your profit. Yes, these extra items will cost you money, but so does having unsold flats.

With your friendly estate agent onside, you can ask them for guidance. Which wow items would customers appreciate most, given you have a limited budget? Remember that they'll know your customers better than you will!

The critical thing to note is to make sure you think about all these things at the outset. Some of these items are integrated into the building and so need to be factored into the Architect's drawings at the start. Some items can be installed after work has commenced, but there's always a benefit in being very clear on what's in or out with your team right out of the blocks. You could easily forget to include something by which time it's twice the price to install. This is because it may involve undoing and then redoing work that has already been completed.

You also avoid a common contractor's grumble of the developer changing his or her mind midway through a project. You may be thinking you'd simply delayed your decision to install premium doors. But the Contractor will see it as changing your mind. The nature of development is that there will be enough unplanned changes during the build already without you adding any more to the list.

19. Marketing Your Units

We're now going to zoom in on the final part of the development journey. However, it's not a part that you should consider last. Marketing is another area where developers often get it wrong. They think about marketing towards the end of the build phase instead of right at the beginning of the project. This may not always be disastrous, but in our view, it misses a big opportunity.

So let's go back to the beginning and plot the ideal marketing plan right out of the blocks.

Start with your estate agent

You're most likely going to be using a residential estate agent to sell your finished units, so let's start with that scenario first. You'll have already met with three or more local agents before you bought the host property. These were the people who gave you their thoughts on the target market, pricing, demand, and specs, and so on. They will also have told you their fees and suggested a marketing plan.

You've now taken ownership of the property, and it's in its raw state, ideally with any equipment, etc. removed so that it resembles a blank canvas. You'll now need to decide which estate agent you'd like to appoint, and you can then give him or her a call and arrange to meet them at the property.

The two key objectives of this first meeting are:

1. To tell them that you'd like them to sell the units for you, subject to agreement on a marketing plan and fees

2. To get them interested and excited about the development. This is important, as you'll want them to feel they've been 'involved' in the project from the outset

Taking the second point first, let's clarify what journey your estate agent will be going on here. You want them to be enthusiastic about the project when they're with potential buyers. In our experience, the best way of doing that is letting them see the development unfold first hand. This means:

1. An on-site meeting at the very start so that they can see the 'blank canvas'
2. A meeting at the end when everything is complete
3. At least one further meeting, preferably around two-thirds of the way through the project where they can see the progress that has been made, but there is still some way to go

The agenda for these meetings is not only to show them how far the project has come – you also need to be talking business at each stage. But by structuring it this way, you get the best of all worlds. In our experience, most agents are very curious to see how things are developing on-site, so you should have no difficulty in getting them to show up.

How to price your units

Pricing is something of an organic process. At the outset, you'll have met with your estate agent to discuss the likely selling prices of the proposed units. However, that was then, and this is now. Quite a few things may have changed since your initial business plan was drawn up. These include:

1. The market may have moved (up or down)
2. Your design or finish may have changed during the build

3. The end product may be better/worse than the agent originally envisaged
4. The selling agent may be different from the agent that initially priced it

Aside from these, there's always a margin for error when an agent tries to price units at the outset. This is because they know very little other than it's a one-bed flat in a particular location with a certain type of finish. You're never going to get as accurate an estimate as you will when the agent is standing in the finished property. This is why it pays to be prudent when setting your initial GDV assumption, and to avoid optimism.

Once your units are close to completion (but not yet finished), you should invite your agent back round. They can then see the (nearly) finished product and can confirm the final target pricing and marketing strategy. We strongly advocate doing your own market area analysis before this meeting. Just do a refresh of the one you did at the outset before you bought the property. This will allow you to see how your assessment has changed in the intervening period. Plus, critically, it will give you a good idea of the current competition. You want to know what's out there on the market in direct competition with your units, and also what similar properties have sold recently. It can also pay dividends to check out the planning portal to see if any pipeline developments could hit the market at the same time.

The reason for having your own assessment is that you want to be able to critique the agent's views during the meeting and to get their take on things. They may suggest you price your units at £150k. But if you've seen one similar down the road on the market at £175k, then you want to ask why the agent thinks that £175k is not the correct price. Some agents will do their homework before a meeting like this, while others will wing it. The problem is that their sample size (particularly if they're winging it) is likely to be small. It might only be based on the units they've sold in the immediate area over the last few months. Your market area analysis will be looking at properties from all agents, both sold and unsold. As a result, you're going to have a bigger sample than the agent, and so between you, you'll have more information to work with.

We should stress that the idea here is not to try and put the agent on the back foot. You're just doing your homework and adding to the pool of information that will allow you to agree on a selling price as a joint effort.

Marketing strategies compared

There are several different marketing approaches you can take when selling your units. Much depends on your target market, market conditions, and the number of units you're selling. Whichever route you choose, it's a decision you should make at the outset of the project and not midway through.

Your marketing activity will need to be geared to getting the best possible price for your units in the quickest possible time. This involves a trade-off since if you charge a premium price for your units, they'll take longer to sell. If you were selling your own home and were in no hurry to move, then holding out for the best price may be the way to go. But in development, this delay will cost you money since you'll need to service the financing costs for longer. Plus, you'll have profit tied up in the units, which may mean you need to delay starting your next project.

On the other hand, if you low-ball the price, it may get you a quick sale, but it will hurt your profits. Hence, we arrive at the middle ground, being able to sell them quickly but without having to take a hit on the selling price

This all sounds great in theory, but how do we make it happen? One of the challenges with the property market is that the marketing of individual properties for sale hasn't changed much in decades. Yes, things have migrated online, but the basic approach is the same. You pick an agent, they draft some particulars, then issue them to their database/publish them online and then wait for the phone to ring. Then it's a series of viewings hopefully followed by one or more offers.

There's nothing wrong with this approach; however, there are a limited number of variables that you can influence:

Reach

Most agents can access the entire market by using online portals like Rightmove, Prime Location, On The Market, and the like.

Experience

Some agents are better than others, plus some may have more knowledge of marketing your type of units in the target area.

Salesmanship

Similarly, some agents are far better salespeople than others; they may perform the same service, but a great salesperson can be far more persuasive when getting customers to buy.

Price

This is the biggest driver, but it's a blunt instrument.

Particulars

Do your words and pictures sing off the page, or do they look like a million and one others? Some agents offer a premium printed brochure for an additional fee, but this is not usually the norm with non-premium properties.

So, what can we do to optimise things? Well, one of the key considerations for marketing your units is timing.

Pre-development

It may be possible to attract a buyer for your units before a single shovel has been taken out of the contractor's van. Typically, this would be an investor as opposed to a homebuyer, and they could be looking to buy the entire development.

Be aware that you will have all your eggs in one basket. That said, you will have contractual protection, plus you haven't lost any sales momentum if the deal falls out of bed.

Also, expect to sell at a discount. This may be offset to some degree through saving on marketing and agency fees as well as finance costs.

Off-plan

What if you could sell the units' off-plan,' i.e., before they were actually 'built'? This would, in theory, get you the quickest outcome since there's no marketing to be done at the back end. But the off-plan approach has its challenges:

1. It's a harder sell. Buyers have limited imagination at the best of times. Convincing them to invest in something that doesn't exist yet generally means you'll face a stiffer challenge
2. You may only be able to show them a building site. Most people will struggle to envisage the transition from an old industrial unit to a swanky new apartment
3. You'll need to invest in some form of computer-generated imagery (CGI). This will support the off-plan sales so your audience has at least some idea of what the finished product will look like. Not a huge expense, but it's an additional workstream and cost you'll need to factor in, plus it's a poor substitute for the real thing

TIP: If you do CGI, do it well. Get it done professionally and be prepared to pay a premium. Don't give it to the cheapest you can find, and never give the task to a budding artist in your circle of acquaintances. Why all the fuss? If you go down the CGI route, then these images will be what sells your units. Numbers and descriptions are all very well, but it's the eyes that buy. If you do an average to good job with the CGI, you won't get any sales. Do an excellent job, and you'll have a reasonable chance of shifting units off-plan.

Post-development

The typical approach; you wait for the units to be fully built before you market them.

1. There are no early-bird advantages; you have to wait until the Contractor has (more-or-less) finished on site so this will mean a longer wait
2. Buyers can see the whole development in its finished state; there's no imagination required

Show-flat

One approach is to create a single show flat where you arrange for one unit to be finished ahead of the others. This is then dressed and used as the show home while work continues on the rest of the project. A couple of thoughts:

1. This can work well when the units are very similar in terms of size, finish, layout, and so on. However, it can be less effective where each unit is different since buyers will be more inclined to wait to see the finished product. They may want to pick the apartment they prefer since they can only glean so much from the show flat
2. You'll need to be very clear with your Contractor about the prioritisation of a single unit if you're to avoid incurring

additional costs. The Contractor will prioritise work in the most convenient and cost-effective way for him. This is unlikely to involve one unit being ready significantly ahead of the others. Negotiation will be needed to see how soon you can get one apartment ready without the scheme incurring extra costs. This approach has the distinct advantage that very little is left to the imagination. Buyers can see what they're getting and will (hopefully) be walking into their dream home

Let's be clear what we mean by 'dressing' first of all. This involves putting furniture and soft furnishings into at least one of the units to create a show home. This is where your potential buyers will be shown around to get a feel of the property. By doing it well, you'll be able to create some wow factor on every viewing that you do.

For larger units, don't go thinking that some fresh, newly painted flats with zero furniture or soft furnishings are going to look more appealing. There may be some people who like a blank canvas, but that's not your typical buyer. Your average buyer has a poor imagination and buys with their eyes. They'll wander around such a sterile apartment struggling to imagine it as their new home. Instead, you need to make it look like a home they'd want to live in from the outset so that there's very little left to their imagination. And not only a home that's liveable in; one that makes them say 'Wow' when they walk in.

Note that we mention dressing larger units since you need to think very carefully before dressing smaller flats. Small apartments can look very cluttered once they've been furnished, so you should consider leaving them empty. That way, they feel deceptively spacious even though they don't look particularly homely.

Dressing your show home needn't cost the earth. You can also re-use the furniture and furnishings time and time again; you'll just need to have somewhere to store it all between projects. Another option is to use professional house dressers who will loan you the fittings until the units are sold. This is a more expensive option, but it does away with the hassle and storage costs associated with the DIY approach.

Alternatively, you could offer to include the furniture and furnishings within the sale. This could be to either sweeten the deal or to charge a premium. Just be aware that this option won't appeal to every buyer, so you won't be guaranteed to avoid storage costs.

Make sure that you dress your home to suit your target market, and whatever you do, make it neutral. Attractiveness is a highly subjective thing. Unless you already know you have outlandish or exotic tastes, you can be tempted to believe that most people like exactly what YOU like. This approach fails on two counts:

1. Your tastes are not neutral even though you may think they are
2. You have minimal design flair even though you may think you're not bad at it (sorry to break this to you, but you'll thank us later)

Luckily inspiration is at hand in many forms. One of the easiest ways is to go and take some photos in someone else's show home. All the major housebuilders have in-house designers who dress their show homes to maximise their appeal. Providing your target market is similar, these homes can be a great source of inspiration. You'll not only be able to see what the experts think works best, but you'll also get to 'feel' how the space is transformed by being dressed effectively.

Take a look for new homes on Rightmove in your area, and you should find plenty of new developments showing off their best show-home look. While you could get lots of ammunition by looking at the website, it's no substitute for having the first-hand 'show home' experience. You'll learn something from it, plus you'll appreciate a sense of 'wow,' which is impossible to get off a web page.

When looking at show homes, pay particular attention to how the rooms are laid out and to the props that they use to sell the space. Notice also how they deploy lighting and fabrics, plus how the colours and tones change from room to room.

Other forms of inspiration can include home magazines and Pinterest. There's so much content available that it can be a bit overwhelming. Feel free to go for fashionable looks, features, and colours when it comes to dressing. You'll get a feel for what's 'in' from trawling the Internet and other peoples' show homes.

Viewing Days

This is where you do a two-week marketing campaign to try and get all potential buyers to view all the finished units on a single viewing day.

1. We prefer this approach for those developments where we have several flats that are similar but different. For example, they may all be one-bed units, but each one is a different shape or size, and some of the features and detailing may be different
2. Prospective buyers will see each of the flats, and because they're all different, they'll have a favourite. As they also know that everyone else is seeing the apartments on the same day, they understand that they'll be sold on a first-come-first-served basis. This may then prompt them to take action to secure the flat they like best before someone else snaps it up
3. It's also very convenient because you can have representatives from the estate agent on site all day. You

could also have a mortgage advisor on hand to work through the financing possibilities with potential purchasers

When to start marketing

That's the million-dollar question! Unfortunately, there's no right answer as each development is different. The best approach is to sit down with your sales agent right at the outset and talk through the options listed above. You should also consider any other ideas that they may have.

We do have one word of caution when it comes to Industrial Conversions. And that is, don't underestimate the impact of customers seeing the finished article. People find it almost impossible to picture the end result, and even those with a vivid imagination are unlikely to do it justice. You don't want people to drive by the incomplete building to take a look. They'll see a tired old industrial building that's now a building site, and it's not going to make them think, "I'd love to live here".

20. Further Learning And Next Steps

Taking things forward

So, there you have it. We hope that this book has given you a sense of what's involved in finding, taking on, and completing Industrial Conversion projects. We also hope that it may have inspired you to take action. But exactly what action should you take if you want to start developing property yourself?

Well, the first thing you need to do is to get yourself educated. Of course, propertyCEO is a property training business, so you probably weren't thinking we'd suggest you go out there and wing it. But whether you choose our training or someone else's, trying to develop property without an education behind you is like jumping out of a plane without a parachute. You may strike lucky and land on something soft and forgiving, but the odds are somewhat against it. Even if you do make it down in one piece, you're likely to have picked up a few bruises on the way. Learning by your mistakes is always more painful than not making any mistakes in the first place. The great news about property is that the training is inexpensive compared to the returns you can make from getting it right. Or for that matter, the costs of getting it wrong.

So, what are the options? Well, this book has focused on the specifics of Industrial Conversions. If you're thinking of taking things to the next stage, you'll want to get educated in the broader subject of property development.

Can propertyCEO help you achieve this? We thought you'd never ask! Well, the answer is, of course, a resounding er... maybe.

Hold on a second. Are we saying that we only <u>possibly</u> might be able to help you? Are we not that confident in our abilities as trainers, then?

Actually, that's not it. The thing is, propertyCEO isn't a volume training company. We don't train thousands of people or offer lots of cheap training workshops or manuals. As we said at the start, we're only interested in training people who will actually develop property. It takes a lot of effort on their part and a lot of effort on ours too. As a result, we only offer a very small range of training packages, but we firmly believe that they're the best property development training available anywhere. They're not cheap, but they're amazing value.

If that sounds interesting, please check out our website at <u>www.propertyceo.co.uk</u> to find out more or to get in touch with us.

And what if you're a would-be first-time developer or have never 'done property' before?

Our programmes happily accommodate people who are looking to take their first steps into property development. The good news is that we make no assumptions about the level of experience you have, so even if that's a big round zero, we'll still be able to help. And if you've already done a bit of property stuff (development or otherwise), then we can help there too.

Some people say that it's wrong to tell people that have no property experience that they could become property developers. Which is a bit like telling someone that because they've never flown a plane, they can never be a pilot. Many people can become pilots if they have the right training. That's why we haven't yet run out of pilots, old, bold, or otherwise. The good news is that a property developer has many more co-pilots to help them fly the plane than a pilot does. In fact, many of the skills they need are already in place. They just need pointing in a different direction.

So, by all means, get in touch with us via the website, and we'll be very happy to share our thoughts on which programme might be the right one for you.

In fact, we often run free masterclasses and training workshops for people who are thinking about getting into property development, whatever their background. You can find out if there's one running at the moment simply by checking out the home page of our website (www.propertyceo.co.uk). If there's a nice big red button on it, then that's probably a good sign!

There you go, that's the hard sell out of the way.

What? You'd like some more?

Ok, if you're asking why you should choose propertyCEO above anyone else's training, then here's a list of ten things that are important to us. If they're important to you as well, then we're probably a good fit in which case we'd love to try and help you:

1. We aspire to excellence in whatever we do. We genuinely want to make the best products and training materials that exist. We're not sure that we always get there, but that's what the sign says above the door, and we always try our very best to live up to it. That goes for everyone in the team. In short, we always aim to exceed people's expectations

2. We don't try and hard sell our courses. If you enjoy the hard sell experience, there are plenty of others out there who can offer this service. Just don't all rush to the back of the room at once ☺

3. Property investment and development is a business, and too many people fail because they had a dream but no idea about business. All of our training courses include an

element of business training as standard so that we can do our part to make sure you stay in business

4. Most people operate at a fraction of their potential because they go through life with the handbrake on, yet they don't realise it. We also include mindset training as standard so that you can achieve your goals more easily. Practical things that you may not know about, but which can make your goals much more achievable. Seriously, the mindset stuff just works – you should check it out if you're not there already

5. We specialise in what we do. We're not trying to become a training brand that offers a million and one different courses. So we'll only teach you about what we know a lot about, not what we think might sell well

6. We'll teach you how to develop property, full stop. You might then decide to pursue a specific strategy or type of project, but ultimately, you'll be learning from us how to develop ANY type of project. Industrial conversions are a hugely attractive proposition, but there are lots of other opportunities out there you should also know about

7. Experience counts for A LOT in both business and property, and we're both getting on a bit. We promise to aim for wisdom, but if we miss, at least you'll get experience

8. We don't outsource our training to secondary trainers. We have a team of professional coaches who specialise in key areas and who interact with our students on that subject. But the core training, the workshops, and the Q&A sessions are all provided by yours truly

9. We think it's important to give something back, which is why we host the podcast, our Open Door sessions, and also provide our free training. Believe it or not, we don't hold back on the advice we give out with our free content, so please help yourself.

10. And maybe above all, propertyCEO is also about having some fun along the way. Life's too short not to enjoy it. If we can help you become financially free and find the life of your dreams, then if you can enjoy the journey too, you've been our perfect customer

Good luck with whatever you do next and thanks for stopping by and visiting us – we hope to see you again soon.

Ian & Ritchie

Alresford, August 2021

Appendix 1

Here's the answer to the 9 dots puzzle; you simply start bottom right:

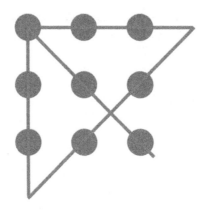

Isn't it strange how we often automatically limit our thinking to operate inside the box? ☺

Appendix 2: List of Podcast Episodes

Season/ Episode	Title	Subject
1.1	Who Needs Property Training?	Training, mentoring
1.2	The Science Of Successful Networking	Networking, mindset
1.3	What Makes Estate Agents Tick	Estate agents, deal sourcing
1.4	Picking The Right Property Strategy	HMO, conversions, buy-to-let, serviced accommodation, new build, development, rent-to-rent
1.5	Build Your Own Time Machine	Productivity, time management
1.6	Finding Finance	Finance, commercial brokers
1.7	Essential Property Business Skills	Business plan, cash flow, leverage
1.8	Outsource Your Life	Outsourcing, productivity, work/life balance
1.9	Avoiding Legal Pitfalls In Property	Professional team, law, solicitors
1.10	How To Find Property Deals	Deal sourcing
2.1	How Passive Is Passive Income?	Property strategies, passive income
2.2	The Part-Time Property Developer	Professional team, training
2.3	Essential Brain Training Part 1	Mindset
2.4	Discovering Industrial Conversions	Industrial conversions, Permitted Development

2.5	How To Win Estate Agent Deals	Deal sourcing, estate agents
2.6	How To Set Goals	Mindset, goal setting
2.7	What Your Contractor Really Thinks About You: Part 1	Professional team, contractors
2.8	How To Structure Your Business	Business plan and structure, group holding co., SPV
2.9	Commercial Conversions	Commercial conversion, planning classes
2.10	Free Money	Solicitors, law
3.1	5 Essential Mindset Tools	Mindset, personal development
3.2	Setting Up Your Property Business	Tax, accountants, business structure
3.3	How To Get Credibility In Property	Professional team, training, leverage
3.4	Managing Risk	Planning, Permitted Development, costs, profit
3.5	Why Use An Interior Designer?	Design, saleability
3.6	Making First Impressions Count	Networking, personal branding
3.7	What Makes A Good Developer	Professional team, mindset
3.8	Lean Startup Learnings	Business skills, mindset
3.9	Ritchie's Stripping Secrets	Stripping out, construction
3.10	Understanding Development Stages	RIBA work stages, design
4.1	Wisebites #1	Personal development
4.2	Nail Your Viewings	Viewings
4.3	Communication Is King	Professional team, relationships
4.4	The Architect's View	Architecture, professional team
4.5	Making Offers & Negotiating	Profit, estate agents, negotiation

4.6	**Nailing Your Personal Brand**	Personal branding, marketing
4.7	**Planning Permission vs Permitted Development**	Planning, Permitted Development
4.8	**Try A Little Tendering**	Construction, contractors, tendering
4.9	**Financial Freedom (And Where To Find It)**	Passive income, property strategies
4.10	**Insurance: What You REALLY Need To Know**	Insurance, brokers

ND Bed Spaces   sq met
1.1   1   39/37
          2   50

2.2   3   61
          4   70

Networking Mindset
    Name of Business

Time Management
Your own personal Time Machine / Ian Child

Printed in Great Britain
by Amazon